The
GROUCHY
HISTORIAN

An Old-Time Lefty Defends Our Constitution
Against Right-Wing Hypocrites and Nutjobs

Ed Asner

and

Ed. Weinberger

Simon & Schuster Paperbacks
NEW YORK LONDON TORONTO SYDNEY NEW DELHI

Simon & Schuster Paperbacks
An Imprint of Simon & Schuster, Inc.
1230 Avenue of the Americas
New York, NY 10020

First Simon & Schuster trade paperback edition October 2018

SIMON & SCHUSTER PAPERBACKS and colophon are registered trademarks of
Simon & Schuster, Inc.

For information about special discounts for bulk purchases, please contact
Simon & Schuster Special Sales at 1-866-506-1949 or
business@simonandschuster.com.

The Simon & Schuster Speakers Bureau can bring authors to your live event.
For more information or to book an event, contact the Simon & Schuster Speakers
Bureau at 1-866-248-3049 or visit our website at www.simonspeakers.com.

Interior design by Paul Dippolito

Manufactured in the United States of America

3 5 7 9 10 8 6 4 2

Library of Congress Cataloging-in-Publication Data
Names: Asner, Edward, author. | Weinberger, Ed, author.
Title: The grouchy historian : an old-time lefty defends our Constitution
against right-wing hypocrites and nutjobs / Ed Asner and Ed Weinberger.
Description: First Simon & Schuster hardcover edition. | New York, NY :
Simon & Schuster, 2017. | Includes bibliographical references.
Identifiers: LCCN 2017024599| ISBN 9781501166020 | ISBN 1501166026 |
ISBN 9781501166037 (ebook)
Subjects: LCSH: Constitutional history—United States.
Classification: LCC KF4541 .A94 2017 | DDC 342.7302/9—dc23 LC record available
at https://lccn.loc.gov/2017024599

ISBN 978-1-5011-6602-0
ISBN 978-1-5011-6604-4 (pbk)
ISBN 978-1-5011-6603-7 (ebook)

To Morris, Lizzie, Nancy, and all the other Asners
—E. A.

To my family—Carlene, Jack, Sam, Max, and Heidi
—E. W.

Contents

The
GROUCHY
HISTORIAN

CHAPTER 1

Introduction:

Why I Wrote This Book

O ye that love mankind! Ye that dare oppose, not
only the tyranny but the tyrant, stand forth!

—Thomas Paine, *Common Sense*, 1776

Nobody thumps the Constitution like a Right-Wing Republican. Conservatives love the Constitution, invoking its very name—even more than the Bible and Ronald Reagan—as all the proof they need that God is on their side. It's not enough that they think they own the Constitution; they act as if they wrote the damn thing.

In fact, frat boys, listening to Republican candidates, have invented a new way to get drunk: every time they hear the word *Constitution*, they down another shot of Jägermeister.*

The Constitution is the cornerstone of the Republican party's agenda, along with small government, less regulation, and making sure the rich pay less taxes than the rest of us.

Republicans are supported by a phalanx of Right-Wing radio and TV hosts who wave the Constitution at us like so many brainwashed Chinese once lofted copies of Chairman Mao's *Little Red Book*.

Mark Levin and Glenn Beck have made small fortunes publishing books that rewrite the Constitution to suit themselves. Rush Limbaugh's website once featured him beside a blow-up of

---

* And if there isn't a drinking game like that, there should be.

the Constitution's Preamble, a wide smile across his face as if he had just scored a prescription for painkillers.* Bill O'Reilly used to give away free copies of the Constitution with every purchase of his "patriot" coffee mug.† That was, of course, before he was fired from his television show where he advocated family values on the one hand while calling female employees and masturbating with the other.‡

From Tea Party politicians to the *Wall Street Journal* editorial board, all share the same distorted view: progressives, with the aid of pinko academics and activist judges, have been on a century-long march to disfigure the Constitution, bend it to their own evil objectives, and undo the social order as ordained by our country's Founding Fathers.

To give you some idea of what I'm talking about, here are samples of quotes from their best and brightest:

> I, as a constitutional conservative, as a believer in Jesus
> Christ . . . readily embrace [Donald Trump's agenda].
>
> —Michele Bachmann,
> former Republican congressperson

> If standing for liberty and standing for the Constitution
> make you a wacko bird, then you can count me a very
> proud wacko bird.
>
> —Senator Ted Cruz

> You can go to our Founding Fathers' early documents and
> see how they crafted a Declaration of Independence and a

---

* A half page down, President Obama is shown gleefully tearing the Constitution to shreds.

† Only $39.95.

‡ According to the claims in at least one settled lawsuit.

Constitution that allows that Judeo-Christian belief to be
the foundation of our lives . . .

—Sarah Palin, who is not who she once was

It is my number one duty as a human being—to earn an
experiment in self-government every day by spotlighting
cockroaches who violate their oath to the US Constitution
and wipe their ass with the US Constitution.

—Ted Nugent, celebrity Trump supporter

And there are a helluva lot more where that came from.

Pissed off by the lies, misrepresentations, and outright horseshit, I
decided it was time to strike back. It was time to reclaim the Constitution. Besides, if the Righties were wrong about everything else—
like health care, climate change, and the corporate tax rate—they
had to be wrong about the Constitution.

First, I did my homework. I read the Constitution and the
amendments; perused *The Federalist** and Madison's notes taken
during the Constitutional Convention; surveyed the lives of the
Founders and Framers†; looked over the Supreme Court opinions
of Antonin Scalia and Clarence Thomas; and even tried to digest
Glenn Beck's *The Original Argument*, Mark Levin's *The Liberty
Amendments*, and Dr. Ben Carson's *A More Perfect Union*—three of
the best over-the-counter sleep aids on the market. To find out how
the mind of a strict constructionist works, I also dipped into Ted
Cruz's autobiography, *A Time for Truth*, a faith-based romance novel
in which the hero falls in love with himself at an early age.

---

* *The Federalist* is composed of eighty-five essays written anonymously by Alexander Hamilton, James Madison, and John Jay. Seven hundred pages in defense of
the Constitution—so who had time for every word? Hell, I'm eighty-six years old.

† The Framers were those who "wrote" the Constitution. All the Framers were
also Founders, but not all the Founders were Framers.

Here is a preview of what I came up with:

> The Framers wrote the Constitution in order to form a *strong* central government, giving sweeping powers to Congress (not the states) and balanced by an equally strong executive branch.
>
> Nothing in the Constitution suggests, let alone enforces, the concepts of limited government, limited taxes, and limited regulations.
>
> The Framers were not divinely inspired. They were lawyers. Do you really know any divinely inspired lawyers? The *only* lawyer ever to be divinely inspired was Saul of Tarsus.*
>
> When the Framers wrote "We the People," they meant themselves.†
>
> Most of the Founders and Framers were Deists. Deism is a religion that believes in a God who really doesn't give a shit.
>
> The Framers did not hate taxation. They needed taxes, desperately. They had a war to pay off.
>
> A strict constructionist is someone who selects *portions* of the Constitution to justify already held beliefs.
>
> Under the Constitution, women had the same rights as a Chickasaw Indian.
>
> The Constitution is as good as the people who swear to protect it.

---

* As Saul, he was a Jewish lawyer. As Paul, he was a Christian tent maker. Later, Saint Paul.

† The Framers created a republic—not a democracy—in which ordinary citizens like us were kept as far removed from the electoral process as possible.

The rest of what I learned is in this book.

For the record: I do not pretend that what I say here is an objective study of the Constitution and the men and events that went into its creation. I come to the subject as a citizen with my own strong point of view, believing that "objective historian" is a contradiction in terms, like "compassionate conservative" or "Fox News."

Nor do I pretend to be a professional scholar—which might explain why not every quote is letter perfect or exactly endnoted.* For that, I have to blame my inexperienced research assistant, who also happens to be me.

But you will be happy to know that I did read some of the best historians and Constitutional scholars in the business. Many of whom happened to beat me to my best ideas.

I know what you're thinking. Why me of all people? Why am I writing a book about the Constitution? Well, why not me? After all, I have played some of the smartest people ever seen on television.

---

* If you don't believe my quotes, look the damn things up yourself.

CHAPTER 2

The Founders and Framers: Who Were Those Guys?

Hamilton had a superabundance of secretions which he could not find Whores enough to draw off.

—John Adams, on Alexander Hamilton

He means well . . . but sometimes and in somethings, is absolutely out of his senses.

—Benjamin Franklin, on John Adams

A curse on his virtues, they've undone his country.

—Thomas Jefferson, on George Washington

The Life of Dr. Franklin was a scene of continual dissipation.

—John Adams, on Benjamin Franklin

Jefferson . . . would soon be revealed as a voluptuary and an intriguing incendiary.

—Alexander Hamilton, on Thomas Jefferson

The Convention is really an assembly of demigods.

—Thomas Jefferson

In the summer of 1787, fifty-five delegates from twelve states*
came to Philadelphia to rewrite the Articles of Confederation. Instead, they decided to write a new constitution for the new nation.
And they had to do it in a hurry. The country had already started.

The delegates were all white men (ranging in age from twenty-
four to eighty-one), well educated, and wealthy property owners.
Thirty-five of the delegates were lawyers. Their attendance—during
the four months it took to write the Constitution—was, at best,
spotty. After all, they weren't getting paid by the hour.

Of the fifty-five delegates, the most influential were George
Washington, Alexander Hamilton, James Madison, and Benja-
min Franklin. Two of the Founders—John Adams and Thomas
Jefferson—were absent, living in Europe as envoys to England and
France. They would show up later to kibbitz.

And now, ladies and gentlemen, I give you the Founders and
Framers. At least the important ones:

George Washington

Legendary war hero George Washington presided over the Constitutional Convention. How much of the day-to-day work on the
actual drafting of the Constitution Washington performed is hard
to say, but as America's most revered leader, we can assume nothing
was done without his ultimate approval.

Washington was both a Deist and a Mason who frequently used
the word *God* while rejecting the divinity of Christ, the Trinity, and
Original Sin.

Born into a modest Virginia family, Washington married the
widow Martha Custis in 1759, one of the wealthiest women in Virginia, whose prime acres were worth (in today's terms) millions of

---

* The Rhode Island delegation, made up entirely of Baptists, boycotted.

dollars. In 1774, he paid taxes on 135 slaves, many of which were part of Martha's dowry.

During the Revolutionary War, General Washington served his country without salary, requesting instead that Congress merely pay his expenses. And so, after the duration of the eight-year war against the British, Washington turned in an expense account in excess of $450,000. (Yes, you read that right.) Not included was the 6 percent interest he added to the total.

Using even the most conservative scale of conversion, George Washington asked for the equivalent of what today would amount to just over $25 million!

The expense account, by the way, included fine dining, stays at the best inns, and out-of-pocket costs for ammunition.

A year after the Constitution was ratified, George Washington was elected the first president of the United States.

Well, *elected* isn't exactly the right word. Washington was the unanimous choice of Hamilton, Adams, and Jefferson and sixty-six other delegates who showed up somewhere to vote in the first electoral college. Hamilton had the fix in making certain Washington would get all sixty-nine votes.

Washington agreed to take the presidency at a sum of $25,000 a year. Which today would be equal to around $1.5 million.

He probably needed the money. Like many of the Founders, Washington lived beyond his means* and was often plagued by debt. (Land-rich, cash-poor, so the saying goes.) He had to borrow the money to make the trip to Philadelphia for his first inauguration.

A major land speculator, Washington at his death owned hundreds of thousands of acres—from New York in the north to the Ohio Valley in the west—much of which he purchased during his presidency.

I'm going to take a shot and say he knew something.

---

* One example: He had a carriage designed in England inscribed with his family crest.

When he died, his estate was valued at $780,000—which tells only half the story. That figure, based on the "prestige value" of his wealth, amounts to $42 million in today's money.

Alexander Hamilton

Before there was *Hamilton*, the Broadway musical, there was Alexander Hamilton, delegate to the Constitutional Convention. Frustrated by the weakness of the state legislatures and the futility of the Articles of Confederation, Hamilton was one of the driving forces behind the formation of the Constitutional Convention. He arrived in Philadelphia with rock-star credentials: former congressman from New York, founder of the Bank of New York, and senior aide to General Washington, the commander-in-chief of the Revolutionary War.

How he got the job with Washington is an interesting story in itself: captain of a company of artillery in 1776, Hamilton was spotted by General Nathaniel Greene, who was immediately taken by the style of the soldier's uniforms, designed—as it turned out—by Hamilton: bright blue coats, shiny brass buttons, and wide white shoulder belts strapped across the chest. As Hamilton later wrote, ". . . smart dress is essential. When not attended to, the soldier is exposed to ridicule and humiliation."

Later in his career, Hamilton outfitted an entire militia. Hamilton ordered the shoes, picked the colors, designed matching coats and shirts, and even chose the fabrics.

As he himself put it, "The jackets ought to be made of some of the stuffs of which sailors' jackets are usually made." Hamilton, as we can see, was indefatigable when it came to details—whether in fashion or writing the Constitution.

Anyway, as I was saying, General Greene was so impressed with Hamilton's military savoir faire that he recommended him to Washington, who, in turn, recognized Hamilton's brilliance and soon appointed him chief aide. Over time, their relationship became described as "father-son."

Curious, at least to me, are the many comments made by his contemporaries as to Hamilton's "effeminacy."

There was even the suggestion that as a young man his relationship with a John Laurens may have been—how to put this?—on the down-low. And from Ron Chernow's biography of Hamilton, we have this remarkable quote from Hamilton's son: "There was a deep fondness of friendship [between the two men] which approached the tenderness of feminine attachment."

Does Hamilton's love for playing dress-up with his soldiers make him gay? Was he, in fact, bisexual or both? Or neither? Who cares? I don't. I just bring it up to piss off the homophobic Right-Wingers.

In 1780, Hamilton married Elizabeth Schuyler, the daughter of Philip Schuyler, one of the wealthiest landowners in the nation. Schuyler's estate extended three miles along the Hudson River and included between 15,000 and 20,000 acres—added to which was another 120,000 acres Mr. Schuyler inherited when he married the even richer Catherine Van Rensselaer.

Though his father-in-law owned slaves,* Hamilton opposed slavery. During the Revolutionary War, he suggested arming slaves to fight the British, freeing them, and compensating their owners. His plan was rejected by the Continental Congress when the delegation from South Carolina vetoed it.

At the Constitutional Convention, he strongly argued *against* the proviso that said the federal government could extend the slave trade for another twenty years. Again, he lost.

When Hamilton was Secretary of the Treasury—some three years after the drafting of the Constitution—he began an affair that almost ruined his career.

As the story goes: an attractive twenty-three-year-old woman named Maria Reynolds appeared at Hamilton's house to ask for

---

* How else could you manage 120,000 acres?

money, saying she'd recently been abandoned by her husband. Since Hamilton's wife was home at the time, he rendezvoused at her lodgings that night bringing a fistful of cash—the first of many such charitable visits.*

In time, it turns out, her husband (and pimp) showed up to blackmail the stunned Hamilton, who, nonetheless, promptly began paying him off.

Like many of the Framers, Hamilton was a Deist, preferring reason to revelation; embracing the morality of Christianity but not its theology. When asked why there was no mention of God in the Constitution, Hamilton replied: "We forgot." Of course, Hamilton forgot nothing.

Nonetheless, on his deathbed—after being shot the day before in a duel with Aaron Burr—he did ask for God's mercy. He also said—with his last gasp—that should he live, he would work to pass legislation to outlaw duels.

Too little. Too late.

James Madison Jr.

Many on the Right claim James Madison is *the* "father of the Constitution." No doubt that, as the cleverest delegate from the powerful Virginia contingent, Madison was pivotal in the drafting (and eventual ratification) of the Constitution and the ten amendments that followed, now known as the Bill of Rights. But he was not the father. As Madison himself wrote: The Constitution "was not like the fabled Goddess of Wisdom, the offspring of a single

---

* Hamilton artfully described their encounter this way: "I took the bills out of my pocket and gave them to her. Some conversation ensued from which it was quickly apparent that other than pecuniary consolation would be also acceptable."

brain. It ought to be regarded as the work of many heads and many hands."

Madison has become the conservative darling because of his later opposition to Washington and Hamilton's idea of a strong federal government, but at the time of the Constitutional Convention, he too (like Hamilton) feared the excesses of state legislatures and fought to deprive the states of their powers, believing—as he said—the local legislatures were "more given to mischief."*

More to the point: Madison once proposed that Congress should have veto power over all state laws.

Historians can find no hint that Madison held any belief in Christian theology. On the contrary, like his fellow Virginian and good friend Thomas Jefferson, he firmly believed in "separation of Church and State." As a legislator in Virginia's House of Burgesses, he had blocked a bill by Patrick Henry that would enact a special tax that would go directly to Virginia's churches. One of many of the disputes Madison and Patrick Henry would have throughout their careers.

Madison grew up on (and later inherited) Montpelier, his father's tobacco plantation of 5,000 acres run by more than two dozen slaves. Madison's grandfather Ambrose had been poisoned to death by one of those slaves, who was quickly hanged.

Events such as those tend a man toward "ambiguity" when it comes to the issue of slavery. And while publicly decrying (I promise I won't use that word again) the "evils of slavery," Madison fully supported the Constitution's view of slaves as property. Privately, Madison saw the answer to the problem in the mass deportation of slaves to Africa.

---

* Which was Madison's elegant way of saying "I trust state politicians as far as I can throw them." And at just over five feet and 100 pounds, there was nothing that Madison could throw very far. Behind his back, the other delegates called him "His Littleness."

In his defense, let me point out that a former slave of his, Paul Jennings, who had served Madison all his life, wrote a memoir called *A Colored Man's Reminiscences of James Madison* in which he praised his owner for having never beat him.

Benjamin Franklin

After Washington, Benjamin Franklin—at the age of eighty-one—was the most celebrated delegate to the Constitutional Convention. Writer, publisher, printer, scientist, and inventor,* Franklin was one of the few delegates who had also signed the Declaration of Independence and the Articles of Confederation.

Surprisingly, Franklin had been a slave owner, having six or seven of them always around to help in his printing shops. He also ran advertisements in his newspapers for their buying and selling. "A Likely negro woman to be sold. Enquire at the Widow Read's."† But, by the time of the Convention, he had become a staunch abolitionist.

Despite being raised by devout Puritans, for much of his life, Franklin was a confirmed Deist.‡ While believing that faith in God should "inform his daily actions," he, like most of the Deists of the time, followed no religious dogma, denying any personal relationship with a savior. As he wrote: "I imagine it a great vanity in me to suppose that the Supremely Perfect does in the least regard such an inconsiderable nothing as a man."

It came then as somewhat of a shock to his colleagues (and his biographers) when he rose at the Convention to suggest that the

---

* Three of his inventions were bifocals, daylight saving time, and the first urinary catheter.

† His mother-in-law.

‡ His parents had once denounced him as a heretic.

delegates begin each session with a prayer. It was a motion quickly and soundly defeated.

Franklin had a reputation as a womanizer. In his autobiography, he confessed this fear of an overwhelming sexual appetite, acknowledging that the "hard-to-be-governed passion of my youth had hurried me frequently into intrigues with low women that fell in my way."*

Of his many illegitimate children, Franklin took credit for only one—a son named William whom he raised almost as his own. William Franklin then had his own illegitimate son, William Temple Franklin, who, in turn, had *his* illegitimate son Theodore.

John Adams

At the time of the Constitutional Convention, John Adams was in Europe as envoy to England, making side trips to Holland to borrow money to pay off the new nation's mounting debts.

When Adams received a copy of the Constitution in London months after it was signed, he read it, as he said, "with great satisfaction." But he had two criticisms: (1) there was no Bill of Rights similar to the ones he had written into the Massachusetts State Constitution, and (2) he would have preferred the president to have been given more powers. Specifically, he did not believe the president should need the "advice and consent" of the Senate to make cabinet and federal appointments. A clear signal that Adams, like Hamilton, believed in a strong central government headed by an executive with vigorous powers:

> If there is one central truth to be collected from the history of all ages, it is this: that the people's rights and liberties, and

---

* Which may give new meaning to some of Franklin's more famous maxims from his *Poor Richard's Almanack*: "Early to bed, early to rise . . ." and "You get what you pay for."

the democratical mixture in a constitution, can never be preserved without a strong executive ...

As a criminal defense lawyer (in 1770), he defended (at great risk to
his career) the eight British soldiers who had killed five Americans
in the confrontation known as the Boston Massacre.* He argued
then (and believed all his life) that it was "of more importance to
community, that innocence should be protected, than it is, that guilt
should be punished ..."†

Of all the Founders, Adams may have been the most churchgo-
ing. But as a Unitarian, he did not believe in the Holy Trinity, the
Holy Ghost, or the divinity of Jesus.‡

Adams was a staunch, lifelong believer in religious liberty. As the
primary author of the Massachusetts State Constitution, he wrote,
"No subject shall be hurt, molested, or restrained in his person ...
for worshipping God in the manner most agreeable to the dictates
of his own conscience." And nary a word about the Judeo-Christian
tradition.

Adams disapproved of slavery and never owned any; still, he preferred that slavery as a political issue of the day be "put to sleep for
a time" because of its "divisiveness" when unity and the common
good of the country were critical to its survival. His wife, Abigail, on
the other hand, was outraged at its evil, denouncing it publicly as a
threat to American democracy.

Adams had become smitten with his third cousin Abigail when
she was seventeen, and their marriage of fifty-five years was one of
the great love stories of the era. Incredible is the fact that they ex-
changed more than 1,600 letters during their lifetimes.

---

* Six were acquitted, two convicted of manslaughter.

† A point ignored when Thomas, Scalia et. al. defend capital punishment as a
principle favored by the Framers.

‡ There were Christians at the time who wouldn't shake hands with a Unitarian.

Which may explain the enduring success of their relationship: they seemed to have been more apart than together.

In one letter, Abigail wrote to her husband: "... to remember the ladies and be more generous and favorable to them than your ancestors. Do not put such unlimited power into the hands of the husbands."

But of course John Adams and the Founders never remembered the ladies.

Thomas Jefferson

Thomas Jefferson, author of the Declaration of Independence, was Minister to France during the Constitutional Convention. It was while in Paris that Jefferson became infatuated with the fifteen-year-old slave Sally Hemings, who had arrived as the companion to Jefferson's daughters. The "affair" between Jefferson and Hemings produced at least three children we know of. James Hemings, Sally's brother, was then also in Paris, where he was sent to culinary school to master the arts of Jefferson's favorite cuisine.

During his lifetime, Jefferson owned more than six hundred slaves. Considered a benevolent owner, Jefferson allowed them to grow their own gardens and raise their own chickens. But he also bred slaves and sold them for profit.*

A proponent of a people's democracy and suspicious of big cities and the mercantile class, Jefferson specifically excluded the voting rights of tenant farmers, day laborers, and, of course, slaves, Indians, and women. Believing himself a man of the people, he designed his

---

* Jefferson never seemed to notice the contradiction between his slave holdings and the inspiring words he wrote in the Declaration that "... all men are created equal ... endowed with certain unalienable Rights, among those are Life, Liberty, and the pursuit of Happiness."

home, Monticello, without a main staircase so he wouldn't be seen "descending" from the upper floor.

In love with all things French, especially their wines, Jefferson later endorsed the French Revolution's Reign of Terror and approved the changing of the name of Notre Dame to the Temple of Reason.

Like so many of the Founding Fathers, Jefferson avoided all forms of organized religion. As a Virginia state legislator, he authored the Bill for Establishing Religious Freedom, which forbids state support of any and all religious institutions.*

He would later write a book titled *The Life and Morals of Jesus of Nazareth*, also known as the Jefferson Bible. It omitted Jesus's miracles, His supernatural powers, and His resurrection.

"In every age," Jefferson once wrote, "the priest has been hostile to liberty ... they have perverted the purest religion ever preached to man into mystery and jargon."

An intellectual prodigy, at ten years old, Jefferson could recite the Ten Commandments in perfect Hebrew. A wit of the day then said: "And at forty-five, Jefferson had broken all ten in fluent French."

Jefferson did not serve in the Revolutionary War (he was Governor of Virginia at the time). When alerted that the British were on their way to Monticello, Jefferson locked up his wine cellar, hid his best silver, and rode off into the woods on horseback.

Seizing the opportunity, twenty-one of his slaves escaped to join the British Army. And who could blame them?

And there you have your Founders and Framers in all their elite glory—the 1 percent of their time. Many spent more than they made. Struggled their entire lives with debt. And, when they could, always married into money.

---

* This bill failed the first time around but was later revived and passed with the help of James Madison.

They were—obvious to say—petty, flawed, inconsistent, and all too human.

Yet compared to many of our feckless lawmakers of today,* those rich white guys were indeed like demigods come from Mount Olympus to walk the Earth. Or at least the streets of Philadelphia.

Not merely politicians, they were (collectively) inventors, architects, scientists, linguists, and scholars who had studied Greek and Latin; who read Voltaire, John Stuart Mill, and David Hume. More interestingly, Voltaire, John Stuart Mill, and David Hume read *them*.†

They were eloquent orators and brilliant writers. They wrote books, political articles, essays, and long, philosophical letters to their wives, friends, and to one another.‡

So who were those guys?

They were men of the Enlightenment who valued reason over dogma, tolerance over bigotry, and science over faith.

And, unlike the current Right-Wing doomsayers and fearmongers, they were all, truly, apostles of optimism.

---

* Paul Ryan and Mitch McConnell come to mind.

† They owned libraries, for godsakes.

‡ Together, Adams, Jefferson, Hamilton, and Franklin wrote more than eighteen thousand letters.

CHAPTER 3

Snapshots of Life
in Philadelphia, 1787

I'd rather be in Philadelphia.

> —W. C. Fields when asked what
> he wanted written on his tombstone

It took three or four days to get to Philadelphia from Boston. Depending on the traffic.

The rich owned 10 percent of the wealth. Not unlike today.

The rich could pay the poor to serve in the military for them. Not unlike today.

Slavery was legal. Philadelphia newspapers carried ads for slaves such as "Good deal on likely negro fellow."

The population of Philadelphia was 40,000—including a large number of prostitutes. Some working out of the Betsy Ross house.

Hanging was prohibited on Sundays. As were other forms of entertainment.

Thieves were punished by branding their hands.*

---

* Much cheaper than putting them in prison.

Because of the high rate of infant mortality, some parents did not name their children until they were two years old.

The punishment for bigamy was thirty-nine lashes and life imprisonment.

People who couldn't pay their bills went to debtors' prisons.

Children—some as young as seven—worked sixty to eighty hours a week in mills and factories.*

The standard treatment for yellow fever was as follows: doctors bled and purged the patient by emptying his bowels four times with a mixture of potions and enemas before draining off twelve ounces of blood to lower the pulse. The process was finished off by inducing mild vomiting. This procedure was repeated twice daily.†

Since toilet paper hadn't been invented, people used a sponge on a stick. Or if you were really rich, corn on the cob.

Women could not vote. Or own property. Except for some fabulously wealthy widows.

The Phillies were in last place.

---

* They were especially valuable in mines where they could crawl into spaces too small for grown-ups.

† This was, of course, before Obamacare, when you still got to choose your own doctor.

CHAPTER 4

Heckling the Right Wing: Their Top Ten Talking Points

and My Top Ten Comebacks

I

THEM: The Framers were all devout Christians.
ME: You think everyone was a devout Christian. You probably think Jesus was a devout Christian.

II

THEM: The Framers were opposed to taxation.
ME: The first day in office, Washington (as President) and Hamilton (as his Secretary of the Treasury) taxed carriages and whiskey, then opened a bank to put the money in.*

III

THEM: The greatest influence on the Constitution was the Bible.
ME: Then why doesn't the Preamble read: "We the Chosen People . . ."?

---

* Okay, maybe not the *first* day.

IV

THEM: To understand the Constitution, you have to read *The Federalist Papers.*
ME: Nobody can read *The Federalist Papers.* Madison and Hamilton wrote the damn things, and *they* couldn't read *The Federalist Papers.*

V

THEM: The Constitution gives everyone the right to own a gun.
ME: The Framers didn't want everyone to have a vote, let alone a gun!

VI

THEM: The Constitution does not grant homosexuals the right to marry.
ME: The Constitution also does not grant the right of homosexuals to win all the Tonys. So what?

VII

THEM: The Framers were a diverse group.
ME: The Framers were as diverse a group as the Mormon Tabernacle Choir.

VIII

THEM: James Madison is the "author" of the Constitution.
ME: The Constitution is the greatest "cut-and-paste" job since the New Testament.

IX

THEM: The Framers believed in term limits.
ME: I'm with you on this: I figure if a congressman can't steal enough money in three terms, he's too dumb to hold the job in the first place.

X

THEM: The only way to interpret the Constitution is to determine what the Framers were thinking when they wrote it.
ME: You can't even figure out how the Framers took a piss in pants without a fly. How do you expect to figure out what they were *thinking?*

I had teenagers. I *never* knew what they were thinking. And we lived in the same house.

Hell, I don't even know what *I'm* thinking half the time.

CHAPTER 5

God and the Constitution, Part I:

Epistle to the Christian Right

Our culture is superior. Our culture is superior because
our religion is Christianity and that is the truth that
makes men free.

—Pat Buchanan, professional Conservative
and Fox News analyst

This is a country built on Judeo-Christian values . . .

—Texas senator Ted Cruz

Greetings Christian Right

I bring bad news. There is no God in the Constitution.

I know that in 1607, the first refugees to our shores built a giant
cross to thank God for their deliverance.

I know that it reads "in God we trust" on our money.

I know that schoolchildren take an oath of allegiance that says
"One nation under God."

But there is no God in the Constitution. Nor is there any mention of His many aliases: Great Preserver of the Universe, Supreme
Judge of the World, or Master Architect.

The Framers *could* have put God in the Preamble but didn't. To
refresh your memory:

> We the People of the United States, in Order to form a more perfect Union, establish Justice, insure Domestic Tranquility, provide for the common defence, promote the general Welfare, and secure the Blessings of Liberty to ourselves and our Posterity, do ordain and establish this Constitution for the United States of America.*

There is no mention of God in the Presidential Oath of Office:

> I do solemnly swear (or affirm) that I will faithfully execute the Office of President of the United States, and will to the best of my ability, preserve, protect and defend the Constitution of the United States . . .

And there is no mention of God in Article 6, which states:

> . . . No religious test shall ever be required as a qualification to any office or public Trust under the United States.

And there were no prayers at the Convention. No opening prayers. No closing prayers. And there was a Baptist convention in town. How hard could it have been to drag one of their preachers in for a quickie?

So, again let me see if I can get through to you: God does not appear in Madison's notes; God does not appear in the Constitution; God does not appear in *The Federalist*.

You can call America a Christian nation all you want, but God—at least for all you strict constructionists out there—does not appear in the text of the Constitution.

For the Framers, this was not an accidental omission. If they wanted God in the Constitution, they knew where to find Him:

---

* I quote it in its entirety in case you think I'm lying.

- Eleven of the thirteen states had religious tests for office. The only two that didn't were Virginia and New York.*
- In New Jersey, New Hampshire, the Carolinas, and Georgia, only Protestants could hold public office.
- The Articles of Confederation (the country's preceding constitution) mentions the "Great Governor of the World."

Instead, the Framers chose to go their own worldly way, not hostile to your religion but indifferent to it.

Your Christian forefathers were a lot smarter than you are. They realized that the Constitution had left out any mention of God. *They* knew at once there was no "God"—Christian or otherwise—in the Constitution. And that's why they—the religious Right of the day—opposed the Constitution.

Here's one such protest from the anonymous pamphleteer "Arisocritis":

> The new Constitution disdains belief of a Deity, the immortality of the soul, or the resurrection of the body, a day of judgement, or a future state of rewards and punishments . . .

In fact, those guys thought the Constitution had gone way too far in protecting religious liberties. As quoted by historian Michael J. Klarman, here's how one delegate put it at the Massachusetts Ratifying Convention:

> . . . A person could not be a good man without being a good Christian, thus rulers ought to take an oath that they believed in Christ or at least in God.

At ratifying conventions throughout the states, the religious Right were horrified at the prospects that "Jews, Pagans, Infidels, and

---

* The states of Madison and Hamilton, respectively.

Papists" might actually hold office. In a Boston newspaper dated January 10, 1788, an anti-Federalist said that "since God was absent from the Constitution, Americans would suffer the fate of ancient Israel "because thou hast rejected the word of the Lord, he hath also rejected thee."

In Connecticut, Christians tried their hand at rewriting the Preamble, aligning it with their own faith:

> We the people of the United States in a firm belief of the being and perfection of the one living and true God, the creator and supreme Governor of the World in His universal providence and the authority of His laws: that He will require of all moral agents an account of their conduct, that all rightful powers among men are ordained of, and mediately derived from God . . .

I know. You get goose bumps just reading it.

In 1863, the Christian Right met at two conventions to blame the Civil War on the godless Constitution. Their solution: another Christian preamble. In other words, the war and the millions of deaths that would follow were the fault of the "heathen" Framers and not the slaveholders trying to preserve a cruel and evil system of oppression.

But at least those Christians got it right. They knew the truth: the Framers had ignored God, Christ, and the Holy Ghost. And that's the way it's been for the last 230 years. Much to your disliking.

So now you've decided to rewrite history to prove—once and for all—that the Constitution is Christian; the Framers are Christian; the Old Testament is Christian; and for all I know, you may think I'm Christian myself.

Let's start with the Constitution and your case for its "religiosity," for lack of a better word.

Look *there*! You point with childish glee at Article I, Section 7:

If any Bill shall not be returned by the President within ten days (*Sunday excepted*),* after it shall have been presented to him, the same shall be a law ...

Yes, the Framers gave the president Sundays off. But they didn't give senators Sundays off. Or members of the House. In my book, this is hardly a come-to-Jesus moment. And if there was some "religious" connotation, why didn't they use the word *Sabbath*?

Then you point to the very end of the Constitution to find this reference to "our Lord":

...Done in Convention of the unanimous Consent of the States present the Seventeenth Day of September in the year of *our Lord*† one thousand seven hundred and eighty-seven and of the Independence of the United States of America the Twelfth In Witness whereof We have hereunto subscribed our names.

But *that*—in case you hadn't noticed—is in the portion added *after* the Constitution, written in the past‡ tense, and is simply how they dated official documents back then. It also follows what is clearly the last line of the Constitution proper:

Article VII. The Ratification of the Convention of nine States shall be sufficient for the Establishment of this Constitution between the States so ratifying the same.

And that is how the Constitution ends. As an actor, I know a last line when I see one.

---

* Italics mine, in case you missed it.

† My emphasis.

‡ The only sentence so written.

We have now concluded our Christian portion of the Constitution: one "our Lord" and one "Sundays excluded." For people who claim to be on the side of God, you are desperately insecure about it.

Having so brilliantly deciphered the Constitution, you then turn to the Founders, scavenging every word they wrote, translating every phrase, inspecting every oil painting, fervently determined to make them over in your own Christian image.

Let's start with:

George Washington

There he is, you shout: the picture of George Washington at Valley Forge, deep in the snow, on his knees—praying.* And just for the record: once while a private at Fort Dix, I too prayed to God. "God," I pleaded audibly, "please don't send me to Korea." And when I ended up in Germany, I never even thanked Him.

And why would I? He's God. What's He need my thanks for? Much later, after my second hip replacement, I had some choice words for both God and my doctors. My conversation with God—which will remain between us—was: if God could do this to one of His Chosen People (me), what did He do to His unchosen ones?

Anyway, my point is prayers are not always a sign of a personal, long-lasting commitment to the Almighty.

But what about Washington's first inaugural? Isn't that proof of the man's Christian faith? Him with his hand on the Bible—the one he brought from home? Yes, but that was, sorry to say, a Masonic Bible. George Washington was a Grand Master Mason—about as

---

* And we know that never happened because, as the historian John Rhodehamel points out, George Washington would never dirty his uniform.

high as you can get in that secret society—and *that* is what he took his oath on. And Masonic Bibles do not acknowledge the Divinity of Jesus Christ.

And what about the oath he took? You know, where he famously *added* "so help me God" at the end? Sorry, but that's how *every* Mason concludes his oath—with the words "so help me God." Don't ask me how I know. It's a secret society.

So every president since Washington, up to Donald Trump, has added "so help me God," not knowing it was Masonic and not God-inspired.

But didn't Washington go to church every Sunday? Yes, and always left before communion because he didn't believe in the Miracles of Christ.

As for the real George Washington and his beliefs, let's hear from a man who should know, his pastor of twenty years, Bishop William White, who said:

> I do not believe that any degree of recollection will bring to my mind any fact which would prove General Washington to have been a believer in the Christian revelation . . . In other words, beyond his generally moral character and the fact that he went to church regularly, there is no other proof that he was a believer.

A less cautious response comes from Bishop White's assistant, the Reverend James Abercrombie, who replied years after Washington's death: "Sir, Washington was a Deist."*

Then there's Thomas Jefferson, who wrote in his journal shortly after Washington's death:

> When the clergy addressed Genl. Washington on his departure from the govmt, it was observed in their consultation

---

* See my earlier definition of a Deist.

that he had never on any occasion said a word to the public which showed a belief in the Xn* religion.

Benjamin Franklin

You people find the best example of Franklin's faith when, during a contentious moment at the Constitutional Convention, he urged his fellow delegates to pray for guidance. A motion unanimously defeated.

You suppose, of course, that Franklin wanted to pray to the same God you do now. But Franklin had a number of names that he used instead of "God." To give only a few: Great Architect of the Universe (a Masonic name); First Cause, and Author and Owner of Our Systems (Deist names); and Powerful Goodness (Franklin's favorite). Benjamin Franklin had more names for God than Jared Kushner has lawyers.

But the one name Franklin never prayed to was Jesus Christ.

That hot afternoon at the Convention when Franklin proposed that everyone pray reminds me of my mother, who always suggested an enema no matter the sickness. It may not help, but "it couldn't hurt."

To know how Franklin really felt about prayer, I refer you to a letter he sent to his brother in 1735. After hearing that 45 million prayers had been offered in all of New England seeking victory over a French fort in Canada, Franklin wrote:

> If you do not succeed, I fear, I shall have but an indifferent opinion of Presbyterian prayers in such cases as long as I live. Indeed, in attacking strong towns, I should have more dependence in *works* than in *faith*.

---

* Jefferson's abbreviation for Christianity.

Still, you cling to Franklin like he was one of yours. Here you are quoting Franklin's letter to the president of Yale University, who had asked him for his views on religion. Franklin wrote back this:

> Here is my Creed. I believe in one God, Creator of the Universe. That He governs it by His Providence. That He ought to be worshipped. That the most acceptable services render Him is doing Good to His other children. That the Soul of Man is immortal and will be treated with Justice in another life respecting its Conduct in this.

For some odd reason, however, you always manage to leave off the rest of the letter:

> As to Jesus of Nazareth, my Opinion of whom you particularly desire, I think the System of Morals and His Religion, as He left them to us, the best the world ever saw or is likely to see; but I apprehend it has received various corrupt changes, and I have, *with most of the present Dissenters in England, some Doubts as to His divinity* . . .*

You can quote endlessly about Franklin's faith in Christian ethics, but none about his faith in Jesus the Christ. Like the other Framers, Franklin was a strong believer that religion—especially Christian religion—was a public necessity to "restrain [men and women] from Vice, to support their Virtue, and to retain in them the Practice of it till it becomes habitual."

Let me put it another way: Franklin believed in Christianity as a religion that kept the people in check, much like the plantation

---

* Italics mine.

owners who gave their slaves an hour off on Sunday to praise the Lord.

But Franklin drew the line at Christ as his personal savior. To clarify the difference, the author Walter Isaacson refers us to Carl Van Doren's biography where he contrasts Franklin with the "fire-and-brimstone" Puritan minister Jonathan Edwards. Where Edwards preached fear and bigotry ("Man was a perpetual Sinner in the Hands of an Angry God"), Franklin exalted "tolerance, individual merit, civic virtue, good deeds, and rationality."

Yes, you can claim Jonathan Edwards—and his famous "terror" sermons of 1733—as one of your own. But not Benjamin Franklin.

John Adams

The best you can come up with for John Adams is this quote from Newt and Callista Gingrich's *Rediscovering God in America**:

> Religion and Virtue are the only Foundations, not only of Republicanism and of all free government but of Social felicity under all governments and in all Combinations of human society.

After that, there is only more of the same as Adams—in a handful of letters—extols the virtues of a Christian morality. Which does not necessarily make him the kind of Born Again you'd like him to be.

In fact, John Adams was a member of the New England branch of the Unitarian Church.† Unitarians did *not* believe in the divin-

---

* News sources indicate that Mr. Gingrich is currently writing a book about Donald Trump's White House. No doubt to be called *One Flew Over the Cuckoo's Nest*.

† The First Parish Church of Quincy, Massachusetts.

ity of Jesus Christ, the infallibility of the Bible, the Holy Trinity, or Original Sin. They not only did *not* believe that Jesus was God, they were certain that Jesus Himself never claimed to be either. Put a hat and a beard on a Unitarian and, in the right light, you might mistake him for a Reformed Jew.

What we do know is Adams's opinion of the clergy: comparing their sermons "preached by the grossest blockheads and most atrocious villains" to the growth of "fungus" meant to "charm and bewitch the simple and ignorant."

And here's Adams—again in his own words—as he seems to address men much like yourselves across the centuries:

> With a power bordering on tyranny, ministers ... were able to ... cultivate with Systems and Sects to Deceive millions and Cheat and Pillage hundreds and thousands of their fellow creatures.

And with a modesty that seems to escape the rest of you, Adams said this: "... The secrets of eternal wisdom are not to be fathomed by our narrow understandings."

Throughout his life, Adams apparently suffered from bouts of melancholy, and when I checked the index of David McCullough's biography, I found nine listings "as a Christian" but more than twenty for "Despair of." John Adams, it seems, spent more time on his knees out of hopelessness than he ever did in prayer.

James Madison Jr.

James Madison—whom you often refer to as the "Father of the Constitution"—remains one tough nut for you to crack. Try as you will, you really have to go digging for anything that remotely suggests that Madison supported a Judeo-Christian constitution.

Oh, there is that time when Madison as president signed into law a "national fast day"—a day of "public humiliation and prayer"—during a bleak moment in the War of 1812. It was a law passed by Congress that I say Madison signed more out of political expediency than his devout faith in a benevolent providence.

And here is a quote—and a solitary one at that—by the Conservative writer Joshua Charles in which Madison called religion "the duty which we owe to our Creator." And that's about it. Interestingly, that quote comes from his "Memorial and Remonstrances *Against* [italics mine] Religious Assessment" in which he opposes state-supported churches.

Elsewhere, we discover the true Madison, who feared "religious bondage that shackled the mind," warning against the "clergy's infernal infamy" and their "diabolical Hells of Persecution."

Madison's entire career—as a politician, lawmaker, and intellectual—was devoted to the separation of church and state:

- His "Memorial and Remonstrances," written in 1785, provides the intellectual basis for Jefferson's "Statute for Religious Freedom." "Religious opinions, beliefs, and practices are *not* the object of civil government."
- At the Constitutional Convention, Madison introduced a provision for the establishment of a national *nondenominational* university.
- As president, in 1811 Madison vetoed a bill that would have given an Episcopal church a charter within Washington, DC, on the grounds it violated the First Amendment.
- Also in 1811, Madison vetoed a law that would have given federal land to the Baptist Church in the Mississippi Territory. Again on the grounds that it would "blur and indeed erase" the "essential distinction between civil and religious functions."

Madison may not have been the father of the Constitution, but he was most certainly the father of the separation of church and state.

And may I remind you folks, it was Madison and his First

Amendment that made *God*'s commandment "Thou shalt have no other God before Me" downright unconstitutional!

Thomas Jefferson

As the author of the "divinely inspired" Declaration of Independence, Thomas Jefferson—of all people—is your go-to guy when it comes to God. After all, he's the one who wrote:

> We hold these truths to be self-evident that all Men are created equal, that they are endowed by their Creator with certain unalienable Rights, that among these are Life, Liberty, and the Pursuit of Happiness.

While "Creator" and (an earlier) "Nature's God" are not much to hang your hat on, it's more than enough for you and your religious Right to convert Jefferson into a divinely inspired man of the Lord.

Never mind that when rebelling against a king, who else higher can you call on for vindication than nature's God? Never mind that in 1820, Jefferson explained his "religious" references this way: "The Declaration of Independence was meant to be an expression of the American mind, and to give that expression the proper tone and spirit called for by the occasion. All its authority rests then on the harmonizing sentiments of the day."

In other words: the Preamble to the Declaration of Independence was not so much evidence of Jefferson's own faith but the rhetorical flourish of a writer trying to make his case.

The Christian Right of Jefferson's time were closer to the truth. For example, the Reverend Dr. John Mason, clergyman of New York, writes (in fear of a Jeffersonian presidency) that he believed Jefferson a "confirmed infidel."

And an anonymous preacher put it this way in the *New-England Palladium*:

Should the infidel Jefferson be elected President, the seal of death is that moment set on our holy religion, our churches will be prostrated, and some infamous prostitute, under the title of the Goddess of Reason, will preside in the sanctuaries now devoted to the worship of the Most High.

The basis for this contempt if not downright hatred of Jefferson (and his secular philosophies) is not hard to trace.

- He had championed the atheistic revolution in France while an "ambassador" to France. Endorsing the decapitation of priests while happily favoring the name change of Notre Dame to the Temple of Reason.
- He wrote and helped pass Virginia's Statute of Religious Freedom.

Which legislates the following:

- the end of tax-supported churches;
- religious tests for office are prohibited; and
- that no man "shall be compelled to frequent or support any religious worship."

After rejecting an amendment that would have included the words "Jesus Christ" in the body of the law, Jefferson's bill was passed on January 16, 1785. Celebrating its passage and its welcome around the world, Jefferson wrote:

It is comfortable to see the standard of reason at length erected, after so many Ages during which the human mind has been held in vassalage by kings, priests and nobles, and it is honorable for us to have produced the first legislature who has had the courage to declare that the reason of man may be trusted with the formation of his own opinions.

Jefferson's Act of Religious Freedom is the guiding influence on the Constitution and the Bill of Rights that, officially, separates church and state. As Jefferson put it: "But it does me no injury for my neighbor to say there are twenty gods, or no god. It neither picks my pocket nor breaks my leg."

That is from Jefferson's *Notes on the State of Virginia*, where he then goes on to give his account of Christian history: "Millions of innocent men, women, and children since the introduction of Christianity have been burnt, tortured, fined, imprisoned ... [all to] make one half of the world fools and the other half hypocrites [in order to] support roguery and error all over the earth."

And don't blame me. Write your angry letters to Jefferson. He's the one who said it. I'm only the messenger.

Despite your paltry claims that the Founders and Framers were devoted, practicing Orthodox Christians, inspired by the Holy Spirit to form a more perfect union, the truth, as it so often does, eludes your grasp.

Here's why:

• Not one of them believed that their souls would rot in Hell for eternity because they were not devout Calvinists, Catholics, Presbyterians, or Something Similar.
• Not one of them believed that they knew who created the universe. Or when.
• Not one of them believed they had been chosen as personal "instruments" in God's grand design for America.

Yet you go on and on, positive you recognize God's hand in the writing of the Constitution. So may I ask—disrespectfully—what God exactly are you talking about? Because you have so many.

There's the Old Testament gods. The merciful God who helped Sarah give birth when she was in her nineties. There's the milita-

ristic God who ordered the Hebrews to skin the Canaanites alive.*
There's the vengeful God who slaughtered every human being on
the planet with His forty days of rain, saving only Noah and his
family.

Then there's your New Testament God, or the Son of God—
now represented by so many denominations, sects, divisions, branches,
and offshoots it's hard to know which Jesus you're talking about.
To name just a few: Protestants, Lutherans, Congregationalists,
Adventists, Mormons, Methodists, Pentecostals, Charismatics,
Evangelicals, Roman Catholics, Greek Orthodox Catholics, Rus-
sian Orthodox Catholics, Ukrainian Orthodox Catholics, Baptists,
Southern Baptists, Anabaptists, and T. D. Jakes.

Finally, there's *your* God—the One who denounces evolution,
homosexual love, and stem cell research.

So let me know. You say God *is* in the Constitution. Fine. Tell
me which One.

Grace be with you all. Amen.

---

* What the Canaanites did to deserve that I'll never know.

CHAPTER 6

God and the Constitution, Part II:

Epistle to the Mormons

The Constitution of the United States is a glorious standard. It is founded in the wisdom of God. It is a heavenly banner . . . We say that God is true; that the Constitution of the United States is true; that the Bible is true; that the Book of Mormon is true; that the Book of Covenants is true; that Christ is true; that the ministering angels sent forth from God are true, and that we know that we have an house not made with hands, eternal in the heavens, whose builder and maker is God.

—*Teachings of the Prophet Joseph Smith*

I am begging you, please do not dismiss the peril that we are in, do not dismiss. Fall to your knees and pray to God to reveal to you what the hour is. Ask the dear Lord, our dear Lord, to show you who the man is that has the integrity, who has the connection, who will fall to his knees at the resolute desk. Who before he asks, doesn't think of a poll, but looks to the Constitution and the holy scriptures. Our Bible and the Constitution both come from God. They are both sacred scriptures.

—Glenn Beck,
radio pundit and Mormon convert, in a speech supporting
Ted Cruz for president during the 2016 primaries

Greetings Mormons

As a member of the Hebrew persuasion, I am not one to question the beliefs of another person's religion. After all, who am I to talk? We Jews were the ones who came up with no dairy with meat, long sideburns, and circumcision.

You have your dogmas, we have ours. In some cases, they are remarkably similar:

> You have your special, "magic" underwear. Orthodox Jews wear what is known as *tzitzit* under their shirts. Both undergarments express devotion to God.

> Your young people leave college for two years to do missionary work in foreign countries. Jewish young people often leave college for two years to come back and live with their parents.

> You oppose divorce because it goes against God's teachings. We oppose divorce because we have found it can put a man and a woman in a financial hole for the rest of their lives.

I have also read where Mormons believe not only that they are descendants of Abraham, Isaac, and Jacob, but also that they can trace their ancestry to one of the ten tribes of Israel—the lost tribe of Ephraim that found its way from Jerusalem to an unknown location in the Americas.

Which makes sense. Jews are notorious for getting lost. Once in Italy, I followed the wrong car into its owner's garage. But how exactly Jews from Palestine ended up in Utah is anyone's guess. And I for one do not see the resemblance. My only explanation is that your people must have stopped off in Sweden for a couple of centuries.

There are, of course, theological differences. As I understand it, when good Mormons die, they get to live on their own planet for all eternity. Jews, on the other hand, believe that when you're dead, you're dead.

Speaking of the dead, I was a little disturbed when I first heard about this "ritual" you had of baptizing more than 400,000 victims of the Holocaust into the Church of Jesus Christ of Latter-day Saints. But then when your elders explained that the dead always retained the right of either accepting their "baptism" or rejecting it, I was much relieved. On behalf of those surviving families, thank you for giving their deceased relatives that option.

Another difference between our two faiths: this business of your polygamy. Ever since Solomon, most Jews have figured out that one wife at a time was more than enough. In this regard, Mormon history is somewhat checkered. While the official policy of your church is to condemn the practice of your earlier members, I've read that there are still pockets of fundamentalist Mormons who cling to the old ways.

Why I'll never know. The concept of "many wives" is beyond my imagining, unless, of course, you live in a house with five bathrooms. And how your wives of yesteryear managed to remain civil to one another, under the same roof, is a miracle unto itself. Once, I ran into an old girlfriend at a wedding, and my wife threw a cup of champagne at me.

I bring up polygamy not to make you uncomfortable. Believe me, we Hebrews (or "stiff-necked people" as you call us in your Book of Mormon) have our own embarrassments. For example: $100,000 Bar Mitzvahs with paid celebrities like the Laker Girls.

No, this issue of plural wives becomes relevant today because of your original justification for it. Let me explain:

The Mormon Bible expressly forbids the right of any man to have more than one wife. And I quote:

Wherefore my Brethren, hear me and harken to the word of the Lord. For there shall not any man among you have save it be "one" wife and concubines he shall have none (Jacob 2:27, The Book of Mormon).

My question to you, then, is how did those first Mormons not only condone polygamy but practice it in such large numbers? Apparently, your founder, Joseph Smith, found a loophole—divine revelation. And on July 12, 1843, Joseph Smith received just such a revelation, which he dictated to his secretary, William Clayton:

> Wednesday 12th this A.M. I wrote a Revelation consisting of 10 pages in the order of the Priesthood, showing the design of Moses, David, and Solomon having many wives and concubines . . .

This revelation went on to state that plural wives "are given unto him to multiply and replenish the earth, according to [God's] commandment and to fulfill the Promise which was given by my father before the foundation of the world, and for their exaltation in the eternal worlds, that may bear the souls of men."

Beside the point is that later, Smith happened to take a fourteen-year-old girl, Helen Kimball, as his twenty-eighth wife.

So, if I've got this correct: whatever is written in the Bible can be contradicted and overruled by divine revelation. A particular of some importance to me that I will get back to later in this letter.

Anyway, I am certain that your young people of today are relieved to know that plural marriages have gone into the dustbins of outmoded beliefs along with the one that said the world is only six thousand years old and therefore dinosaur bones must have come from another planet.

Now, if I may, allow me to consider your views on the United States Constitution. From the founding of your religion up until the present, you have always made yourselves absolutely clear.

This from *Doctrines and Covenants*:

> In the Book of Mormon, the Prophets predicted that God would create an America so that the Lord's Church [yours]

could be built there. . . . And for this purpose have I [that is, God] established the Constitution of this land, by the hands of wise men [meaning the Framers] whom I raised up unto this purpose, and redeemed the land by the shedding of blood.

And this from one of your Apostles, Dallin H. Oaks:

. . . No wonder modern revelation says that God established the US Constitution and that it should be maintained for the rights and protection of all flesh . . .

And finally, this from the president of the Church of Jesus Christ of Latter-day Saints, Gordon B. Hinckley:

Both the Declaration of Independence and the Constitution of the United States were brought forth under the inspiration of God to establish and maintain the freedom of the people of this nation. I said it, and I believe it to be true. There is a miracle in its establishment that cannot be explained in any other way.

I think I've made my point. Or rather, you've made yours: the Constitution and the Declaration of Independence—as sacred as the Gospels—are divinely inspired. Which leads me to ask: How exactly did that work?

- Were all fifty-five Framers equally inspired? Or just the thirty-nine who signed?
- Were some Framers more inspired than others?
- Was Madison, say, who never missed a session, as inspired as Robert Morris, who missed almost all of them?
- Were the hundreds of men who ratified the Constitution also divinely inspired?

- Who first came up with "the three branches of government"? John Locke, James Madison, or God?
- Were the congressmen who reworked Madison's Bill of Rights in 1791 inspired as well?
- What about Charles Pinckney and Nathaniel Gorham when they cowrote the Fugitive Slave Act. Were they also inspired?
- Were all of them inspired when they decided to call each slave three-fifths of a person? Or had God left the room for a minute?
- Did the Framers *know* they were inspired? Did they know they were doing God's work?
- Did they retain their own identities? Their intellects? Their individual wills? Or were they merely conduits, messengers from a heavenly power?
- And if they *did* know they were divinely inspired, how come they never mentioned God in the Preamble or the Presidential Oath of Office?

I don't mean to needle, but I'd really like some answers. And don't tell me that God works in mysterious ways His wonders to perform. I get that. But you are making some serious claims for yourself and, as best as I can figure, they are based on your *own* divine inspiration.

You seem to know precisely what God is up to. You have His ear and He has yours. And not just a few of your more exalted members—your prophets, your presidents, and your apostles—but *every* Mormon, assuming he meets the moral requirements.

It is one of the basic tenets of your theology: your personal relationship with the Holy Ghost from whose Spirit you receive revelation for your own direction, your family's, and, it seems, our nation's.

When a man speaketh by the power of the Holy Ghost, the power of the Holy Ghost carrieth it unto the hearts of the children of men.

If only the rest of us were so lucky. Jews too speak to God. Only the other day, I happened to call on Him while passing a kidney stone. But hearing back—at least the same day—is another story.

Again, let me say I am not writing to question your faith. That is a matter between your God and your conscience—the very essence of your First Amendment rights.

Except when those rights might potentially encroach on mine do I feel compelled to express concerns. And especially troubling is my recent discovery of yet another prophecy by your founder, the Prophet Joseph Smith Jr.

I refer to "The Rider on the White Horse" prophecy. For those unfamiliar with it, let me try to explain as objectively as possible. The reference to "The Rider on the White Horse" comes from the Book of Revelations:

> Then I saw heaven opened, and behold, a white horse! The one sitting on it is called Faithful and True, and in righteousness he judges and makes war. His eyes are like a flame of fire, and on his head are many diadems, and he has a name written that no one knows but himself. He is clothed in a robe dipped in blood, and the name by which he is called is The Word of God.

Smith's prophecy—made in Illinois in 1843 and based on that portion of the Book of Revelations—goes like this: Mormons, Smith prophesized, "would go to the Rocky Mountains and be a great and mighty people . . ." and that "the United States Constitution would 'hang by a thread' until restored by that Rider on the White Horse."

Perhaps Smith saw himself as that man on the White Horse when he ran for president of the United States in 1844 as an independent candidate, advocating the overthrow of the US government in favor of a Mormon-dominated country.

Not that any of you dare talk like that today,* but the precedent has been set, and who's to say that at this very minute there isn't some Mormon (or like-minded fellow) slouching his way to the White House to fulfill the prophecy Smith failed at: to repair our "tattered" Constitution and establish, as Smith said, "a theodemocracy where God and the people hold the power to conduct the affairs of men in righteousness."

So, yes, it worries me—your apocalyptic vision of the United States and its Constitution—and the role you have chosen for yourself to defend and protect it.

Especially when that is coupled with (as I mentioned earlier) your unyielding faith that God is primed to reveal Himself to you at a moment's notice.

I mean, how can an ordinary guy like me even challenge your interpretation of the Constitution when you claim God is on *your* side? Two against one, I call it, and frankly un-American.

One last comment before I close. The history of America is littered with the crap of politicians and pundits, prophets and preachers who speak for God. It's a sad and sorry list:

In 1692, in Salem, Massachusetts, Cotton Mather—Puritan minister—engineered the executions of twenty people (fourteen women) accused of being witches. All in the name of God.

In 1707, the Governor of North Carolina defended the taking of Indian land this way: "It at other times pleased All Mighty God to send unusual Sickness amongst them [the Native Americans] as the Small pox, etc., to lessen their Numbers ... I shall further add one late more immediate Example of God's more immedi-

* In 2012, when then-candidate Mitt Romney was asked about this "White Horse prophecy," he replied categorically, "No comment."

ate Hand in making a consumption upon some Indian nations in North Carolina.

In 1739, a Baptist minister in Rhode Island explained his followers' good fortune this way: "By driving out and killing the Indians as punishment for their sins, God was pleased to make ready a place prepared as an asylum for our early settlers."

In 1820, an editorial defending slavery argued that Africans were descendants of Ham and "their slavery an accomplishment of Noah's prediction" which was *"divinely inspired"* [italics mine], thus "the present condition of the African is inevitable; all efforts to extinguish black slavery are idle . . ."

More recently, we have this example from the Reverend Jerry Falwell, explaining to Pastor Pat Robertson God's motives for allowing the tragedy of 9/11:

> I really believe that the pagans and the abortionists and the feminists and the gays and the lesbians who are actively trying to make that an alternative lifestyle, the ACLU, People for the American Way—all of them who have tried to secularize America—I point the finger in their face, and say, "You helped this happen."
>
> To which Robertson responded: "Well, I totally concur."

Oh, and just one other question before I forget. If Thomas Jefferson was divinely inspired when he wrote the Declaration of Independence, as you say, what was he when he wrote the following letter to a General Alexander Smyth on January 17, 1825?

Dear Sir,

I have duly received four proof sheets of your explanation of the Apocalypse with your letters of December 29th and January 8th; in the last of which you request that so soon as I shall be of opinion that the explanation you have given is correct I would express it in a letter to you. From this you must be so good as to excuse me because I make it an invariable rule to decline ever giving opinions on new publications in any case whatever. No man on earth has less taste or talent for criticism than myself and least and last of all should I undertake to criticize works on the Apocalypse. It is between fifty and sixty years since I read it **and I then considered it as merely the ravings of a maniac no more worthy nor capable of explanation than the incoherences of our own nightly dreams . . .**

And there, I believe, you have the real Thomas Jefferson. Divinely uninspired.

Peace be with you. Amen.

CHAPTER 7

The Writing of the Constitution:

Notes from the Constitutional Convention as Recorded by Billey, Slave to James Madison, May 6 to September 17, 1787

If they [slaves] were of our own complexion,
much of the difficulty would be removed.

—James Madison

Introduction

I first came across the name of "Billey" (no last name) in Lynne Cheney's affectionate biography of James Madison, *A Life Reconsidered.*

Billey appears briefly as the slave who accompanied Madison to Philadelphia in 1787 (doing, no doubt, the sort of things slaves did for one's master) during Madison's four-month stay at the Constitutional Convention.

A couple of hundred pages later, I was to learn that Billey was educated, well read, and far more literate than you would expect of a slave at that time. How exactly Mrs. Cheney relayed that information I'll withhold in the interests of good storytelling. Let me just say that my curiosity about Billey had been thoroughly piqued, and as I struggled to find a new way to describe the "writing" of the Constitution and Madison's critical part in it,* I thought it might be

---

* For how could any book on the Constitution not comment on its authorship?

interesting to imagine this: What if Billey, like Madison, had kept a journal of those days? And, even better, what if such a journal had not only been found but I was in sole possession of it?

Since, of course, that was impossible, I decided to write it myself. So here it is, for what it's worth: "Notes from the Constitutional Convention as Recorded by Billey, Slave to James Madison, May 6 to September 17, 1787."

May 6th, 1787
This is my first entry into my diary which I intend to keep as a record for posterity so that future generations—most especially my own—may learn of one slave's views of the events now occurring at this most crucial time in the new nation's history.

For the record: my name is Billey, and since there is no exact evidence of my birth, I think I am about 38 years old.

I was born at the seat of the Madison family home in the Piedmont region of Virginia, where my mother Jane (passed these many years) worked in their tobacco fields.

It was because of her sacrifice and encouragement that at an early age I began to show a capacity for learning. At about 16 years of age, I became personal servant to Mr. Madison, who was then a sickly boy and needed full-time observation and caring.

And it is he, Mr. Madison, who I must thank for allowing me attendance at his tutoring, access to his library and many books, and the opportunity to speak, read, and write far above my station.

It is, I assume, because of my level of literacy that Mr. Madison selected me to accompany him to Philadelphia, where he believed I could prove helpful, as it was his intention as a delegate from Virginia to keep a detailed record of the daily events at the Convention—given its historical significance.

While I would not have the ability to transcribe those

notes personally, it was Mr. Madison's thought that I had the necessary skills in their copying, filing, and organization.

That, of course, was in addition to my regular chores of washing and pressing his clothes, polishing his boots, of which he was most particular, running his errands, and the dispensing of the various remedies, tonics, elixirs, et cetera, that Mr. Madison took regularly to protect himself against his assortment of illnesses, real and imaginary, to which he was prone.

It is also my secret intention, if I may so admit, that at the conclusion of the Convention, whenever that may be, to ask Mr. Madison if he could see his way to granting me my freedom based on my enterprise, diligence, and devotion. A freedom, it is obvious to note, I most fervently desire.

May 7th, 1787

After many treacherous miles, Mr. Madison and I arrive, finally, in Philadelphia. Its streets, worse than country roads, are an irregular mix of gravel and unpaved stones. Mr. Madison, as short as he is, bumped his head thrice on the carriage ceiling within the last mile alone.

Mr. Madison has reserved rooms at the boardinghouse owned by Mrs. House, a widow, who lives there with her daughter Mrs. Trist—also a widow. The sheer number of widows per square foot in Philadelphia must give a married man pause, but as Mr. Madison and I are both unattached, the fact is of little consequence.

Mr. Madison first stayed with Mrs. House when he served here as a member of the Continental Congress, and he and Mrs. House, as well as her daughter, are old and good friends—not that that prevents Mrs. House from charging an arm and a leg for her rooms and three meals a day.

As there is but one hotel in the city, and Philadelphia has not much decent lodgings elsewhere, Mr. Madison is fortunate to have such spacious quarters: a bedroom and adjoining sitting room large enough for a good-sized desk. Many delegates—not expected to arrive in weeks—will be forced to sleep two to a bed. Which I suppose is the source for that quip that politics makes strange bedfellows.

May 8th, 1787

My first night in Philadelphia was spent accompanying Mr. Madison to dinner at the residence of Dr. Benjamin Franklin. He lives in a three-storey brick house, the first floor of which could fit easily into the entry hall of Mr. Madison's plantation home at Montpelier.

The guests at this dinner, beside Mr. Madison and the host, included members of the Pennsylvania delegation, who I had the opportunity to identify and observe as I was requested during the evening to attend to the elderly Dr. Franklin. In partnership with one of Dr. Franklin's own servants, an irritable octoroon named Will, I had the responsibility of taking the right side of Dr. Franklin while Will took the left as we would lift, keep steady, and transport Dr. Franklin from one location to the other.

As I would learn, it was a formidable guest list—each man more resplendent in his appearance than the "last." There was one named Gouverneur Morris who they called "Guv." Mr. Morris was distinguished by the fact that he had one good leg and one peg. I was not sure of the wood, but I guessed it was oak, as pine would be too ordinary for a gentleman of his stature. Rumor has it that the leg was shot off when an angry husband caught Mr. Morris running from his wife's bedroom. In my opinion, a moment's pleasure is hardly worth the lifetime loss of a limb. An hour and a half, perhaps, is another story.

There was also a man named Mr. James Wilson, who I detected had been born in Scotland. His eyeglasses were as thick as his accent. Mr. Wilson's spectacles were so thick, in fact, I am certain that at a distance greater than five feet, Mr. Wilson could not have identified me as negro.

The last of the attendees was a Mr. Robert Morris (no relation to Gouverneur Morris), who was thought by some to be the richest man in the country—with more acres to his name than God.

It was a relaxed and convivial evening, and when the gentlemen were not discussing their plans for the Convention, they were regaled by stories from Dr. Franklin, whose body may have grown old and heavy, but whose mind remained alert and lively.

Many of Dr. Franklin's tales involved detailed escapades with sundry French women (many at the same time)—the images of which I feared would haunt my dreams for years.

Dr. Franklin also read from a mock proposal he had once written to the Royal Academy of Brussels,* suggesting they take up a serious inquiry as to the causes and cures of farting. As the men (with the exception of Mr. Madison) laughed themselves red in the face, Dr. Franklin continued with his solution to the problem: a drug added to one's food in order to render such breaking of wind as agreeable as perfume. The laughter continued unabated.

I have often been amazed at the low level of humor among distinguished white men. Tonight was no exception.

On the walk home, I asked Mr. Madison if he thought the night had gone well for him. He replied that it had. I was much appreciative to be taken so into his confidence as he explained that the Pennsylvania delegation—along with Virginia's—had arrived at an agenda to ensure the complete transformation of the present form of government.

---

* Editor's note: A scientific spoof written by Franklin on May 19, 1780.

As he put it: "If things go our way, the government we now have will be no longer."

What import that may have had for me I did not ask, since I had no government. All I knew was that the government had me.

May 13th, 1787

Today, the sounds of cannon fire greeted the arrival into the city of General George Washington.

The General—who was to stay at the same lodgings with Mr. Madison—arrived here before noon with a caravan of carriages, one for the General and three for his servants and luggage.

After a quick tour given to him by Mr. Madison and our landlady Mrs. House, the General decided he would stay elsewhere.*

I was not surprised. Mrs. House's lodgings are much too modest for a man as grand as the General. He would need one room just to hang up his uniforms.

I have seen the General on numerous occasions, and each time have come away impressed with his bearing, stature, and sense of authority. Even his slaves believe they are better than anyone else's.

May 14th, 1787

Today was to be the first day of the start of the Constitutional Convention. Yet by 10:00 this morning, the only delegates to have arrived, besides Mr. Madison, were General Washington and Edmund Randolph, Governor of Virginia.

Nonetheless, Mr. Madison arranged to visit the site of the

---

* Editor's note: Washington ended up staying at the mansion of the financier, and his good friend and sometime business associate, Robert Morris.

Convention—Independence Hall—and asked me to accompany him. There, we were admitted to the Assembly Room on the first floor, where the delegates were to meet. It was not as spacious as I had imagined, with one desk abutting the next. I tried to picture it crowded with men—large and beefy men at that—smoking their cigars, spitting out their excess tobacco juice, and passing their water—God knows where. I thought of Dr. Franklin's drug to perfume farts, and if ever there was a need for such an invention, this would be the time.

Mr. Madison pointed to the desk where he intended to sit, front and center and adjacent to the platform where the presiding officer was to stand. I placed, as he had asked, fresh quills, ink, and sand for blotting inside the desk. It was his intention to take exact notes of everything that was said for the duration of the Convention—a feat I would have deemed impossible for any man other than Mr. Madison.

As we were about to leave, Mr. Madison stopped and with some pride told me that it was in this very room the Declaration of Independence had been signed. Mr. Madison keeps a copy of it framed in his office in Montpelier, and I have from time to time perused the document, especially struck by the phrase that "all men are created equal." What, I wondered, did that mean?

Still, I could not help but admire the rhetoric of it and would happily frame a Declaration of Independence on my own wall as soon as I got myself a wall.

May 18th, 1787

This afternoon, after session, Alexander Hamilton, Mr. Madison's colleague, arrived from New York. Mr. Hamilton, at least for the time, plans on staying here at Mrs. House's in separate quarters down the hall from Mr. Madison.

After a brief get-together with Mr. Madison, Mr. Hamilton, who is to be a member of the important Rules Committee, hurried off to the City Tavern to meet with delegates who gather there regularly for drink and talk.

That Mr. Madison and Mr. Hamilton are so joined in purpose attests to their like-minded ideas, for in style, character, and personality they are complete opposites. Where Mr. Madison is quiet and soft-spoken, placid if not stoic, reserved if not shy, Mr. Hamilton is gregarious, worldly, and self-assured.

Where Mr. Madison is plain, Mr. Hamilton is most handsome with features a pretty woman might envy.

Where Mr. Madison wears only black coats and breeches day in and day out, Mr. Hamilton is debonair in dress even to the point of frilly.

And where Mr. Madison is modest, Mr. Hamilton is exceedingly vain. Commenting on that vanity once to Mr. Thomas Jefferson—in my presence—Mr. Madison said of Mr. Hamilton, "He is so vain, he carries a locket with a snippet of his own hair inside."

May 28th, 1787

Before retiring for the night, Mr. Madison enjoys a simple refreshment—usually warm milk and two plain buttered crackers. Tonight as he chewed, swallowed, and digested his crackers, savoring each bite as if dining on an elaborate entrée prepared by one of Mr. Jefferson's master chefs, Mr. Madison described Dr. Benjamin Franklin's grand entrance today at the Convention.

Because walking Philadelphia's irregular cobblestone streets disturbed his kidney stones, Dr. Franklin was carried in a sedan chair designed by Dr. Franklin himself. The chair, situated on a small platform with flexible rods, was held by four sturdy prisoners of the nearby Walnut Street Jail, apparently freed for the afternoon for just such purpose.

Since one of the prisoners was much taller than the other three, the chair, from time to time, tilted precariously to one side, and there were fears that Dr. Franklin might topple out. But to the huzzahs of the crowd that had gathered to watch the spectacle, Dr. Franklin arrived in one piece, safe and sound.

May 29th, 1787

Today, the Convention busied itself with the adoption of the Rules. While 19 were passed, there were only two that Mr. Madison described as essential. The first was that the entire proceedings of the Convention—from debates to votes—would be held in complete secrecy. So, as Mr. Madison explained, there would be no outside political pressure brought to bear on the delegates. To that end, all windows and doors were to be sealed as well.

The second rule stated that the delegates could, at any point, insist on as many reconsiderations as they wished. To put it another way: nothing was ever to be finally agreed on, no matter the earlier voting, until the very end of the Convention.

Even to someone like myself—unfamiliar with the practices of such a Convention—this rule struck me as unusual as it protected, if not rewarded, backroom deals, collusion, inconsistency, and confusion.

Which is why, perhaps, the reason for the first rule.

May 30th, 1787

This day after supper, I was burnishing the silver for Mrs. House when a gentleman of great importance, Virginia Governor Edmund Randolph, came to call on Mr. Madison. Since neither of the gentlemen paid me no mind, I continued my work, remaining to overhear their conversation.

They discussed the various and sundry resolutions that

the Governor was to introduce the following morning at the Convention.*

These resolutions had been devised by Mr. Madison during the previous months and were already known to the delegates from Virginia.

It was decided between them—Mr. Madison and Governor Randolph—that it would be the Governor, not Mr. Madison, who would introduce these resolutions to the Convention.

Governor Randolph was a hearty bear of a man with great speaking powers. Mr. Madison, on the other hand, was an indifferent orator and given to an innate shyness—perhaps because Mr. Madison had always been sensitive to his lack of height. One of the smallest men in the Commonwealth, Mr. Madison had been referred to (behind his back) as His Littleness, a name that unfortunately followed him here to Philadelphia.

Those of us in servitude to him at Montpelier had our own private (most private) joke that Mr. Madison was so diminutive, he was always the last person on the plantation to know that it was raining.

The Resolutions that Governor Randolph was to introduce—in the hopes that they would serve as a blueprint for the rest of the Convention—were the following:

The government was to consist of three branches: Legislative, Executive, and Judiciary.

The Legislature would be made up of two houses: the lower to be elected by the people—which included white men with property—and a higher, second house, which would be selected by the lower one. They would make the laws. Which the Judiciary were to interpret and the Executive was to enforce.

It was Mr. Madison's concept—influenced by his readings

---

* Editor's note: This is what became known as the Virginia Plan.

into the histories of republics from the Greeks and Romans to the present—that these three branches would provide the necessary checks and balances on each other so that one branch would not come to dominate or tyrannize the rest.

All in all, it seemed to me a most reasonable form of government allowing those like myself to sleep easy at night, knowing that the country was in the hands of a few eminent men who knew so much more than the rest of us.

While Mr. Madison's plan was not in any way radical in its concept, what would come as a surprise to some of the delegates was the fact that they would be hearing for the first time that the true purpose of the Convention was not to amend the Articles of Confederation (as previously supposed) but to write a new and fundamentally different Constitution.

After Governor Randolph departed for home—fully rehearsed—Mr. Madison retired early in anticipation of the important day ahead. I then laid out Mr. Madison's wardrobe for the morrow, one of my easier tasks, since Mr. Madison never varied in his choice of attire.

I then stepped outside to smoke my pipe—a pleasure I had developed since I was a boy, as had many negroes who grew up on tobacco plantations. To some, smoking tobacco is considered exceedingly vile and nasty. To them I say: not nearly so much as the picking of it.

It was a clear night. The sky filled with stars. And so quiet you could hear the distant howls of cats in heat. And men folk too.

June 8th, 1787

Over the years, Mr. Madison has made it a habit of keeping his feelings to himself. Never did I see any open displays of anger or joy, for that matter. Whatever Mr. Madison was thinking never made it to his face.

But having spent so many years in his company, I could

sense that today things had not gone as he would have liked. My suspicions were confirmed when Mr. Madison told Mrs. House that he would not be dining that night and asked instead that I bring a tray to his rooms.

When I arrived with the tray—a pot of tea, two slices of bread, a wedge of cheese with olives—Mr. Madison was at his desk transcribing today's notes. Afterwards, he went right to bed, even earlier than usual.

It was difficult then to resist the temptation not to read what Mr. Madison had set down on paper, if only to determine the cause of his discomfort. Within the span of two pages, I had found my answer:

Earlier in the Convention, as part of his original plan, Mr. Madison had introduced a clause that would give the national legislature the right to negate all and any laws passed by the states.

Now, as one who played no part in this government, I had not made it a practice to study its politics, figuring those laws which most affected me would make themselves known soon enough. But in this instance, I could tell that this clause of Mr. Madison's was not likely to prove popular, especially among the states. Still, it was dear to his heart and one that Mr. Madison had pursued with some vigor.

Only the other day, he explained his reasoning in a lengthy conversation with Mr. Hamilton: such a clause was necessary in a new government, he argued, to control the excessive power of the states. Mr. Madison had seen the ignorant brutality of a local state legislature led by one rabble-rousing orator,* selfish in his own interests and not the people's.

In defense of that clause, Mr. Madison rose today to address the delegates, and I copy now his remarks that he himself transcribed from his own speech: "The order and

---

* Editor's note: Reference to Patrick Henry.

harmony of the political system will be destroyed unless the national legislature can negate* the laws of each individual state."

Unfortunately, Mr. Madison did not prove persuasive, and the clause was defeated by a vote of 7 states against and only 3 for.

After tidying up, I looked in on Mr. Madison—fast asleep. Rather than calm and at peace, his face showed a grim determination as if, even in his dreams, he were working on some way to resurrect his most cherished law.

For supper, Mrs. House gave me the meal that Mr. Madison had no appetite for: a mutton roast with French beans.

Later, while digesting that meal, I came to better sympathize with the nature of Mr. Madison's internal complexities. Fortunately, by morning, my grief had dissipated.

June 11th, 1787

It has grown suffocating hot. When Mr. Madison returned from the Convention today, I could see on his forehead where beads of sweat had crystalized the white powder he used to color his hair.

Later, as I prepared his bath, adding salt and vinegar to the cool water to reduce the bites from the ever-present Philadelphia flies—bites, I may add, that were in places Mr. Madison could not reach to scratch himself—I asked about this day's proceedings.

Mr. Madison informed me that there had been debates and votes taken on the issue of representation in the lower house of Congress. Otherwise, he seemed hesitant to explain further.

I suppose it is for that reason I decided, as I organized his papers, to read Mr. Madison's notes for myself. As I understood the situation: the problem facing the delegates was how

---

* Editor's note: That is, veto.

to determine the number of representatives proportioned to each state. After discarding the idea that representatives would be decided by revenue (or taxes) as impractical, there emerged a compromise between the Northern and Southern states by which the allocation of seats in the House of Representatives (as they were calling it) was to be based on population. Then came this part that quickly caught my attention: "other persons" were each to be counted as three-fifths of one person. This resolution passed by a vote of 9 to 2 with only New Jersey and Delaware objecting.

Clearly, the mention of "other persons," in contrast to those who were "white and free," referred to slaves. Why they couldn't call us by our real name I have no idea. And, while not discounting the honor to be mentioned by such distinguished people in such an historic document, I was not certain one way or the other if it did me good or harm.

As for the mathematics of the thing—it never being my best subject—I was left more confused than clarified.

If I was three-fifths of a person and my sister Stucky was also three-fifths of a person, did we together add up to one whole person with a fifth left over? And what about my second cousin, Anthony, who was missing one leg and one arm— the result of a mill accident? Did the absence of 50 percent of his extremities reduce his three-fifths by that amount? It was a great puzzlement all around.

Reading further, I noticed that Mr. Madison did not participate in the debates. Which came as no surprise. Mr. Madison has always been most quiet on the subject of slavery, except when practicing it himself.

Later when I looked in on Mr. Madison, he was in his bed, tossing and turning, fighting a losing battle against the terrible heat that came blasting through his open window like a furnace.

Lucky for me I got to sleep in the basement.

June 14th, 1787

Since childhood, Mr. Madison has been afflicted with an illness that is difficult to diagnose but has in common many of the symptoms of epileptic seizures: loss of consciousness, trembling of the extremities, et cetera. This comes unexpectedly and then is gone again within minutes. It is an illness, name unknown, that has been a cause of alarm for both Mr. Madison and his family.

One such episode occurred a few years ago, one morning, as Mr. Madison was about to commence shaving himself, as was his practice every third day, not being especially hairy. For obvious reasons, since that day, Mr. Madison had entrusted that task to me.

I cannot help but feel flattered that Mr. Madison places such trust in me that I have been assigned this delicate responsibility. It is not every slave owner that will trust a colored man with a straight razor.

This is especially significant when you consider that Mr. Madison's grandfather, Mr. Ambrose Madison, was poisoned to death by one of his slaves, no relation to me. Thank God.

I mention all this as a way of explaining how this morning I came to stand behind Mr. Madison, putting hot towels to his face. After which I applied my special shaving cream—a mixture of soap cake, butter, and warm water—brushing his whiskers, though few and far between, in a swirling motion until each individual hair was properly moisturized by the rich and foaming lather.

After a few hones of the steel razor—of English design, a gift from Mr. Madison's father—I began to shave, keeping my first three fingers on the back of the blade, though I often changed my grip, adjusting to each new area as I proceeded.

I always start on the right side of Mr. Madison's face, drawing his tender skin upward to make a smooth shaving surface.

To take Mr. Madison's mind off the procedure, I asked, quite casually, about the Convention and its progress.

As I skillfully moved the razor from his cheek to under his right jaw, Mr. Madison informed me of the disagreements between the small and large states. He was not at all pleased with a resolution* from the New Jersey delegation with a plan to counter his own.

"Imagine," he said, barely moving his mouth as I drew down his upper lip, "that after all this time, there are delegates who still think we are here merely to redo the Articles of Confederation."

"Hard to believe," I responded, concentrating on the crevice below his nose.

"Indeed," said Mr. Madison, "the thought of leaving the provision of 'one State, one vote' unaltered and denying Congress the power to tax exceeds all foolishness."

I assented as if I understood exactly what he meant while I moved dexterously to the left side of his face, holding my one hand just above his ear.

"Imbecility," Mr. Madison muttered.

"I trust you will set them straight," I said congenially.

"I will dismember this New Jersey plan of theirs piece by piece. And when I am done," he continued, "New Jersey will not know what hit them."

That Mr. Madison was now confiding in me as he would almost an equal filled me with no end of satisfaction.

I was now coming to the most difficult part of my endeavor: Mr. Madison's neck. My fierce concentration was essential when approaching the aforesaid surface. One nick and I could find myself back at Montpelier storing horse manure for the winter.

I now raised Mr. Madison's head, elevated his chin, and

---

* Editor's note: What was to be known as the New Jersey Plan.

made one final pass over his Adam's apple, against the grain, and I was done.

To conclude, I wiped his face with a wet towel, then dabbed his cheeks with an eau de cologne that Mr. Jefferson had sent him from Paris. His skin felt as smooth as a baby's behind.

Mr. Madison stepped out from the chair. "Thank you, Billey," he said.

Whenever Mr. Madison called me by my name, I knew he was pleased with my work and, smiling widely, I responded, "You are most welcome, Mr. Madison."

Within the hour, Mr. Madison was on his way to Independence Hall and the business of the Convention. And from the look on his face as he left, I could foretell when he got there that New Jersey would wish it had never been born.

July 4th, 1787

The Convention is in recess for the holiday. Mr. Madison has given me the day off—well, not the whole day, but a goodly portion of it.

Today, Philadelphia is loud in celebration. Fireworks. Speechifying. Church bells that won't shut up.

There was a parade this morning. A marching band. Militia on horseback. Butchers in white aprons leading oxen to their slaughter. And up front—city politicians smiled and waved at people in the crowd, pretending they knew who they were.

By night, the taverns filled to overflowing. Men drunk like nobody's business.

I miss the quiet 4ths back home. I miss my sister Stucky. Also Lucy, George, Hannah, and Bob.

I miss the supper. The biscuits and the gravy and the parts of the pig that people up here never heard of.

Independence Day. Too bad it comes but once a year.

July 23rd, 1787

Today, the New Hampshire delegation finally arrives. About which Mr. Madison says, "I am not altogether certain that anyone knew they were missing."

July 26th to August 3rd, 1787

After turning all the business of the Convention to a committee called the Committee of Detail,* the Convention adjourned for 10 days.

The adjournment could not have come at a better time as the heat grew stifling, and the Philadelphia flies bigger, more numerous, and more persistent. Of all the living things in the world God did not need to take onto Noah's Ark, these flies head the list.

Many delegates, who were too far to go home, left for cooler climates. However, Mr. Madison stayed at the boardinghouse, working at his desk every day—reading, writing, and planning for the weeks ahead, always concentrating on the business of the Constitution. Despite the flies, the heat, and his vulnerability to sickness, Mr. Madison's determination never flagged.

I only hope that this Constitution he is giving birth to— so to speak—will not be so dependent in the future on men like him. For there I see is the danger: the politicians who will come after Mr. Madison will not have half his wit and none of his conviction. And when that day comes, as I am sure it will, the nation will end up in as big a shambles as it is now.

---

* Editor's note: This committee consisted of James Wilson (Pennsylvania), Edmund Randolph (Virginia), John Rutledge (South Carolina), and Oliver Ellsworth (Connecticut).

August 4th, 1787

Tonight, Mr. Madison hosted a small dinner party at his lodgings for Mr. John Rutledge of South Carolina and Governor Edmund Randolph, two of the members of the Committee of Detail who have been working through the recess, trying to stitch together the various resolutions and articles—finished and unfinished—into a first draft of the Constitution.

For Mr. Madison, the dinner was all business as he sought to learn, in advance, what the Committee might propose the following day to the Convention as a whole.

As I was engaged in clearing dishes, refilling wineglasses, and swatting the Philadelphia flies that would swoop and settle onto heads of the participants, I was able to glean most of what the Committee of Detail had accomplished through the conversation of its chairman, Mr. Rutledge.

In an effort to end the impasse that the Convention had found itself in, the Committee had reached several compromises: (1) It had granted states certain rights previously denied under Mr. Madison's original plan, and (2) It specifically enumerated Congressional powers, thereby preventing Congress from enacting any laws beyond those named.

Throughout the presentation, Mr. Madison remained stoic. But knowing him as I did, I could tell by his most minuscule gestures that he was not pleased: arranging spoons, forks, and knives equidistant from each other, dabbing his napkin to his lips unnecessarily, and smoothing the little hair on his head to a point above his forehead.

Immediately after Mr. Rutledge and Governor Randolph left, Mr. Madison was at his desk working to draft what I would learn was a new resolution to counter what had just been proposed.

After Mr. Madison retired for the evening, I read Mr. Madison's addition to the enumeration of powers: Congress shall have the power "to make all laws which shall be necessary and proper for carrying into Execution the Foregoing Powers vested in this Constitution in the Government of the United States, or in any Department or Officer thereof."

Even someone as uninformed as myself understood that with that one clause, Mr. Madison had given Congress all the "necessary" powers it would need.

Later that night, I looked in on Mr. Madison before retiring. He was peacefully asleep, the faint trace of a self-congratulatory smile on his little lips.

August 12th, 1787

Today is Sunday. It is a day that Mr. Madison usually spends quietly letter writing, reading, and taking long walks. Not that there is that much else to do in Philadelphia on Sunday. Nor the rest of the week, for that matter. Philadelphia is so boring a city that many delegates have begun sending for their wives.

But today is different. And I accompany Mr. Madison on the five-mile carriage ride to "The Hills"—Mr. Robert Morris's mansion in the country outside Philadelphia. It is a sprawling estate with separate housing for at least a half dozen slaves in Mr. Morris's employment. Not a large number in comparison to Mr. Madison, but for me a surprising amount for a businessman from the North.

Mr. Madison is there to attend a supper hosted by Mr. Morris for several delegates to the Convention. These include General George Washington, James Wilson of Pennsylvania, a Mr. William Blount of North Carolina, Rufus King of Massachusetts, and Charles Pinckney of South Carolina, all of whom were present when we arrived.

While the event seemed on the surface to be a social occasion, it would later be made clear that it was strictly political, having to do with critical votes in the upcoming sessions.

Mr. Morris and his staff had prepared a feast for his guests. A sit-down dinner with three courses but many dishes: Besides the nuts, dried fruits, and pickles, there was fresh-caught perch, fried rabbit, kidney pie, fricassée of chicken, and seared loins of boar meat. All accompanied by flagons of red wine, ale, hard cider, and beer. For dessert there was a huge whiskey cake made from one of George Washington's family recipes.

Mr. Madison, who is moderate in his appetite, ate well but not—like the others—overly well.

As I was quickly put to work (for no reason that I could see, Mr. Morris having ample slaves on hand) clearing, washing, and stocking the endless supply of dishes that streamed from the kitchen to the dining table and back again, I was privy to portions of the gentlemen's conversations.

Much of it in the beginning centered on a tour taken the previous day to the iron foundry in New Jersey owned by the host, Mr. Morris. Mr. Blount, delegate from North Carolina, had been especially impressed by the amount of nails produced there and the efficiency of the negro laborers, as well as the boys, as young as 12, who were able to turn out as many as 15 pounds per day.

Mr. Morris was humorously questioned as to his profits from such an enterprise, which he in turn playfully refused to divulge.

After supper, the men adjourned to the outside porch for cigars, brandies, and Spanish ports. And it was then that the true purpose of the festivities was revealed.

Apparently, a critical point had been reached at the Convention—an impasse between the large and small states over representation in Congress. (Whatever Mr. Madison had done to dismantle the New Jersey Plan had only angered the small states, which now threatened to quit the Convention entirely.)

To head off this revolt, a committee had been formed, with Elbridge Gerry of Massachusetts as its chairman, that was soon to announce its recommendation—a compromise suggested by the Connecticut delegation.*

This compromise, as I understood it, was this: there would be two bodies of Congress. A lower house, based on representation, and an upper house (called the Senate after the old one in Rome), with an equal number of representatives per state with its members elected by the state legislatures. A solution favored by the small states but that had been objectionable to Mr. Madison.

It soon became apparent that the men lounging there with their cigars and liquor favored the compromise and were now urging Mr. Madison—the most prominent resister—to go along with them.

Mr. Madison tried to stand his ground until General Washington—who had been silent most of the day—said that the Convention was at serious risk should Delaware and New Jersey, among others, carry out their threats to abandon the Convention. Faced with the choice between an unsatisfactory compromise and the termination of the Convention itself, Mr. Madison reluctantly agreed to support the measure.

It was a long carriage ride back to Philadelphia, made longer by Mr. Madison's complete and utter silence. Out of the corner of my eye, I could see him staring straight ahead, unblinking and deeply troubled, as if envisioning some future crisis that might befall this new nation he was working so hard to construct.

Then again, it could have been the fried rabbit, as yet unsettled in his stomach.

---

* Editor's note: Which would be known as the Connecticut Compromise.

August 14th, 1787

The terrible heat continues. Tempers are on edge. Debates grow contentious. Personalities displace the issues. There is a rumor that one delegate from Georgia will need to sell a slave to pay his hotel bill. General Washington grinds his gums.

And amid the resolutions regarding a Standing Army, control of State Militias, and the salaries Congressmen are to pay themselves (some suggesting as high as $4.00 a day), there is still talk from delegates to disband the Convention and admit to failure.

Meanwhile, the buzzing swarms of Philadelphia flies that have plagued us all—coloreds and whites equally—multiply in size and number. Now, these are no ordinary houseflies, or horseflies, either. No sir, these are flies that are an entire breed unto themselves. Old Testament flies right up there with such vindictive pestilence as locusts and lice.*

Their size alone distinguishes them. Seeing one, you are not sure to swat at it or pull a knife.

Worst of all, these creatures are as common at night as they are in the daytime. A man asleep is as good a place for them to rest as a rotten orange.

So—to ensure Mr. Madison's much-needed, uninterrupted sleep, I have today fashioned a tent-like apparatus of lace netting that fits over Mr. Madison's bed and for which he is most appreciative.

I only wonder if by making myself indispensable in this way, I hurt my case later when I request my freedom.

It is a thought that keeps me awake this night while Mr. Madison snores away in peace.

---

* Editor's note: Two of the ten plagues God visited on Egypt.

August 24th, 1787

It was late at night, long after Mr. Madison had gone to sleep, when assembling his day's notes I discovered that the session had been spent on the slave trade. Or as the delegates preferred to call it, "the importation of such persons."

There were those delegates who wished to end it immediately and those, mostly from the South, who insisted they needed to enjoy another 20 years to import slaves from Africa, tax free. After which, they would agree to shut down the trade once and for all.

I could only marvel at the optimism of these men who trusted the slave trader—who made his fortune in the buying and selling of human souls—to suddenly shut down his business because of this paper law they were now enacting.

After what seemed a dispassionate debate (which also involved much talk about navigation), three New England states joined the Southern ones to extend the slave trade (by a vote of 7 to 4) until 1808.

Virginia and Mr. Madison voted against. Speaking to the delegates in opposition, Mr. Madison said this, as he himself recorded:

> . . . that 20 years will produce all the mischief that can be apprehended from the liberty to import slaves. So long a term will be more dishonorable to the national character than to say nothing about it in the Constitution.

Reading that, I must admit, I was proud to be owned by such a wise and foresightful man.

August 29th, 1787

This night, after finishing transcribing his notes, Mr. Madison bathed and dressed to attend a supper at the house of

Dr. Benjamin Franklin. What other delegates would be attending and the business to be discussed I did not learn.

From my last experience at Dr. Franklin's residence, I was relieved that I was not asked to go, thankful that there would be others to lift the great man (in more ways than one) from chair to chair.

While as a rule Mr. Madison enjoys the company of Dr. Franklin, he is also made somewhat uncomfortable by the ribald stories Dr. Franklin tells of his conquests of various women the globe over, often in details better left to the imagination.

When it comes to the matter of women generally, Mr. Madison has always been conservative to the point of prudishness. And he is as uneasy about the topic of sex as he is about slavery. Two subjects he has never considered ripe for frank and open discussion.

I mention the latter not only because it is one I retain some personal interest in, but because it has, once again, become a matter of debate at today's session.

Apparently, General Pinckney from South Carolina and Mr. Gorham from Massachusetts have introduced a law that would require fugitive slaves who had run off from their masters to be returned like common criminals.

Some delegates from the North objected to this, primarily on the grounds of the cost they would incur in retrieving said slaves. And who cannot see the fairness of their argument?

After all, why should one party in a free state bear all the expense when it is the party in the slave state that reaps the benefit? Surely, if it were a runaway horse that was being brought back, you can be assured a portion of the costs would be assumed by the grateful owner.

The debates that ensued from this quarrel made me realize for the first time how valuable—in hard currency—we slaves really were; and it bore no resemblance to the discounted prices we were now going for at auction.

For example, at auction a strong, young, childbearing girl could be had for as low as 25 dollars. But if she ran off, the cost of getting her back would run to more than a hundred. What with the tracking, the capture, the housing, and the feeding—not to mention transportation.

So by my reckoning, such as it is, that would mean a slave is worth at least a hundred dollars apiece, and *then* when you think that there are near a million of us,* that would mean, being charitable, that together we are worth more than 100 million dollars!

I cannot wait to write my sister Stucky back in Virginia and tell her that we're rich!

September 5th, 1787

Why Mr. Madison chose to bring with him five pairs of boots, each one identical in style, quality, size, and color, is a question a man in my position cannot openly ask. That he wants each pair regularly polished—whether worn or not—is also beyond my comprehension.

Nonetheless, it is a chore that I am performing with my customary artistry when Mr. Madison returns from the Convention, quietly vexed, and hurries to his desk to transcribe his notes.

As he did so, he expressed his disdain at the day's results. I am complimented that he takes me into his confidence and, while continuing to shine away with rag and brush, listen attentively.

The matter of the day was the method of choosing the Executive or President. The Convention had rejected Mr. Mad-

---

* Editor's note: The figure was actually closer to 700,000 slaves in the thirteen states.

ison's plan that he be chosen by Congress, and instead had come up with a complicated process in which each state would choose individual electors whose votes would then elect the President. Each elector, Mr. Madison went on, would get two votes—one for President and one for Vice President.

"Would that not mean," I asked, "that a President could end up with a Vice President whose political views were totally opposed to his?"*

Mr. Madison gave me a long look and said, "Exactly. You have discerned that which supposedly more learned heads than yours could not." After a pause, he added, "Well done, Billey."

It took me a minute to realize that Mr. Madison was talking about his boots.

September 10th, 1787

As it now seems likely that the Convention will conclude within the week, there is a flurry of activity on my part and Mr. Madison's.

General Washington has already sent out invitations for a farewell party in celebration for the 17th of this month, and knowing that the General would never wish to lose his deposit for the private room at the City Tavern, I am assured that day will be the Convention's last.

It is in that belief that I have begun preparations for Mr. Madison's return to Montpelier: refitting his carriage, shoeing the horses, et cetera. Meanwhile, Mr. Madison has been working days and nights (while the Convention is in brief recess) with the Committee of Style (as it is called),

---

* Editor's note: Which is what happened when John Adams was elected President and Thomas Jefferson his Vice President.

which is comprised of Mr. William Samuel Johnson of Connecticut, Mr. Gouverneur Morris of Pennsylvania, Mr. Rufus King of Massachusetts, and of course Mr. Madison.

These men have been entrusted with the arranging and ordering of all the Articles, Clauses, et cetera, previously proposed into what will hopefully be the final draft of the new United States Constitution. Given the makeup of that Committee, I have every reason to believe that Mr. Madison's influence—which had seemed to wane in recent weeks—will be evident in the final outcome.

Copies of the draft, which compresses the previous 22 Articles into 9 and states them in clear, concise, crisp language (according to Mr. Madison), will be printed and presented to the entire Convention on the 12th of this week.

There is also (again according to Mr. Madison) a Preamble to be written by Mr. Gouverneur Morris, and if it is composed with the same enthusiasm with which Mr. Morris hops after married women on his one good leg, I am certain it will catch the attention of this new nation.

September 12th, 1787
While I was preparing Mr. Madison's bath this evening, he informed me of a particular in the newly written Constitution of which he was most proud: there would be no religious test for office. Which meant, as I understood it, that any white man in the country with sufficient property, with or without religious affiliation, could hold national office, even President.

As this was a matter that I take no concern in, I feigned my enthusiasm.

I have always found it curious that Mr. Madison never shared his family's Christianity. And once when I expressed my own faith in the Lord Jesus Christ as my Savior, Mr. Mad-

ison gave me this book to read by a Scottish philosopher*
who said, as best as I can remember, that the human mind
goes only so far. The rest is a mystery, so don't believe anything that cannot be double-checked by reason.

Anyway, it went something like that. Only for around 600
pages.

While I have since come to acknowledge that Mr. Madison is sincere in his indifference to the Christian faith, I
could not help but think at the time that this was just his way
of discouraging a black man from getting into Heaven.

September 15th, 1787
My day has been spent in packing, a chore complicated by
Mr. Madison's considerable accumulations since we first arrived in Philadelphia five months ago—though I must admit
it seems like years.

Over that span, Mr. Madison has acquired books, buckles
(15 exactly and why I have no idea), new boots, pairs of silk
hose, undergarments, political pamphlets of all stripes, and
a plentitude of jars, ointments, tinctures, elixirs, et cetera—
many devoted to his gastrointestinal ailments.

It was in the midst of my duties that I heard from the adjoining room Mr. Madison engaged in conversation with
an unannounced guest, Mr. George Mason, delegate from
Virginia.

Mr. Mason had come to ask Mr. Madison to support a resolution he planned to introduce the following day, calling for
what he described as a Declaration of Rights to be added to
the Constitution.

For my part, as this might add days if not weeks to the
Convention, it came with some relief when I heard Mr. Mad-

---

* Editor's note: No doubt David Hume.

ison politely decline. As Mr. Madison pointed out, there was no need for a Declaration of Rights since the Constitution took no rights away.

Mr. Mason, however, was not persuaded, and from the tone of their exchange, it was evident that the relationship between the two men was not as cordial as it once had been.

In addition, Mr. Madison noted that the Constitution was now in its final draft, the delegates were in a rush to return to their homes, and there was no appetite among them for further and lengthy debates.

Mr. Mason then departed in a mood more sour than when he first arrived.

As for those Declarations of Rights, as Mr. Mason had proposed—that is, freedom of speech, of religion, and of the press, along with the Right of Persons to be secure in their own homes, among others—as glorious as they may have sounded to those entitled to them, I sided with Mr. Madison in that there was nothing that important worth staying in Philadelphia for an extra week.

Later that night, as I smoked my pipe in the alleyway behind the boardinghouse (perhaps for the last time), I imagined what my own Declaration of Rights would be if I could write them myself:

The Right to live where I liked.
The Right to choose my work and who I worked for.
The Right to marry without permission.
The Right to say what I was thinking.
And the Right to look any man in the eye when I said it.

Whether a Declaration of Rights or pipe dreams, that was another story.

September 17th, 1787

Mr. Madison returned from the Convention to announce that the Constitution had been signed. In the parlor, he told Mrs. House and her daughter Mrs. Trist of the special events of the day.

The women—both of whom had been kept in the dark about the Convention because of the rule of secrecy—listened raptly as Mr. Madison described Dr. Franklin's urging for a unanimous vote in favor of the new Constitution. And although three delegates—Mr. Mason, Governor Randolph, and Mr. Gerry—declined to sign their names, the other 39, including General Washington, did so happily.

Mr. Madison said that Dr. Franklin even cried when he fixed his name to it. Though I could not help but wonder if out of patriotism or kidney stones?

In his chambers, Mr. Madison prepared for the gala party that General Washington was giving in celebration that night at the City Tavern. After I helped Mr. Madison repowder his hair—as was his wont on these special occasions—I thought, given his genial mood, that this was as good a time as any to broach the subject of my freedom.

As I asked Mr. Madison to consider the possibility of letting me go, I also made it clear that I was more than willing to work out any financial arrangement necessary to pay him back. I then suggested the terms of paying him $20 per year for a period of five years.

If Mr. Madison had been surprised by my request, I could not tell from his face, which remained neutral. "I will think about it," he said, walking off.

But knowing Mr. Madison as well as I did, I feared from his tone that my freedom was not as close at hand as I had hoped.

Maybe I had sold myself too cheap.

Afterword

The day the Constitution was signed—September 17, 1787—seems as good a day as any to end Billey's imaginary journal. And now, as the saying goes, for the rest of the story as related by Lynne Cheney in her biography of Madison:

James Madison stayed in Philadelphia for another week, during which time he sold Billey to a local resident (name unknown) under the conditions that after seven years Billey would be granted his freedom.

Madison later wrote to his father (Madison Sr.) that he did so rather than bring Billey back with him to Virginia on the grounds that Billey might have been "tainted" by the liberties he experienced while in Philadelphia.

After Billey's period of servitude, he was freed (adding the last name of Gardner) and, surprisingly, went to work for James Madison as his business agent.

It was on assignment for Madison that Billey's ship went down in the Atlantic. Billey's body was never found. And it was James Madison who notified Mr. Gardner's family of his death.

CHAPTER 8

Charles Beard's Economic Interpretation of the Constitution, Part I: Meeting the Framers

> Hardly a prominent man of the period failed to secure
> large tracts of real estate, which could be had at absurdly
> low prices, and to hold the lands for the natural advance
> which increasing population would bring.
>
> —Albert Beveridge, *The Life of John Marshall**

> The Founders were an exceptional group of men and
> women, among the greatest to have ever walked this land.
> They worked hard and aimed high. They dedicated their
> lives to establishing a country that would be a moral and
> political example to the rest of the world.
>
> —William J. Bennett, *Our Country's Founders:*
> *A Book of Advice for Young People*

In May 1787—at the start of the Constitutional Convention—the country did not have a pot to piss in. Here's a little of what I'm talking about:

---

* Marshall was Chief Justice of the Supreme Court from 1801 to 1835.

- The Revolutionary War had cost more than $200 million.* Almost all borrowed, very little paid back.
- States including Virginia, Rhode Island, and the Carolinas were printing their own paper money, causing skyrocketing inflation.
- Thousands of Tories (British Loyalists), who had their property and wealth confiscated, were now suing in state courts for compensation.
- State legislatures were passing laws that helped small farmers and businessmen reduce their debt at the expense of their creditors.†
- Ex–Revolutionary War soldiers and suppliers held millions of dollars of paper IOUs that were now worth pennies on the dollar.
- The government (or what there was of it) did not have the funds to redeem bonds, paper IOUs, or securities at their face value.
- Debt and land speculation had become the rich man's favorite pastimes.

Riding to the rescue were the Framers, ready to draft a Constitution that would establish Justice, ensure Domestic Tranquility, and secure the Blessings of Liberty.‡ That is, if you take their word for it.

And who wouldn't? It has, in fact, been the basic tenet of Conservative legal theory that the Framers were infallible patriots— men of God—who acted solely to establish national unity, economic development, and the civil liberties of all citizens.

Any critique of the Framers—and their motives—has always been met with angry accusations of un-Americanism.

---

* That's in *their* money, not ours.

† This caused, as James Madison put it, a serious class struggle between those with property and those without.

‡ I'm paraphrasing the Preamble.

I'm afraid I am now about to open myself up (forgive the image) to just such charges.

For years, I believed what I was taught. Then, in preparation for this book, I read *An Economic Interpretation of the Constitution of the United States*, written in 1913 by Professor Charles A. Beard. And here, in his own words, is Beard's thesis:

> The members of the Philadelphia Convention, which drafted the Constitution were, with a few exceptions, immediately, directly, and personally interested in, and derived economic advantages from, the establishment of the new system.

I know what you're thinking. Blasphemy. Professor Beard had the balls to suggest that our beloved Framers studied their pocketbooks as much as they did their John Locke or Montesquieu.

Not surprising, then, that Beard's book was quickly attacked in editorials, banned from school libraries, and all but dead and buried by historians and Constitutional scholars. By the '60s, Beard's economic interpretation was so out of favor that the renowned historian Richard Hofstadter wrote this:

> Today, Beard's reputation stands like an imposing ruin in the landscape of American historiography. What was once the grandest house in the province is now a ravaged survival.

I humbly but strongly disagree. Maybe you will too, as I retell Beard's theories in my own way. Because despite his complex methodologies, inconsistencies, and oversimplifications, Beard makes a helluva case. His healthy skepticism a much-needed antidote to the Right Wing's poisonous idolatry.

First, an important note: Beard is no radical socialist. He is, in fact, an avowed patriot, with a deep, abiding respect for the Founders, stating: "It was a truly remarkable assembly of men that gathered in Philadelphia on May 14th, 1787 . . . It is not merely patriotic pride that compels one to assert that never in the history of assemblies has there been a convention of men richer in political experience ... or endowed with a profounder insight into the ... essence of government."

Which in no way contradicts his main point about the writers of the Constitution as a "small and active group of men immediately interested through their personal possessions in the outcome of their labors."

Beard begins by dividing the Framers into five financial categories:

1. Plantation owners and slaveholders.
2. Those heavily invested in lands for speculation.
3. Bankers and money lenders.
4. Bond holders—those who held "paper"—i.e., creditors who owned government securities and military debt.
5. Wealthy merchants, manufacturers, and ship owners.

To make his point that all of the delegates fit into one or more of the above categories, Beard gives us a thumbnail sketch of every delegate and where his economic interests lie.

Beard lists all fifty-five delegates to the Constitutional Convention, highlighting their financial backgrounds and interests. I will do the same (in abbreviated fashion), adding as I go a few tidbits of my own.

Now it's time to meet all fifty-five delegates, as Beard saw them, warts and all. Mostly warts.*

---

* I've included all fifty-five because I was afraid if I left some out, you'd accuse me of hiding something. Those of you who get bored reading about other people's money—skim.

Abraham Baldwin

LAWYER, PLANTATION OWNER, GEORGIA

One of the eminent attorneys in Georgia. Some portion of Baldwin's fortune was invested in public securities. Fierce advocate for the extension of the slave trade, as many Georgians were in the business of selling their excess slaves to other states.

Richard Bassett

LAWYER, DELAWARE

By inheritance, he came into 6,000 acres of the best land in Delaware. Owned mansions in Wilmington, Dover, and Bohemia Manor. Bassett secured a charter in Delaware for the First Bank of North America.

Gunning Bedford

LAWYER, DELAWARE

Son of a substantial landowner. As Governor of Delaware, he organized the Bank of Delaware. One of the first members of the Electoral College that elected Washington as President. Appointed by Washington to the Federal Court.

John Blair

LAWYER, VIRGINIA

Scion to one of the wealthiest, most powerful families in Virginia. His father was once the Royal Governor. A confidant of George

Washington. They even rode home together after the Convention.*
Later appointed to the Supreme Court by Washington. In September (after the signing of the Constitution), Blair cashed in nearly
$10,000 ($140,000 in today's money) worth of paper on the United
States loan.

William Blount

POLITICIAN, NORTH CAROLINA

In 1789, Blount, son of one of North Carolina's largest landowners,
was connected with land speculation on a grand scale by way of his
involvement with the Yazoo Companies. This would later be known
as the Yazoo Land Scandal,† a fraud perpetrated by the Georgia
General Assembly in the mid-1790s. As Governor of the Southwest Territory, Blount was a leading force in getting Tennessee into
the Union, personally acquiring millions of acres in the process. His
risky land speculations led to serious debt and, in turn, to a conspiracy with Great Britain to seize Louisiana from Spain. In 1797, when
the conspiracy was revealed, he was expelled from the US Senate.

David Brearly

LAWYER, NEW JERSEY

Owned 1,600 acres of downtown New Jersey, 100 acres of river-view
property along the Delaware, and 3,000 acres near Lawrenceville.
Prominent attorney who specialized in public securities. Served on

---

* Both almost drowned when their carriage went off a bridge.

† The Yazoo Land Fraud Scandal transferred 35 million acres of what is now Alabama and Mississippi to land speculators for $500,000. The deal was done with
bribes and gifts of land to State officials.

the first Electoral College that elected George Washington the first President. Appointed to the Federal Court by Washington in 1789.

Jacob Broom

MANUFACTURER, DELAWARE

A man of diversified financial resources, Broom owned cotton mills and was one of the original stockholders of the Insurance Company of North America (organized at Philadelphia three years after the Convention). He was also one of the original shareholders of the Delaware Bank, founded by fellow delegate Gunning Bedford. He owned extensive manufacturing plants, which he sold in 1802 to the DuPonts at enormous profit. A personal friend of George Washington, Broom is on record at the Convention arguing that the President should serve for life.

Pierce Butler

POLITICIAN, PLANTATION OWNER, SOUTH CAROLINA

One of the country's wealthiest men. He was a plantation owner said to have as many slaves as any man in America. He was also director and major stockholder of the first United States Bank. Late in life, Butler squandered his fortune and was saved from bankruptcy by his sale of 436 slaves outside of Savannah, at the time the largest slave auction in the history of the United States. He was also briefly imprisoned for treason.

Daniel Carroll

POLITICIAN, PLANTATION OWNER, MARYLAND

Described by his fellow delegate William Pierce as "a man of great fortune," Carroll was also a major stockholder of the Potomac Company.* Carroll made another fortune, having the good luck to just happen to own a large portion of the land on which the nation's capital—Washington, DC—was eventually located.

George Clymer

SHIPBUILDER, MERCHANT, BANKER, PENNSYLVANIA

Clymer was one of the foremost shipbuilders in the nation and augmented his fortune by marrying the wealthy daughter of a fellow shipbuilder. Clymer helped create the Bank of Pennsylvania and later was president of the Philadelphia Bank. At the time of the Convention, he was one of the largest holders of government bonds and securities. In partnership with his fellow delegate Robert Morris from Philadelphia, Clymer increased his wealth by accumulating large portions of land. He served in the first Congress in 1789.

William R. Davie

LAWYER, PLANTATION OWNER, NORTH CAROLINA

Owned a plantation with a number of slaves at Tivoli, North Carolina. As a prominent lawyer, he is said to have drawn up all the

---

* The Potomac Company was founded in 1785, two years before the Convention, as a major construction company created to build canals on the Potomac River to improve navigation for commerce. George Washington was its major investor and its first president.

wills of "eminent men" made during his time in that part of the state. Occupation at the time of the Convention: investing and land speculation.

Jonathan Dayton

LAWYER, NEW JERSEY

At the time of the Convention, Dayton was the agent and business partner of John Symmes,* together purchasing more than 500,000 acres of land in Ohio (hence Dayton, Ohio). Dayton was also active in buying up military certificates† and government securities for less than their full value. In 1800, after the Constitution guaranteed full payment of all military certificates, Dayton used those certificates to purchase 15,000 acres of public lands. Later, Dayton became involved with Aaron Burr in a conspiracy to invade parts of the United States.‡ Dayton was arrested and, along with Burr, tried for treason.

John Dickinson

LAWYER, PLANTATION OWNER, DELAWARE

Slaveholder. Owner of one of the largest plantations in Delaware. In 1770, he tripled his wealth when he married the heiress Mary Norris.

---

* John Cleves Symmes is also known for his "Hollow Earth" theory in which he proposed that the Earth was not only hollow but habitable. At one time, called the "Newton of the West," Symmes soon became ridiculed, but not before President John Adams almost approved an expedition to explore the hollow Earth beneath Ohio.

† Paper IOUs given to Revolutionary soldiers that were almost worthless at the time of the Convention.

‡ A preposterous scheme in which Burr and Dayton were to lead a military invasion to conquer (and then sell) what is now the Southwest United States.

His business associates at the time of the Convention were the land speculators Robert Morris and George Clymer of Philadelphia.

Oliver Ellsworth

LAWYER, CONNECTICUT

Ellsworth had the good fortune to marry the daughter of William Wolcott, from one of the oldest, richest families in the state. Wolcott had once been Royal Governor of Connecticut. Tax records of the time indicate Ellsworth lent money at interest and was a large stockholder in the Hartford Bank of Connecticut. In 1788, he profited greatly by the rise of credit that followed the establishment of the new government. He was also one of the first citizens in the country to cash in on his government securities. Later appointed by Washington as Chief Justice of the Supreme Court.

William Few

LAWYER, PLANTATION OWNER, GEORGIA

Successful enough at his law practice to purchase a plantation in Columbia County, Georgia. No record of how many slaves came with it. Records indicate that he was connected to the Georgia Union Company, one of the subsidiaries involved in the Yazoo Land Fraud. Charges that Few was one of those bribed were never proven. However, he did leave Georgia (reasons unknown) for New York, where he increased his small fortune of $100,000 (around $1.4 million today) by becoming one of the directors of the Manhattan Bank, later called Citigroup.

Thomas Fitzsimons

MERCHANT, PENNSYLVANIA

Identified by historians of the time as the man who "laid the foundations of the commercial and financial systems of the United States." At one time, he was President of Philadelphia's Chamber of Commerce, Director of the Delaware Insurance Company, and Director of the Bank of North America. Later, his business dealings with the infamous financier and fellow delegate from Philadelphia Robert Morris seriously crippled his financial resources.

Benjamin Franklin

STATESMAN, PHILOSOPHER, AUTHOR, SCIENTIST, LANDOWNER, PENNSYLVANIA

Much of Franklin's wealth was in property: houses and land. His interest in land started when he lived in London and tried to put a consortium together for a land grant of 20 million acres (!) in what is now Ohio. But the deal fell through. It would have been one of the biggest land grabs in history. Later, in the United States, Franklin was one of the principal shareholders in the Ohio Company, whose goal was to purchase and sell 12.5 million acres of Ohio County land. During the Convention—in addition to providing an inspiring presence—he supervised the construction of several rental properties in downtown Philadelphia. At his death, he owned, at least, much of Nova Scotia, 3,000 acres in Georgia,* and "lands near Ohio."

---

* Deeded to him by the Georgia legislature as his *per diem* for a speech he gave.

Elbridge Gerry

MERCHANT, MASSACHUSETTS

The Gerry family was among the wealthiest in Massachusetts, with trading connections in the West Indies, Spain, and cities all along the North American coast. Gerry was also a speculator in public lands, a shareholder in the Ohio Company, and a partner with Timothy Pickering, one of the leading land operators of the period. Much of his gains in trade were offset by losses in the value of paper currencies, which he held (and speculated in) in great amounts. He supported, and became a major investor in, Hamilton's First Bank of the United States. He died rich in land but with little else, having to pay off his debts from his salary as the fifth Vice President of the United States (1813).

Nicholas Gilman

POLITICIAN, NEW HAMPSHIRE

Prior to the Convention, Gilman had accumulated a considerable amount of public securities. He also owned large sums of deferred stock in the new government and dealt extensively in the speculation of military certificates.* There is evidence that on the day the Convention adjourned, he wrote the President of New Hampshire, advising him to buy public securities at their prevailing low prices.†

---

* Paper money paid to veterans of the Revolutionary War that could be bought from them at a fraction of their face value.

† State papers of New Hampshire, as quoted by Beard.

Nathaniel Gorham

MERCHANT, POLITICIAN, MASSACHUSETTS

In 1786—a year before the Convention—Gorham and his syndicate (which included Robert Morris) bought large portions of land in Western New York State for $1 million,* paid for by below-par Massachusetts scrip, known as consolidated securities. To claim title, Gorham and his syndicate had to extinguish all Indian rights to the land. In 1790, Gorham defaulted in payment, selling almost all of his unsold lands to Robert Morris, who then resold them. Gorham did manage to hold on to 500,000 acres that became known as the Morris Reserve.

Alexander Hamilton

POLITICIAN, NEW YORK

Rumors of Hamilton's speculation in public securities have never been proven, despite the fact that he was accused of criminal violations when Secretary of the Treasury by the House of Representatives in 1793. In 1797, more charges appeared, accusing Hamilton of employing his "high" authority in the interests of his friends and family. That Hamilton himself profited by inside information at any time in his career seems doubtful given the condition of his estate at the time of his death. Surprising, given the fact that in 1780, Hamilton married the daughter of Philip Schuyler, who owned 20,000 acres along the Hudson River. Hamilton on his own bought large tracts of land near Oswego in upstate New York. He died after his duel with Burr some $55,000 in debt.

---

* Today about $14 million.

William C. Houston

LAWYER, NEW JERSEY

Of whom Beard writes: ". . . was of no consequence in the Convention, and little is known of his economic interests." Shortly after the end of the Revolutionary War, Houston and others joined an enterprise to stake out land northwest of the Ohio River. What came of that investment, however, Beard didn't say.

William Houstoun

LAWYER, PLANTATION OWNER, GEORGIA

Slaveholder. One of the more obscure delegates. He arrived at the Convention late (June 1) and left early (July 23). Due to the paucity of records of the Georgia Loan Office, Beard says: "It is impossible to say whether he was the benefactor through the appreciation of public securities." Married later (1788) into one of the more prominent real estate families in New York (the Bayards), from which the street in Manhattan takes its name.

Jared Ingersoll

LAWYER, PENNSYLVANIA

Described by his contemporaries as a man of "considerable wealth." He is listed as a business partner on various ventures with the financier Robert Morris.

Daniel of St. Thomas Jenifer*

PLANTATION OWNER, POLITICIAN, MARYLAND

President of the Maryland Senate and Manager of the state's finances, slaveholder, and owner of a 16,000-acre plantation in Maryland. The number of slaves he owned is not known, but in his will he instructed that they all be freed *six* years after his death, which came in 1790. Good friend of Robert Morris and George Washington.

William Samuel Johnson

LAWYER, CONNECTICUT

Wealthy lawyer who at the time of the Convention represented various mercantile houses in New York City. As a member of the first Senate, Johnson was named by Thomas Jefferson as one of the many "*operators*† in securities." Johnson's son Robert speculated extensively in stocks after the establishment of the new government, holding nearly $50,000 worth of various securities.

Rufus King

LAWYER, MERCHANT, MASSACHUSETTS

The King family was one of the largest landowners in Massachusetts (more than 3,000 acres) and the largest exporter of timber from Maine. Along with Gouverneur Morris and Robert Morris, King was suspected of engaging in a plan (1788) to purchase most of the debt the

---

* Apparently, every male in the Jenifer family was named "Daniel." St. Thomas was the name of his plantation.

† Emphasis mine. Jefferson means, of course, those operating on inside information.

United States owed to France, hoping for a full return on their money after the government was formed. Rufus King was also among those Jefferson accused of holding enormous bank stock and public securities while Director of the first United States Bank. Later, a US Senator.

John Langdon

MERCHANT, SHIPBUILDER, NEW HAMPSHIRE

Landon made his fortune building ships and sailing them (as "privateers") against the British during the Revolutionary War. He was a close friend and business associate of Robert Morris, arguably the largest land speculator in the world. Suspected, as a Senator in the first Congress, of buying government certificates of public debt for as low as 7¢ in the hopes of reselling them at face value.*

John Lansing Jr.

LAWYER, NEW YORK

Lansing was against the idea of the Convention from the start and left early. But (as Beard says) he was there long enough to learn what the effect of an efficient government would have on "Continental securities." And in January 1791, immediately after the establishment of the new financial system, he appeared at the New York loan office to cash in his paper. Then Beard adds, "All the members of the Lansing family in Albany seem to have taken advantage of the opportunity to augment their fortunes."† On December 29, 1829, he left his Manhattan hotel room to mail a letter at the docks. Either murdered or drowned, he was never seen again.

---

* Face value unknown.

† Beard cites manuscript from the Treasury Department, New York Loan Office.

William Livingston

SECURITIES LAWYER, NEW JERSEY

The Livingston family was one of the largest landowning families in New York and New Jersey. Former Governor of New Jersey.
Shortly after he died in 1790, his son became one of the largest security holders in New York City. One entry (1791) in the Treasury
Records shows the son cashing in $70,000 worth of paper. About
$10 million today.

James Madison Jr.

LAWYER, PLANTATION OWNER, VIRGINIA

Madison's father was a tobacco farmer who owned more than 5,000
acres of prime Virginia real estate. The number of slaves Madison
inherited from his father was in the hundreds. Madison was not indifferent to land speculation. In the 1780s, he speculated on land in
New York's Mohawk Valley with his business partner—and later
President of the United States—James Monroe. During a visit to
George Washington at Mount Vernon in October 1785 (two years
before the Convention), Madison discussed the Mohawk Valley
Project, at which time Washington counted himself in. Unfortunately, Madison died broke, having to sell off his slaves—a few at a
time—to pay off his debts.

Alexander Martin

LAWYER, PLANTATION OWNER, NORTH CAROLINA

Martin was among the well-to-do planters and slave owners in the
state. Beard's search in the Treasury Department, plus the papers of
North Carolina, produce no records of any of his transactions. One

other note: While Martin was serving under Washington as a Colonel during the Revolutionary War, his soldiers mistook the Continental Army for the British, killing several Americans. After the debacle, Martin was court-martialed and charged with cowardice. Though not convicted, Martin resigned his commission, claiming stress. Later elected to the US Senate.

Luther Martin

LAWYER, MARYLAND

Martin's fortune was modest compared to those of other delegates. He owned only six slaves. However, among his clients were men of "great wealth and influence," including Philadelphia's Robert Morris. An anti-Federalist, he refused to sign the Constitution in sympathy with the country's debtors. What is not generally reported is that *he* was one of those debtors. Like other wealthy men of the time, Martin dabbled in properties confiscated from Loyalists during the Revolution and borrowed money to do so. Along with other "pro-paper" investors, it was in his interest to see his debts retired. Which is why he showed up in Philadelphia. To his dismay, the delegates there were all creditors. Later in life, Martin was destitute, ravaged by alcohol, and homeless—until taken in by Aaron Burr.

George Mason

PLANTATION OWNER, VIRGINIA

Mason's family fortune was based on tobacco plantations. The number of slaves he owned has not been calculated. In 1769, he came into possession of more than 2,000 additional acres in Kentucky. As a member of the Ohio Company (along with George Washington and Benjamin Franklin), he attained a grant of 600,000 acres of land in Southwest Ohio. At his death, Mason left his son another 15,000 acres of the best land bordering the Potomac River.

James McClurg

PHYSICIAN, VIRGINIA

A confidant of George Washington and James Madison, Mc-Clurg was picked to take the place of Patrick Henry in the Virginia delegation.* McClurg left the Convention early and never returned. But he apparently impressed George Washington enough for the general to name McClurg as an "advisor" in his first administration. While renowned as a physician, McClurg also had a reputation as a financier: on February 17, 1791, he presented certificates in the amount of $26,819 (more than $300,000 today) at the local loan office in Virginia. He was also an investor and one of the Directors of the first United States Bank.

James McHenry

POLITICIAN, MARYLAND

McHenry was a confidant of George Washington and served on his staff at Valley Forge. McHenry made his fortune in lending and investments and was one of the original stockholders of the Insurance Company of North America. An entry in the Treasury's records of 1797 shows him holding at least $700,000 in public securities. Later, George Washington appointed him Secretary of War.

---

* Patrick Henry, a states rights guy, warned the delegation that the Northerners were going to take their "n****rs away."

John Francis Mercer

LAWYER, PLANTATION OWNER, MARYLAND

John Mercer was a prominent Virginia attorney before moving to
Maryland in 1786. A landowner with six slaves. He was also an attorney for George Washington as well as his business partner in
various land deals. Mercer was, by marriage, George Mason's uncle.
Mason, of course, was the wealthy landowner and fellow delegate to
the Convention. After serving as Governor of Maryland, Mercer retired to Philadelphia for his health. He died shortly thereafter. People should not move to Philadelphia for their health.

Thomas Mifflin

BUSINESSMAN, PENNSYLVANIA

A Major General in the Revolutionary War and once aide-de-camp
to George Washington. Later, as quartermaster, he was accused of
embezzlement and selling supplies to the highest bidder. But no
charges were formally brought. Mifflin made his fortune with his
brother in various commercial enterprises. He died heavily in debt
in 1800. Brought down—like other Federalists—by the bankruptcy
of his friend Robert Morris.

Gouverneur Morris

LAWYER, MERCHANT, PENNSYLVANIA

Gouverneur Morris was selected to be a delegate from Pennsylvania by his friends George Washington and Robert Morris,* even
though he lived in New York. According to Beard, he belonged "by

---

* No relation.

birth to a powerful, landed aristocracy." Morris added to his fortune through various commercial ventures with Robert Morris, including East Indian voyages on a large scale and huge shipments of tobacco to France. He met a bizarre end on November 6, 1816, when he tried to dislodge a blockage in his urinary tract with a whale bone from his wife's corset, bleeding to death.

Robert Morris

FINANCIER, PENNSYLVANIA

Of all the delegates, Robert Morris had the most widely diverse economic interests: his land speculation ran into the millions of acres. He owned every kind of Continental security and traded stocks in the tens of thousands. According to Beard, "No man of his time ... [was more] involved in the personal affairs of so many eminent men ... all closely identified with the new system of government."* Morris owned and directed ships trading with the East Indies and West Indies, engaged in iron manufacturing, and speculated in lands near the Potomac once he learned that the new capital would be established there. Washington named Morris, known as the "Patriot Financier," his first Secretary of the Treasury, but Morris was unable to accept because he was too busy with his own affairs. Other financial skullduggery on the part of Robert Morris included:

- 1765: Actively involved in the slave trade.
- 1779: Charged with profiteering and improper transactions during the Revolutionary War.

---

* These included the following delegates: Alexander Hamilton, Gouverneur Morris, John Langdon, Thomas Fitzsimons, Robert Clymer, and of course George Washington.

- 1791: Purchased (from Massachusetts) 11 million acres of Western New York State for the (bizarre) sum of $666,666.66.*

After a purchase of more than 6 million acres in the rural Southwest, Morris was forced to declare bankruptcy and later imprisoned three years in Philadelphia for debt. During the four months of the Constitutional Convention, Robert Morris's houseguest was his good friend and business associate George Washington.

William Paterson

LAWYER, MERCHANT, NEW JERSEY

Beard can find no record of Paterson's financial interests. He later became one of New Jersey's first Senators.

William Pierce

PLANTATION OWNER, POLITICIAN, GEORGIA

Married well in 1783 to the daughter of a wealthy South Carolina planter. Later moved to Georgia, where he acquired confiscated property—including a plantation—from a British Loyalist. Seriously in debt, Pierce left the Convention early (July) to avoid a duel with one of his foreign creditors. The duel was eventually settled by (of all people) Alexander Hamilton.

Charles Pinckney

LAWYER, PLANTATION OWNER, SOUTH CAROLINA

South Carolina Governor at the time of the Convention, first cousin of fellow delegate and signer Charles Cotesworth Pinckney. Mar-

---

* Perhaps the first and last financial joke ever made about the Antichrist.

ried the daughter of Henry Laurens, wealthy and powerful merchant and slave trader. A landowner with considerable acres, Pinckney, according to census records of 1790, owned fifty-two slaves. Holder of government securities on a grand scale. At the Convention, he claimed to be the youngest delegate, lying about his age, which was really twenty-nine, not twenty-four as he purported. Died impoverished after turning his affairs over to an unscrupulous business manager. Fearing he might be buried alive, Pinckney ordered in his will that he be left out of the ground for at least several weeks.

Charles Cotesworth Pinckney

LAWYER, PLANTATION OWNER, SOUTH CAROLINA

Considerable landowner in the city of Charleston, with a country estate at Pinckney Island, and the owner of forty-five slaves. As a lawyer representing rich merchants and manufacturers, he took a strong stand against any weakening of public and private debt.

Edmund J. Randolph

LAWYER, PLANTATION OWNER, POLITICIAN, VIRGINIA

Governor of Virginia at the time of the Convention, he was also one of George Washington's personal attorneys. For his loyalty, Washington made him his Attorney General and later Secretary of State.* While SOS, he was charged with defrauding the US Treasury. In his defense, Randolph argued that his property only came by way of "inheritance amounting to some 7,000 acres of land, several houses, and near 200 negroes."

---

* He was forced to resign as SOS when a mysterious (potentially traitorous) letter he wrote to the French Minister was intercepted.

George Read

LAWYER, DELAWARE

Son of John Read, one of the founders of the city of Charleston, Maryland. His father also developed the "ironworks" of the Principio Company, in which George Washington had a stake. As one of the first US Senators from Delaware, he supported the assumption of state debt, establishment of the national bank, and the imposition of excise taxes. Beard sums him up this way: "Read had felt personally the inconveniences of depreciated paper . . ."

John Rutledge

LAWYER, PLANTATION OWNER, SOUTH CAROLINA

His biographer writes of him: "He was employed in the most difficult causes and retained with the largest fees that were usually given."* A former Governor of the state, Rutledge had a successful law practice that only increased the already considerable fortune he inherited from his mother. During the Convention, he was active in the promotion of slavery as it was then practiced. In 1795, President Washington selected Rutledge as the second Chief Justice of the Supreme Court. Rumors of his drinking and mental instability led to his rejection by the Senate. His reputation and finances in tatters, he attempted suicide in Charleston on December 20, 1795. At his death, five years later, he had been reduced to owning only one slave.

---

* He twice defended clients who were accused of abusing their slaves.

Roger Sherman

LAWYER, CONNECTICUT

One of the few delegates who rose from poverty to affluence, Sherman made enough in his lifetime to become a major benefactor of Yale University. With other far-seeing businessmen of the day, Sherman seemed to have invested in public securities. After Hamilton's fiscal system went into effect, he immediately cashed in—according to Beard—$8,000* worth of paper at the loan office of his native state.

Richard Dobbs Spaight

LAWYER, PLANTATION OWNER, NORTH CAROLINA

He was among the largest planters in North Carolina and is recorded as owning more than seventy-one slaves. Friend and confidant of George Washington. Former Governor of North Carolina, Spaight was killed by a political rival in a duel in 1802.

Caleb Strong

LAWYER, MASSACHUSETTS

Successful lawyer born into a distinguished family. Whether he inherited his wealth or accumulated it in the practice of law is not made clear by his biographer, Senator Henry Cabot Lodge. In May 1787, *during* the Convention, Beard finds him purchasing "certificates of issue," which he then cashed into federal securities in September 1791. One of the first Senators in Congress from Massachusetts and a close advisor to George Washington.

---

* Which would be around $125,000 today.

George Washington

PLANTATION OWNER, VIRGINIA

Described by Beard as one of the richest men in the country at the time of the Constitutional Convention.* Washington had added to his already considerable wealth by marrying the widow Martha Dandridge Custis, who came along with 17,000 acres and more than one hundred slaves. Like his business associate Robert Morris, Washington was a great speculator in land. In 1769, he petitioned the government for 200,000 acres of land promised him and his soldiers. When he received a portion of that, he divided it up, taking the best land for himself and giving his soldiers what was left. At his death, it was said he owned more than 50,000 acres from New York through Maryland to Kentucky and beyond. Washington was also a moneylender of considerable proportions, and one who suffered the "paper money" laws of the Virginia legislature. As Beard concludes: "If any one in the country had a just reason for being disgusted with the imbecilities of the Confederation, it was Washington. He was paid his personal expenses . . . in paper that steadily depreciated."

Hugh Williamson

MERCHANT, NORTH CAROLINA

In 1777, he entered the "mercantile business" with his brother and "engaged in the West Indies trade." Williamson was also active in Western land speculation and in 1787 wrote this to Madison: ". . . having claims to a considerable quantity of land in Western Country, I am fully persuaded that the value of these lands must be increased by an efficient Federal Government." At the beginning of Hamilton's funding of the US government, Williamson personally

---

* Other historians give the honor to Benjamin Franklin.

delivered two trunks of deferred stock to Hamilton's New York office in 1793.

James Wilson

LAWYER, PENNSYLVANIA

James Wilson, a close ally of James Madison, was a prominent Philadelphia lawyer who represented fellow delegates and financiers: Robert Morris, George Clymer, and Thomas Mifflin. Wilson was one of the Directors of the Bank of North America and one of the original stockholders of the Insurance Company of North America. He was also a principal investor in the Georgia Land Company, a highly speculative concern (tainted with fraud), in which he personally owned 750,000 acres. He was appointed to the Supreme Court by Washington in 1789. And while still a member of the Court, retained his interest in the Georgia Land Company, which had then persuaded the Georgia State Assembly to sell more than 40 million acres of land in what is now Alabama and Mississippi for $500,000. Many of Georgia's legislators* were offered shares in the company or bribes to secure the sale. His last days were troubled by financial difficulties. He was twice imprisoned for failure to pay his debts.

George Wythe

LAWYER, LAW PROFESSOR, PLANTATION OWNER, VIRGINIA

Law professor and mentor to Thomas Jefferson. A slaveholder, he eventually emancipated all his slaves, laying aside funds for their future needs. On May 25, 1805, he became gravely ill and went to see his doctor, fellow Virginia delegate James McClurg, who diagnosed

---

* A few of whom were later murdered by irate citizens.

the illness as cholera and prescribed bloodletting. When Wythe died shortly thereafter, it was discovered he had actually been poisoned with arsenic by his sister's deranged grandson.

Robert Yates

LAWYER, NEW YORK

A man of modest means, especially for a lawyer. He left the Convention early, in protest, along with his fellow New York delegate John Lansing, when he figured out what the other delegates were up to: a completely new form of government. He refused to enrich himself—unlike so many of his business associates—by speculating in confiscated properties. He died poor.

And there you have all fifty-five delegates. Whether they were all Framers—given how little some actually did—I leave up to you. Me, I'm not sure. One thing is for certain: they are not the saints living in the imagination of the Right Wing, acting out God's will.

Roughly speaking: more than forty held government bonds. More than twenty were moneylenders. Over fifteen were slave owners. The rest an assortment of land and debt speculators. And most dabbled in more than one category. George Washington, for example, was a slave owner, a moneylender, a land speculator, and the largest holder of government IOUs in the country.

Who was *not* at the Convention is as interesting as who was: unrepresented were small farmers, shopkeepers, Revolutionary War veterans, laborers, indentured servants, and, of course, slaves, Indians, and women.

What we have instead is a small circle of capitalist elites with George Washington at the center. They were (if we're to believe only half of what Beard tells us) a rogues' gallery of scoundrels, scalawags, moneylenders, stockjobbers,* embezzlers, and, as it would turn out, traitors. Not to mention lawyers. Men, it would be fair to say, drawn to the power of their own purses.

Beard does make two notable exceptions: Madison and Hamilton. Madison for his unique national perspective and Hamilton for his disinterest in his own personal fortunes.

Whether the Framers' lives after the Convention are relevant or not, it is an undeniable fact that many of them ended up broke, destitute, and land poor: William Pierce, Thomas Mifflin, Pierce Butler, Luther Martin, James Madison, Alexander Hamilton, Charles Pinckney, John Rutledge, Robert Morris, George Washington, James Wilson, Jonathan Dayton, William Blount, and Thomas Fitzsimons.†

Now, as a man who's made some dumb investments himself, I sympathize.‡ And I, for one, do not believe that their financial missteps should disparage either their character or their achievements. But you would think, at least, their sad examples would give some Supreme Court Justices pause the next time they ask: "What were the Framers really thinking?"

---

* Jefferson's word for inside traders.

† The list could also include Founder Thomas Jefferson, who had to sell his library to defray expenses at his Monticello plantation.

‡ My former stockbroker, E. F. Hutton, had me heavily invested in Eastern Airlines, Woolworths, and the Enron Corporation.

Charles Beard's Economic Interpretation of the Constitution, Part II: Following the Money

A covenant with death and an agreement with Hell.

—William Lloyd Garrison, abolitionist,
as he set fire to the Constitution on July 4, 1854

As I said earlier, Beard divided the Framers into five financial categories: government bond holders; moneylenders and debt speculators; land speculators; wealthy manufacturers and merchants; and plantation owners and slave owners. The question now is: Can we discover what the Framers incorporated into the Constitution that benefitted each of those groups? Not that I'm saying each and every Framer used the Constitution to put money into his pocket. But I am suggesting the direct connection between certain Articles of the Constitution and the Framers' own financial interests.

Here are a few examples as I try, using Beard's blueprint, to connect the dots.

The power to lay and collect taxes (Article I, Section 8). This taxing power was, according to Beard, the "basis of all other positive powers." The revenues collected would allow the government to then pay off all its debts, including those owed to holders of US bonds.

And how quickly did the government want its money? Two

weeks into office, Alexander Hamilton asked Madison for suggestions of the least-unpopular taxes. A year later, apparently ignoring
Madison's advice, Hamilton imposed a so-called "whiskey tax" on
farmers who distilled their grain into whiskey.*

When farmers in Western Pennsylvania protested—often
violently—Washington and Hamilton personally led an army of
13,000† specially recruited militiamen to suppress the rebellion.

**The power to raise and support a standing army (Article I, Sec-
tion 8).** This was no small thing, considering the country's fear of
standing armies, given the British occupation. But an army—their
own army—could now be used to collect taxes (as in the whiskey rebellion), put down slave revolts, and, most important, uproot Native
Indians from the new territories. Soon, huge tracts of land could be
made available for agriculture and settlement, increasing tenfold the
investments of land speculators.

To put that into terms everyone can understand: Imagine having
a house next to one owned by Ted Nugent. Now picture how your
property value increases the day he moves away.

**All debts contracted and entered into before the adoption of the
Constitution shall be valid against the United States (Article
VI).** Beard's calculation is that this Article put some $40 million
into the hands of the debt speculators, many of whom, of course,
were Framers.

While some have questioned that huge amount, it's not hard to
see how much money there was to be made.

To give you some idea how this all worked, I'll quote David O.
Stewart as he calculates Abigail Adams's‡ profits:

---

* The country's most popular beverage.

† Hamilton designed their uniforms.

‡ Abigail Adams, wife of then Vice President John Adams and a speculator in
securities.

Imagine an investor purchasing a hundred dollars' worth of certificates at 20 percent of face value, with a promise of six percent interest. If those certificates were honored, the investor would receive six dollars per year in interest or a 30 percent annual return on her investment of twenty dollars. If the certificates were later redeemed at face value, the investor would receive an additional 500 percent return on her initial payment. Small wonder that Mrs. Adams bought them.

Not even Russian bankers promised Donald Trump that handsome a return on his money.

No person held in service or labour . . . shall be discharged for such service or labour but shall be delivered up on claim of the party to whom that service or labour may be due (Article IV, Section 2). Known as the Fugitive Slave Act, this was a classy way of saying that slaves who had run off to free states had to be returned to their rightful owners. A gift to slave owners, this section had to be most relevant to George Washington. At the Battle of Yorktown (1781) when his troops captured the British, Washington discovered to his amazement* that among the British soldiers were a half dozen of his own runaway slaves. They were quickly returned in bondage to Washington's plantation at Mount Vernon.†

The migration or importation of such persons . . . shall not be prohibited by the Congress prior to the year one thousand eight hundred and eight . . . (Article I, Section 9). Another boon to slave owners. This Article allowed the slave trade to continue another twenty years.

It seems clear by their language that the Framers were slightly

---

* I'm assuming.

† Thomas Jefferson also had runaway slaves captured at the Battle of Yorktown, who were then, of course, sent back to Monticello.

embarrassed by the word *slaves*, preferring the nicety of "such persons." And for good reason. The history of slavery in the United States is a tragic, shameful story—and worth remembering.

The historian Howard Zinn, among others, recounts the horrors: By the time of the writing of the Constitution, at least 10 million slaves had been brought to the Americas. They were packed into ships, chained together in dark, wet slime at the ships' bottoms, under conditions from which perhaps one of every three died. The number who died upon arrival is a mystery but has been estimated to be at least equal to the number who survived. Infant and child mortality rates were twice as high among slave children as among Southern white children.

But the planter elite needed slaves to maintain their economies, and the Framers obliged.

From the Ratification of the Constitution until 1808 when Congress finally abolished the slave trade, an additional 160,000 slaves were imported into the country. After the ban, illegal smuggling continued: cargoes of human beings were often dropped off into the Atlantic Ocean by slaveholders to avoid detection.

After 1808, *domestic* slave trading increased: the needs of the cotton plantations in the Deep South for more slaves drove up the demand, and more than a million slaves were sold from the upper South—Virginia and Maryland—to the Deep South, [meaning] Georgia and the Carolinas.

For years I had heard the expression "being sold down the river," but it was only the other day that I discovered it referred to the slaves sold to slave owners in Louisiana and the terrible fate that awaited them there among the sugar plantations.

Of course, it's easy to blame the Framers for the perpetuation of slavery in the United States. So I will.*

---

* For the record, in the seventy years between George Washington and Abraham Lincoln, for fifty of those, a slaveholder was President of the United States.

. . .

I'm sure the Framers saw no conflict between their interests and the nation's. After all, they saw themselves *as* the Nation. And I'm sure George Washington considered his speculation in land beneficial not only to himself but to America, believing that westward expansion would bring prosperity not to a few but to the Country. And I'm also sure that the Framers' belief in a strong central government, in order to protect their own wealth and property, was in their minds good news for everyone else.

But Beard's basic question persists: Did the Framers "represent distinct groups whose economic interests they understood ... or were they merely under the guidance of abstract principles of political science?"

It's a fair question needing to be asked, even if we can never be sure of the answer. For me, all I can say is: *Nobody spends his August in Philadelphia unless he's up to something.*

Likewise: two Chief Justices of the Supreme Court—John Marshall and Roger B. Taney, who ruled the Court from 1801 to 1864—were slave owners.

CHAPTER 10

The Chapter of Leftovers: Part I

Much of the writing of the Constitution was done by twelve committees. The important ones were the Rules Committee, the Committee of Detail (which did the first draft), and the Committee of Style (which did the last draft). Then there was the Committee of Leftovers.

Since the historians have little to say about the Committee of Leftovers,* I assume it cleaned up after the other committees on all issues that had been left up in the air.

And so in honor of that committee, I call this my Chapter of Leftovers: bits of facts and trivia that I could find no place for in the other chapters. For example:

In fear that their letters would be intercepted, Madison and Jefferson wrote in code, usually when discussing political opponents like John Adams and Patrick Henry.

At the time of the writing of the Constitution, the one state that allowed women to vote was New Jersey. Women lost that right in 1807.

The Constitution states that Congress need only assemble once a year.

---

* Sometimes referred to as the Brearly Committee, after its chairman, David Brearly of New Jersey.

In 1791, the first Senate suggested that the president of the United States be addressed as "His Highness the President of the United States of America and Protector of their Liberties."

The delegates to the Constitutional Convention were not paid. But eleven delegations got *per diems*: $4.00 a day for New Jersey—the highest—and 40 shillings per day for Delaware—the lowest.

The "publisher" who first printed the copies of the Constitution in 1787 did not get paid until March 1793.

As a member of the Continental Congress in 1787, James Madison was paid $6.00 per day.

George Washington's dentures were made from hippopotamus tusks. Whether from the same hippopotamus or several is not clear.*

At the time of the Convention, the age of consent in Virginia was 10 years old.

---

* And what kind of book about the Constitution could leave off some mention of George Washington's teeth?

CHAPTER 11

Open Letter to Senator Ted Cruz Written in the Style of 1787

If you shot Ted Cruz on the floor of the Senate, and the
trial was in the Senate, nobody would convict you.

—Senator Lindsey Graham of South Carolina

To the Right Honorable US Senator from the State of Texas, Theodore Cruz:

I am prompted to write this upon Discovery of a Foreword you penned to *The US Constitution for Dummies*. In it, you make Assertions about our American Constitution that I, as one of the country's Citizens, feel compelled to respond to.

Before I proceed, however, with the main Body of my Argument, I would like to observe that none of my Comments is meant to be taken—in any way—as "Personal."

Unlike our current President, I am not given to reckless, unfounded Assaults on a man's Good Name.

I refer, of course, to the Calumny perpetrated by the aforesaid President when he repeated, as gospel, the Conspiracy Theories promulgated in the worthless Pages of that so-called Magazine known as the *National Enquirer* in which your Father was named in connection with Lee Harvey Oswald's assassination of John F. Kennedy.

I should mention that I myself am not a Reader of that Scandal Sheet, finding in it small Lies heaped upon greater Ones. Though I will confess that when idling at my local Supermarket, I have been drawn to its Pages, especially when they feature compelling Essays like "Who's Gay and Who's Not?" as well as various close-up Photographs featuring the Cellulite of assorted well-known Personages.*

That you were able to deflect the scurrilous Attacks made on your Father (and later your Wife) with such Equanimity and then to endorse the Man who repeated them only attests to the forgiving, faith-based Charity of your Good Nature.

Others might judge you harshly for choosing Sycophantism over Loyalty to your own Family, but not I. I leave that a matter to be decided eventually between You and your Maker. All I know is that a lesser Man, such as myself, would have certainly harbored a Lifetime of Grudges and Recrimination.

But I digress. As I stated earlier, this Missive is only meant to respond, as best I can, to the five Assertions you made in your Foreword regarding our nation's Constitution.

1. Assertion: The Constitution was written to limit government.

An Assertion I find strange though oft repeated.

Why indeed would the Framers want a Constitution when they already had "Limited Government" under the Articles of Confederation? A Government, in fact, that was so limited, there was no Executive Branch, and populist State Legislatures printed their own Money: a Country on the verge of Anarchy without a Nickel to its Name.

The Preamble to the Constitution (which you once said you memorized) makes clear the Goals of the Constitution: ". . . to establish Justice, insure Domestic Tranquility, provide for the common

---

* I myself often feared I'd be caught by their paparazzi at a pool party in my Speedo with my inner thighs exposed, looking like they've just been bashed by a sack full of quarters.

defence, promote the General Welfare, and secure the Blessings of Liberty to ourselves and our Posterity." Now how, may I ask, do you do all that with a "Limited Government"?

Surely as a Constitutional Scholar you know that when Delegates favoring "Limited Government" tried to make their Case, it was James Madison who argued against them. And I quote: "It was impossible to *confine* a Government to the exercise of express Powers; there must necessarily be admitted Powers by Implication . . ."

And here's Madison again defining the very Purpose of the Constitutional Convention: ". . . since the greatest Danger to the Nation is that of Disunion of the States, it is necessary to guard against it by sufficient Powers to the Common Government."

2. Assertion: James Madison is the "Primary Author" of the Constitution.

As much as I regret disrelishing you of this Assertion, the Word *Author* in regard to Madison is erroneous.

Madison did help draft and introduce the Virginia Plan, which served as a rough Outline for what would become the Constitution. During the Convention, however, the Virginia Plan was seriously revised by, among others, the Committee of Detail, of which Madison was not even a Member.

Besides, the Virginia Plan itself did not originate with Madison but was an Amalgam of Constitutional "Ideas" taken from the British Government and various State Constitutions, like those of Virginia and Massachusetts.

Almost all of Madison's pet Provisions for the Constitution were rejected, including the one he considered the most important: the Power of Congress to *negate (veto) any and all Laws* passed by the State Legislatures.

So much for Madison's Belief in a Limited Federal Government.

And if you don't believe me that Madison was *not* the Author of the Constitution, maybe you'll believe Madison when he wrote to his friend William Cogwell in 1834: "You give me Credit to which I have no Claim calling me the Writer of the Constitution of the US. This was not like the fabled Goddess of Wisdom, the Offspring of a single Brain. It ought to be regarded as the Work of many Heads and many Hands."

3. Assertion: The Rehnquist Court "repudiated many Years of Judicial Hostility to expressions of Faith."

Specifically, you refer to the State of Texas, *Van Orden v. Perry*, which upheld, by a Vote of 5–4, that a Display of the Ten Commandments at the State Capitol was constitutional.

What you failed to mention is that on the very same day—June 27, 2005—by another 5–4 Vote, that same Supreme Court ruled that a similar Display of the Ten Commandments on Kentucky State Grounds was *unconstitutional*.

In other words, Rehnquist's "repudiation of Judicial Hostility" lasted an hour and a half.

Worrisome to me is you seem to have forgotten that the First Amendment itself states:

... Congress shall make no Law respecting an establishment of Religion ...

You neglect as well Jefferson's Statement that the Amendment thus built "a Wall of Separation between Church and State."

You also choose to ignore what James Madison (your favorite) said after the House and Senate hired chaplains in 1789: "The establishment of the chaplainship in Congress is a palpable violation of equal rights as well as of Constitutional principles." Like a woman of ill repute hanging out of a second-floor window, you display some parts while hiding others.

4. Assertion: The 2008 Supreme Court Ruling (in *D.C. v. Heller*) "held that the Framers' Second Amendment protects the Right of an Individual to keep and bear Arms" ... giving Force to the original Understanding of the Framers.

In this Matter, you further trifle with the Facts. Allow me then to inform you (notwithstanding your anticipatory Disdain) of the following:

> That the Heller Ruling applied only to a specific DC Law—the most restrictive in the Nation—in which a Security Guard was barred from keeping a Handgun in his own Home for his Self-Protection.

> That in his Majority opinion, Justice Scalia said this: "The right to own a Gun is not *unlimited*, just as the First Amendment's Right to Free Speech is not ... Thus, we do not read the Second Amendment to protect the Right of Citizens to carry Arms for any sort of Confrontation ..."

> And that State and Federal Courts have upheld almost every Gun Regulation challenged since *Heller*. As one Wag put it, "*Heller* is firing blanks."

5. Assertion: The Constitution explicitly authorizes Capital Punishment as stated in the Fifth Amendment.

To make your Point, you mention the Fifth Amendment but don't quote it. Let me do it for you: "No Person shall be held to answer for a capital or otherwise infamous Crime, unless on a Presentment or Indictment of a Grand Jury."

Now, as I understand the Amendment, this does not in any way *authorize* Capital Punishment. It merely acknowledges it. In writing the Fifth Amendment, the Framers were trying to *protect* the Rights of the Accused, *not*, as you disingenuously imply, establish or enshrine the Punishment itself.

Of course, the Framers were well aware of Capital Punishment. In the Public Square, not far from where they were meeting, there were occasional Hangings. But nothing in their Debates or Deliberations shows they relished the Proceedings.

And shouldn't any Discussion of Capital Punishment include a Mention of the Eighth Amendment, which forbids "cruel and unusual Punishments"?

And shouldn't you—Constitutional Scholar that you are, concerned with the Framers' Original Intent—try to imagine *their* View of, say, the Execution of one Joseph Rudolph Wood III, which took place in Arizona on July 23, 2014? Executioners began pumping a combination of Midazolam and Hydromorphone into his Veins and Groin at 1:57 p.m. His Death was announced at 3:49 p.m.

This was just one of a long line of botched Executions states like Arizona, Texas, and Oklahoma have become famous for.

Maybe you should go to One sometime and decide for yourself how James Madison, Thomas Jefferson, and Alexander Hamilton would have judged those Executions: "Cruel and unusual Punishments" or "hip-hip huzzah"?

. . .

In Summary, Sir, I find your Assertions about the Constitution to be nothing more than an assorted pack of Half-Truths, misstated Facts, and downright Lies: Dissembling and Disinformation employed by you in the Service of your own misguided Principles of Justice.

I have read where your former Harvard Law Professor, Alan J. Dershowitz, once proclaimed you "a brilliant Legal Mind."* Have you since then lost all Sense of Reason? Has your once-brilliant Mind been o'erthrown by Political Expediency? So poisoned by Ambition that Truth-Telling has become an obsolete and neglected Vocation beyond your Lexicon?

For you, Sir, have become in no uncertain way:

• Monarch of Mendacity
• Devotee of Deception
• Prince of Pretense

If one of the great Dangers to our Democracy is the pestilence of Sophistry, then you now border on Treachery, if not Treason. To put it blunt but fair, you, Sir, are a dangerous Man and one not to be trusted with the Reins of Government.

I recognize the severity of my Words, writing as I do in so public a Forum, but I hereby stand behind each and every one of them.

I also recognize that you—as a Man of Honor—may choose, as is your Right, to demand Satisfaction from me for their issuance. In which case, I will be most assuredly willing to oblige should that be your course of Action.

As you well know, there are still States in the Union that permit

---

* Professor Dershowitz is best known as a member of the legal "dream team" that represented O. J. Simpson.

Men such as ourselves to go into the Woods with Dueling Pistols and try to kill each other.

I await your Response.

Your Seconds can contact my Seconds at William Morris Endeavor, Beverly Hills Office.

Whilst This Vital Flame Exists Within Me, I Remain Your Most Staunch Adversary,

Edward Asner

CHAPTER 12

The Constitution According to Ben Carson, MD

> ... In the book [*Gifted Hands*], he said terrible things
> about himself. He said ... that he's got basically a patho-
> logical disease ... Now, if you're pathological, there's no
> cure for that, folks.
>
> —Donald Trump, on Dr. Ben Carson

> Trump likens Carson's pathology to that of child molester!
> —CNN news item

> Ben Carson has a brilliant mind and is passionate about
> strengthening communities and families within those
> communities.
>
> —President Donald Trump naming Ben Carson to lead
> the Department of Housing and Urban Development

The famous neurosurgeon and successful author Dr. Ben Carson ran
in 2016 to be the Republican nominee for President of the United
States. He follows in a long but undistinguished line of Republican candidates who seem more interested in book deals, a job on
Fox News, or high-paying speaking engagements than in actually
becoming President. Newt Gingrich, Sarah Palin, Mike Huckabee,
Rudy Giuliani, and Herman Cain are some who come to mind.

Likable, mild-mannered, and soft-spoken, Dr. Carson is as nice a guy as you'd want to meet—until you find out what he really thinks. Then he gets a little . . . quirky.

Here's what I'm talking about:

On Homosexuality: Carson believes homosexuality is a choice. To back that up, he asserts, "A lot of people . . . go into prison straight and when they come out, they're gay."

I can only assume that Thoreau, Gandhi, Nelson Mandela, and Martin Luther King Jr. are the rare exceptions.

On Ancient Egypt: Carson has said that the pyramids were *not* tombs but *silos* built by Joseph, the son of Jacob, in preparation for the famine as described in the Book of Genesis.

Since the pyramids are not hollow (and therefore could not store grain), either Genesis or Dr. Carson doesn't know what the hell they're talking about.

On Evolution: Carson has stated that the Theory of Evolution was "encouraged by the Adversary" (i.e., Satan) and that only God can make a man. He also claims that Natural Selection, carbon dating, and the Big Bang Theory are all "fairy tales."

Unlike, of course, Jonah in the Whale and Noah on the Ark.

Over the years, Carson has been accused by some as the teller of tall tales—inventing a colorful history of himself as a young man who went from the dangerous, drug-infested ghettos of Detroit to Yale and the operating rooms of Johns Hopkins by dint of hard work, natural smarts, and extraordinary eye-hand coordination.

In his autobiography, *Gifted Hands*, he describes his epiphany: When a friend went to change a radio station, Carson tried to stab the friend in the stomach. But the blade broke on his friend's belt buckle, saving—in effect—both their lives.

As later malpractice suits attest, Dr. Carson has not always been so lucky when it comes to knives.

Anyway, this incident drove him somehow to Scripture, and he has been a changed man ever since.*

And now that we know something about the man, let us consider Dr. Carson's book on the Constitution, *A More Perfect Union: What We the People Can Do to Protect Our Constitutional Liberties.*

Every chapter begins with a quote from the Bible. For example: Chapter 9 on "the Legislative Branch" has this epigraph—"Everyone must submit to governing authorities. For all the authority comes from God, and those in positions of authority have been placed there by God." (Romans 13:1)

It's as if subliminally linking Scripture with the Constitution will suggest that, like the Ten Commandments, the Constitution was written by the Finger of God Almighty and not by fifty-five super-rich white guys sweltering through a Philadelphia summer without air-conditioning and flushing toilets.

To "hammer" home this theme, Carson informs his readers that the Constitution was "steeped in a Christian understanding of politics." He supports that vague claim by finding two (and only two) obscure delegates with supposedly Christian credentials—Richard Bassett, a Methodist from Delaware, and Abraham Baldwin of Georgia—while ignoring the Christian indifference of Alexander Hamilton, James Madison, and Benjamin Franklin.

For the record, Bassett (one of the wealthiest men in Delaware) was rarely present at the Convention, and there is no record of him (in Madison's notes) ever opening his mouth. And Baldwin, while a chaplain during the Revolutionary War, quit the ministry to become

* Dr. Carson's temper was so violent, he claims, that as a boy he tried to hit his mother over the head with a hammer.

a lawyer. The profession of choice for those looking to make really big bucks.

It is precisely because the Framers did *not* see themselves as chosen by God* (and inspired by His Divine Will) that they were able to draft a Constitution based on practical and political compromise.

Carson's view of the Framers as "Men of God" is as misguided as his sense that the Framers were "diverse" and "egalitarian."

On the contrary, they were collectively the richest men in the country: marrying into money like Hamilton; inheriting vast plantations like Charles Pinckney, James Madison, and George Mason; or making fortunes for themselves in business, banking, and land speculation like Gouverneur Morris, Robert Morris, and Benjamin Franklin.

Most were career politicians who represented the elite class of their time while denying the vote to women, Native Americans, slaves,† small farmers, workers, and shopkeepers. Only white men over the age of twenty-one with sizable amounts of property—or cash on hand—got the right to vote. A butcher was dead meat.

From the Preamble to the Amendments, Carson examines the Constitution through the prism of a worldview all his own. For example: he takes the words "... secure the blessings of Liberty to ourselves and our posterity" as proof of the Framers' stance against abortion.‡ An argument he supports by telling us that "*children*§ still in the womb" have the same rights as any other US citizen, including "due process" and "equal protection of the laws." He does stop short, however, in not giving fetuses the right to a driver's license.

---

* Unlike the former President of the United States George W. Bush.

† Carson is curiously sympathetic to the Framers, who called slaves three-fifths of a human being. Which leads me to ask: Does Dr. Carson even know he's black?

‡ Elsewhere, Carson compares Planned Parenthood to slave owners, both equally guilty for killing black people.

§ My emphasis, his word.

Like many anti-abortion activists, Dr. Carson seems to think that Life begins at Erection.

No surprise then that Carson believes the Second Amendment gives all US citizens (including, no doubt, those still in the womb) the right to own whatever weapons they choose, from military assault rifles to bazookas.

What is eye-popping, jaw-dropping, and mind-bending is his rationale:

> ... German citizens were disarmed by their government in the late 1930s, and by the mid-1940s Hitler's regime had mercilessly slaughtered six million Jews and numerous others whom they considered inferior. Through a combination of removing guns and disseminating deceitful propaganda, the Nazis were able to carry out their evil intentions with relatively little resistance.

In other words—to paraphrase the NRA—the only thing that can stop a Gestapo with a gun is Anne Frank with a gun.

When it comes to the Fourteenth Amendment, which gives all citizens "equal protection of the laws," Carson quarrels with the Supreme Court's recent ruling that homosexuals have the right to marry. For Carson, this opinion sabotages the Constitution's Preamble, which ensures "domestic tranquility." Because, according to Carson, the *mainstay* of tranquility is marriage between one man and one woman.

Perhaps as a happily divorced man, I am not the best judge of the "tranquility" of other people's marriages, but here are some statistics that Dr. Carson should know about:

> Each year, more than 10 million women and men are victims of intimate partner violence.

> Each month, the National Domestic Violence Hotline receives an average of 25,000 calls.

Each day, three or more women are murdered by their husbands, according to the American Psychological Association. And usually by a gun.

And those are just the heterosexuals.

In 1987 at Johns Hopkins, Dr. Carson was the lead neurosurgeon of a seventy-member team that separated twins joined at the back of the head but who had separate brains. Immediately after the twenty-hour surgery, Carson gave a press conference announcing the operation's triumphant success.

In a story by the *Washington Post*, the surgery "launched the stardom" of Carson, who "walked out of the operating room that day into a spotlight that has never dimmed."

Carson's press conference led to book deals, worldwide fame, and a second, even more lucrative career as a motivational speaker.

What has been less reported is the fate of the twins, who soon were institutionalized, one more helpless than the other. In 1993, their mother plaintively asked, "Why did I have them separated?" Perhaps Dr. Carson should have remembered his Bible, specifically Matthew 19:6: "What therefore God hath joined together, let no man put asunder."

CHAPTER 13

Rewriting the Constitution:

Mark Levin and the Asner Amendments

I don't know why your husband doesn't put a gun to his
temple. Get the hell out of here.

—Radio show host Mark Levin to a
woman caller who defended President Obama

For those of you unfamiliar with Mark Levin, host of the syndicated
radio show *Mark Levin,* he has the politics of Billy Sunday, the car-
toon voice of an animated chipmunk, and all the charm of a . . . well,
Mark Levin.

In his *The Liberty Amendments*, Mr. Levin proposes eleven
amendments to the US Constitution. It is Mr. Levin's claim that
over the last two centuries, the Constitution has become "mangled"
by a "delusional governing elite." And only Mr. Levin knows how to
restore it to its original glory.

In more than three hundred pages, Mr. Levin cherry-picks his
plodding way to what he says is a more preferred form of government. Despite prose that mimics the style of a civics term paper at a
mid-level university (the kind that might award an honorary degree
to Hugh Hewitt), the book sold more than a million unread copies
and made no. 1 on the *New York Times* Best Sellers List.*

---

* For what it's worth: Mr. Levin's latest book is called *Rediscovering Americanism,*
Mr. Levin being one of our foremost Americanismists. I can't recommend the
book, but the cover (featuring Mr. Levin hunched in front of an American flag,

Not that Mr. Levin doesn't love the Constitution the way it is. Oh, but he does and with a passion not unlike Othello's when he strangled Desdemona. It's just that the Constitution could be so much better if only he had his way with it.

Here now are five[†] of Mr. Levin's eleven suggested revisions to our present Constitution—his so-called Liberty Amendments:

Levin Article I. Senators are to be elected by the *State* Legislature and not directly by the people.

Levin yearns for the good old days when politicians elected *other* politicians while ignoring the Democratic concept of "one person, one vote" established by the Warren Court in 1963.

Levin Article II. Supreme Court decisions can be overturned by a three-fifths vote by Congress.

Let me see if I can get this straight: Congress passes a law that the Supreme Court rules is unconstitutional, which *then* goes *back* to the now even higher court—the Congress—which passed the law in the first place.

Levin Article III. The federal government shall not collect more than 15 percent of a person's annual income.

That means, according to the impartial Tax Policy Center, a deficit of $8.6 trillion over the next ten years. Unless, of course, you eliminate Medicare, Social Security, and the Departments of Education, Housing and Urban Development, and Energy. Which is, of course, Levin's idea in the first place: to starve the government out of existence.

---

clenched-jawed and reeking of Trump-like machismo) can be used to scare small children into eating their vegetables.

[†] Trust me, getting through five will be more than enough. And yes, they're out of order.

It also means that multimillionaires such as Levin would pay the same amount of taxes as the minimum-wage employee at Jack-in-the-Box who microwaves your bacon.

As listeners of his radio show are well aware, Mr. Levin, like most rich Republicans, is fixated on taxes. And somewhere he has gotten the idea that his idolized Framers were against taxes.* Perhaps he should go back and read the Constitution, because there it is in Article I, Section 8:

> Congress shall have Power to lay and collect Taxes, Duties, Imposts, and Excises to pay the Debts and provide for the common Defense and *general Welfare of the United States* . . . [italics mine].

Perhaps Levin should also read *Hylton v. United States* (1796)—the very first Supreme Court decision—in which it ruled that Congress's tax on horse-drawn carriages was constitutional. The case was argued on behalf of the government by Alexander Hamilton, Founder and Framer.† Levin should read as well Washington's Farewell Address, a portion of which defends taxation.

Levin Article IV. Amendment to protect the vote: Every citizen shall produce valid photographic identification documents as a requirement to vote.

Levin offers a more sophisticated but no less sinister attempt to suppress black voters than the Literacy Test Louisiana used in 1964.

For the record, I give you the following:

---

* Is he kidding? The Constitution was written so the new government could start collecting taxes.

† And Levin must have been horrified by Benjamin Franklin's defense of high taxes, especially on luxury items: "A person has the natural right to all he earned that was necessary to support himself and his family," he wrote, "but all property superfluous to such purpose is the property of the public . . ."

The State of Louisiana

Literacy Test (This test is to be given to anyone who cannot prove a fifth grade education.)

Do what you are told to do in each statement, nothing more, nothing less. Be careful as one wrong answer denotes failure of the test. You have 10 minutes to complete the test.

1. Draw a line around the number or letter of this sentence.

2. Draw a line under the last word in this line.

3. Cross out the longest word in this line.

4. Draw a line around the shortest word in this line.

5. Circle the first, first letter of the alphabet in this line.

6. In the space below draw three circles, one inside (engulfed by) the other.

7. Above the letter X make a small cross.

8. Draw a line through the letter below that comes earliest in the alphabet.

ZVSBDMKITPHC

9. Draw a line through the two letters below that come last in the alphabet.

ZVBDMKTPHSYC

10. In the first circle below write the last letter of the first word beginning with "L".

11. Cross out the number necessary, when making the number below one million.

10000000000

12. Draw a line from circle 2 to circle 5 that will pass below circle 2 and above circle 4.

13. In the line below cross out each number that is more than 20 but less than 30.

31 16 48 29 53 47 22 37 98 26 20 25

14. Draw a line under the first letter after "h" and draw a line through the second letter after "j".

a b c d e f g h i j k l m n o p q

15. In the space below, write the word "noise" backwards and place a dot over what would be its second letter should it have been written forward.

16. Draw a triangle with a blackened circle that overlaps only its left corner.

17. Look at the line of numbers below, and place on the blank, the number that should come next.

2 4 8 16 ___

18. Look at the line of numbers below, and place on the blank, the number that should come next.

3 6 9 ___ 15

19. Draw in the space below, a square with a triangle in it, and within that same triangle draw a circle with a black dot in it.

20. Spell backwards, forwards.

21. Print the word vote upside down, but in the correct order.

22. Place a cross over the tenth letter in this line, a line under the first space in this sentence, and circle around the last the in the second line of this sentence.

23. Draw a figure that is square in shape. Divide it in half by drawing a straight line from its northeast corner to its southwest corner, and then divide it once more by drawing a broken line from the middle of its western side to the middle of its eastern side.

24. Print a word that looks the same whether it is printed frontwards or backwards.

25. Write down on the line provided, what you read in the triangle below:

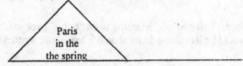

26. In the third square below, write the second letter of the fourth word.

27. Write right from the left to the right as you see it spelled here.

28. Divide a vertical line in two equal parts by bisecting it with a curved horizontal line that is only straight at its spot bisection of the vertical.

29. Write every other word in this first line and print every third word in same line, (original type smaller and first line ended at comma) but capitalize the fifth word that you write.

30. Draw five circles that have one common inter-locking part.

I know I'm exaggerating. But as much as Levin rationalizes his voter ID laws, his intent is no different than Louisiana's: strip the voting rights of black and Latino minorities. At least the founder of the Tea Party, Jim DeMint,* is honest when he acknowledges that voter ID laws have one motive and one motive only: help Republicans win office. As he wrote:

> In the states where they do have voter ID laws, you've seen ... elections begin to change towards more Conservative candidates.

And as reported by the *New York Times*, Republicans in Wisconsin were "like really giddy" over the suppression effects of their voter ID laws.

Levin Article V. Any law passed by the House and the Senate could be overruled by three-fifths of the fifty state legislatures.

And how long do you think that process would take? Long enough, I suspect, that there'd be no laws passed at all. Which, again, may be Levin's idea in the first place.

Anyway, you get what Levin is up to: a Limited Government, run by the rich for the rich, Devil take the hindmost, and screw you, pal, I've got mine.

Mr. Levin's amendments tell us all we need to know about his definition of *liberty*. And it is certainly not the same as the Framers'.

As Hamilton wrote in his first *Federalist* essay: "The vigor of government is essential to the security of liberty."

Mr. Levin—who bills himself as "radio's biggest personality who is now taking television by storm"—is serious enough about his amendments that he has not just written his book, he has taken to the streets.

Speaking to a group of Republican state legislators, Levin called

---

* Former Republican Senator from South Carolina and former president of the Heritage Foundation, a Republican think tank. And former employer of Clarence Thomas's wife.

for a convention of the states (under Article V, Section 3) to "take the country back" ... You have a duty under the federal Constitution," he barked, "to save the Republic."

The state legislatures that James Madison warned us against Mark Levin now wants to run the country.

Midway through the dark woods of Mr. Levin's book, I stumbled onto an idea. *His.*

If he could come up with *his* amendments, why couldn't I with mine? I'm as big an ignoramus as he is.

So here they are—the six Asner Amendments to the Constitution of the United States:

Asner Article I. The Senate. No state shall be awarded two senators from states that do not have populations equal to that of the Bronx, Brooklyn, and Queens.

Let me explain: North and South Dakota, Wyoming, New Mexico, Idaho, and Montana *together* do not exceed six million people. Those boroughs in New York City have *more than* six million. So why should those states get twelve senators and New York only two? I say—lump those states into one. It makes sense, is democratically fair, and, I'm sure, Madison would agree.

Asner Article II. Freedom of Speech. Congress shall make no laws abridging Freedom of Speech *except* in the case of Fox News, where the following words, phrases, and opinions shall be forever banned:

1. "Politically correct."
2. "The War on Christmas."

---

* Article V, Section 3 states that amendments to the Constitution can be ratified by three-quarters of specially called state conventions. Something that has never been done in the history of the United States.

3. "Women who sue rich newscasters for sexual harassment are only looking to make a quick buck."
4. "Climate change is a hoax perpetuated by the Chinese to ruin America's economy."
5. "Why won't Democrats say the words 'radical *Islamic terrorist*'?"
6. "Sharia Law is coming to America."
7. "Fake news."
8. "If that kindergarten teacher only had a gun, no one would be dead."

Asner Article III. Reproductive Rights. Neither Congress nor the states shall pass any law abridging a woman's right to control her own body.

I'm a firm believer that the only time a woman should give up control of her own body is during orgasm.

Asner Article IV. Health Care. Every person residing in these United States shall be entitled to free health care, with the exception of tummy tucks and hair transplants. Funds for free health care shall be provided by federal taxes levied on all secret and foreign bank accounts held in the name of US corporations.

Asner Article V. Gun Rights. Congress shall pass any and all laws necessary to abridge the rights of crazy people to possess firearms.

Asner Article VI. Guaranteed Minimum Income. The government guarantees a basic income of $10,000 per year for an American family of four.

I know—this sounds like another harebrained idea from a bleeding-heart liberal. In fact, it is a concept that was supported by the Right-Wing economist (and one of Mark Levin's political heroes) Milton Friedman and was, believe it or not, almost introduced to the public by Richard Nixon back in the sixties. The thinking be-

hind a basic income ("social security for all") is that it would reduce poverty, cut down or destigmatize intrusive welfare, keep kids
in school, and help those who lost their jobs to outsourcing.*

Okay, so it'd probably cost a couple of trillion. To get the money,
we could stop building nuclear submarines, tax religious cults like
Scientology, and end billion-dollar subsidies to ExxonMobil.

There. That wasn't so hard, was it?

---

* A guaranteed minimum income was also introduced in 1795 (*Agrarian Justice*)
by the patriot, Revolutionary War hero, and Founding Father Tom Paine.

CHAPTER 14

Immigration and Ann Coulter:

A Review That Was Never Published in the New York Times Book Review

God said: "Earth is yours. Take it. Rape it. It's yours."

—Ann Coulter

We know who the homicidal maniacs are . . . We should invade their countries, kill their leaders, and convert them to Christianity.

—Ann Coulter

For her admirers, *¡Adios, America!: The Left's Plan to Turn Our Country into a Third World Hellhole*—is a take-no-prisoners, biting commentary on America's immigration policy and the undesirables that come with it.

And for Ann Coulter, there is no one more undesirable than the Mexicans. To put it simply: Ann Coulter hates Mexicans. Here's how much:

Mexicans specialize in corpse desecration, burning people alive, rolling human heads onto packed nightclub dance floors, dissolving bodies in acid, and hanging mutilated bodies from bridges.

Lost a friend to drugs? Thank a Mexican.

The main difference between decapitation in Syria and Mexico is that Mexicans also behead women, children, and innocent bystanders.

But it's not just their crime sprees, decapitations, and a failure to enjoy consensual sex that bothers Ms. Coulter. Mexicans are also serial litterbugs.

Here she is from her chapter "Keep America Multicultural":

Sending their poorest, most backward people to the United States is obviously a big help to Mexico, but it's pretty rough on America's landscape ... But it is also a fact that the vast majority of the Teddy Kennedy immigrants come from peasant cultures that have no concept of "litter."

In other words, the only reason Mexicans have picnics is to leave their trash behind when they go. You'd think they'd have the decency to bring along their leaf blowers.

Here she is quoting one resident of a Los Angeles neighborhood overrun by Mexicans:

"Mexicans just do not clean up after themselves. It is as if they have never thrown a piece of trash away in their lives ..."

Clearly, "littering" is in the Mexican DNA, like a bushy moustache.

I'm surprised that Ms. Coulter forgot another and more serious charge: Mexicans cook with lard! Not only do they litter our national parks, pollute our lakes and rivers, they clog our arteries!

I sympathize with Ms. Coulter because, as much as I hate to admit it, I've had my own problems with Mexicans. And this is as good a time as any to tell you about them:

• During dinner at Dos Caballeros, a mariachi band came to my table and played "La Cucaracha" back to back.

- I once lost $500 at a cock fight in Tijuana.
- A young woman I slept with in college called me Speedy Gonzales behind my back.
- I once dated a Mexican waitress who left a bite mark on my right shoulder that took a month to heal.
- At the common urinal at Dodger Stadium, a Mexican with a Fernando Valenzuela jersey pissed on my shoes.
- A Mexican gardener of mine macheted my pet snake.
- I got the shits in Acapulco.
- At a Screen Actors Guild meeting, the late Ricardo Montalban told me to go fuck myself.

So, Ms. Coulter, as you can see, you're not alone. I too bear the scars—physical and emotional—from Mexican immigration.

But Mexicans are not the only group of immigrants turning our nation into the cesspool it's become. Let me run down her list for you, paraphrasing (and taking liberties) as I go:

- *Somalian* immigrants have so degraded the state of Minnesota that it reelected Al Franken to the Senate.
- *Indian* rapists have disguised themselves as high-tech geeks employed by Mark Zuckerberg.
- *Ugandan* immigrants have brought crime as well as a penchant for circumcising anything they can get their hands on.
- *Pakistani* cab drivers work part-time chauffeuring ISIS-inspired terrorists.
- *Hmong* immigrants believe that animal sacrifices will cure type 2 diabetes. (You can almost hear her warning America: Watch out for your puppies!)
- Women from *Ecuador* are known for cutting off their husbands' penises in retribution. The Ecuadorian immigrant Lorena Gallo was quoted by Coulter as saying she chopped it off because "he always have orgasm and he doesn't wait for me to have orgasm. He selfish."

Perhaps in Ecuador, chopping off your husband's penis is as common as chicken for Sunday supper. I wouldn't know myself. The only Ecuadorian I knew worked for me as a housekeeper. And if I remember, she wouldn't go anywhere near my penis. She wouldn't even rinse out my tub.

But on behalf of American husbands everywhere, I thank you, Ms. Coulter, for standing up for our penises even when they won't stand up for themselves.

Ms. Coulter is especially hard on the Hmong tribal people from Vietnam. According to Ms. Coulter, the Hmongs are rapists, mass murderers, as well as notorious for not returning their overdue library books. She also accuses them—in horror—of lying in court!

Ms. Coulter is more than a little miffed that the Hmongs got in the country in the first place. "Thank you, Teddy Kennedy," she writes, blaming the late Senator for the fiasco.[*]

Here, I'm afraid I must respectfully step in and set the record straight. As much as Ms. Coulter knows her Mexicans, her Ecuadorian women, and her Pakistani cab drivers, she really hasn't studied up on her Hmongs. Perhaps she's too young to remember the Vietnam War and the Hmongs' role in it. In the 1960s, the CIA trained and recruited the Hmong people in Laos to fight against the North Vietnamese. Over 60 percent of Hmong men fought on our side. They formed a secret army made up of divisions, battalions, and special guerrilla units that attacked the North—all under the direction of the US military. Hmong civilians as well risked their lives rescuing and hiding downed American pilots.

It was a story long untold but now fully acknowledged: the Hmongs made monumental sacrifices on behalf of the United States' war effort in Vietnam. In the course of that dreadful war, the Hmongs were always our most dependable and trusted allies.

---

[*] More on her beef with Ted Kennedy coming up.

Following the withdrawal (and defeat) of American forces in 1975, Hmong refugees fled the country because of the ethnic cleansing, military attacks, and arrests at the hands of the Communists. Thousands were persecuted, tortured, and killed.

In the 1980s, because of their service to the American cause, Conservatives in Congress (along with former President Bush aide Michael Johns) fought to grant Hmong refugees immediate immigration rights. Despite President Clinton's threat to veto the legislation, the Republicans succeeded. And I'm with those Republicans on this. It seems the least we could have done for the most persecuted people on Earth.

This is a surprising position by Ms. Coulter, since no doubt she does not come by her facts frivolously. I'm sure all her statements are well researched: decades-old news clippings, the Breitbart website, Jeff Sessions's tweets, and a Ted Cruz press release.*

She is also especially impressive when it comes to statistics. For example: she can come within one decimal point in telling us how many Mexican heads of households living on food stamps once held up a liquor store using only a gardening tool.

It would be a false impression, however, to say that Coulter is opposed to *all* immigrants. She seems particularly fond of the policies in the eighteenth century when America let in mostly British and Dutch. Still, she does not totally disapprove of later-arriving immigrants like the Irish, Italians, and Jews.

Again, let me summarize, in my own biased ways, her evaluations:

Despite their flaws, the Irish—at least—didn't rape anybody because they were too drunk all the time.

Italians only killed each other.

---

* He said mockingly.

And the best thing about the Jews was their uncanny ability to assimilate. So good at it were they that there are now stretches on the Upper West Side of New York where, if it weren't for their excessive amounts of gold jewelry, you could not tell a Jew from a Gentile.

Ms. Coulter has special kudos for the Jews who gave us the film industry, especially for those ideal portraits of Christian life in the suburbs where Kate Hepburn, Cary Grant, Donna Reed, and Bing Crosby celebrated America as it was meant to be: white, rich, and witty.

For his unique contributions, Ms. Coulter singles out Irving Berlin, the Jewish songwriter who gave us "Easter Parade," "White Christmas," and "God Bless America." Then she adds in that unique way of hers: "Try to imagine an immigrant in La Raza doing any of that!"*

Another of Ms. Coulter's bugaboos is the subject of "anchor babies," the derogatory term to describe children born in the United States whose parents are illegal citizens. It is Coulter's claim that every year hundreds of thousands of these babies are born in this country—fraudulently—in order for the parents and their extended families to acquire citizenship. Hence the term "anchor."

Coulter blames this revolting phenomenon on Supreme Court Justice William J. Brennan Jr., who, she says, "cooked up" anchor babies when he "slipped in" a footnote into a ruling in 1982.

For Coulter, "anchor babies" as a Constitutional issue is right up there with, and I quote, "abortion, sodomy, gay marriage, and unicorns."

But before I address the Justice Brennan Constitutional issue, let me ask: How valid is it as an immigration strategy for parents to

---

* For those keeping score at home, it's Jews 3, Mexicans 0.

drop their anchor babies in this country in order to become citizens? The answer: almost impossible. Why? I'll tell you:

Because according to law, the parents would first have to leave the country, then wait for the child to reach *twenty-one* to even apply for citizenship.

And if it was discovered (as it would be) that the pregnant parent had been here illegally when she gave birth, there'd be a ten-year ban for that parent to reenter the country.

So—parents who think having an anchor baby is a good way to gain US citizenship are as wrong about the laws as Coulter is.

Now, let's look at that infamous footnote Justice Brennan snuck into the Supreme Court case back in 1982.*

The case Coulter refers to is *Plyler v. Doe*, in which the Supreme Court struck down (by a 5–4 vote) a Texas state statute that denied funding for education to undocumented immigrant children.

The Majority opinion was written by Justice William J. Brennan Jr. (appointed to the Court by that crazy Leftist Dwight D. Eisenhower) and concurred with by Justice Thurgood Marshall (appointed by Lyndon Johnson), Harry Blackmun (a Nixon appointee), John Paul Stevens (appointed by Republican Gerald Ford), and Lewis F. Powell Jr. (also appointed by Richard Nixon).

Here in part is what the ruling said:

> The deprivation of education takes an inestimable toll on the economic, intellectual, and psychological well-being of the individual and poses an obstacle to individual achievement . . . The undocumented status of those *innocent* children does not establish a sufficient rational basis for denying them benefits that the State affords other residents . . . Under the current laws and practices, the illegal alien of today may well be the *legal* alien of tomorrow . . .

---

* A similar claim has been made about that footnote by a host of Right Wingers, among them Beck, Cruz, and Limbaugh.

In a nutshell: the Supreme Court ruled that Mexican children were people too, and that Texas could not screw them out of an education because, as the Fourteenth Amendment says: "No State . . . shall deprive *any person* of life, liberty, or property . . . nor deny to *any person* within its jurisdiction the equal protection of the laws."

And it was not a footnote! It was a ruling! [*]

Coulter blames our current immigration laws, and their disastrous results, on one archvillain: Senator Ted Kennedy. Maybe because he died in 2009 and can't defend himself.

But for Coulter, if you want the one guy who "wrecked our country," it's Ted Kennedy and his 1965 Immigration and Nationality Act. The act—a Cold War response to the oppressive regimes of the Communists—replaced the strict quota of our 1920s immigration policies.[†]

Trouble is, in 1965 Ted Kennedy was a freshman Senator with little influence, and while he supported the bill, it surely wasn't *his*. (Actually, it was called the Hart-Celler Act.) It was, in fact, passed overwhelmingly in the Senate by a margin of 76–18 and in the House 318–95, with a higher percentage of Republicans in favor than Democrats.[‡]

The bill was signed into law by President Lyndon B. Johnson on October 3, 1965, stating at the time that the quota system it was replacing violated "the basic principle of American democracy, the principle that values and rewards each man on the basis of his merit as a man. It has been un-American in the highest sense because it

---

[*] A common mistake among lawyers, confusing a ruling with a footnote. Usually to their own benefit.

[†] Since the Act banned the immigration of all homosexuals, it's surprising Ann Coulter isn't more favorably disposed to it.

[‡] In total, 74 percent of Democrats and 85 percent of Republicans supported the bill.

has been untrue to the faith that brought thousands to these shores even before we were a country."*

It should be noted that President Johnson signed the Act on Liberty Island at the base of the Statue of Liberty. Which suggests this might be as good a time as any to remind Ms. Coulter and her ilk what is inscribed there:

> *. . . Here at our sea-washed, sunset gates shall stand*
> *A mighty woman with a torch, whose flame*
> *Is the imprisoned lightning, and her name*
> *Mother of Exiles. From her beacon-hand*
> *Glows world-wide welcome; her mild eyes command*
> *The air-bridged harbor that twin cities frame.*
> *"Keep, ancient lands, your storied pomp!" cries she*
> *With silent lips. "Give me your tired, your poor,*
> *Your huddled masses yearning to breathe free,*
> *The wretched refuse of your teeming shore.*
> *Send these, the homeless, tempest-tossed to me,*
> *I lift my lamp beside the golden door!"*†

But what is most disappointing about the Coulter book is not the misstatement of facts nor its empty and endless sarcasm, or even the overabundance of exclamation points!‡ What is most disappointing is that it's the same old crap—regurgitated! To mix a metaphor.

Hating foreigners, you see, is a tradition as old as our Constitution and often more honored. Even some of our beloved Founders hated foreigners:

---

* Remarks at the signing.

† "The New Colossus" by Emma Lazarus, 1883.

‡ One grows hoarse just reading them.

Benjamin Franklin thought German immigrants were too stupid to learn English.*

John Adams wished for some kind of magic globe he could place over the country to keep out Catholics.

George Washington disapproved of all immigrants unless they were "useful mechanics."

Our hatred of immigrants—especially those of another color—can be read in the history of our immigration laws:

The Alien and Sedition Acts of 1798 imposed a fourteen-year ban on all French and Irish immigrants.

In 1875, the Page Act banned criminals, prostitutes, and Chinese.

The Naturalization Act of 1906 required all immigrants to learn English before becoming citizens.

In 1907, in what was known as the Gentlemen's Agreement, all Japanese workers were banned from entering the United States.

In the same year, the Expatriation Act said that women who married foreigners lost their citizenship.

In 1921, the Emergency Quota Act limited immigrants from anywhere other than Western Europe.

---

* In a pamphlet written in 1751, Franklin compared Germans to "Blacks and Tawneys" who could never acquire the "complexion" of America's first settlers, thereby weakening the colonies' social structure.

In 1929, the Natural Origins Act again reduced immigration from Eastern and Southern Europe, specifically targeting Polish and Italians.

In 1941, strict quotas on Jews trying to escape Nazi Germany gave them no place to go.

With those laws, there was always the accompanying discrimination and violence toward immigrants too frequent and graphic to catalog here.

The sad truth is that Ann Coulter is just the latest voice in a long jingoistic line of anti-immigrant rhetoric. Her slurs may be different. Her targets may be different. But it's the same old message: the white majority in this country is endangered by the rising wave of foreign and darker immigrants. Everything she says is as dated as her hatred, without a new thought in the carload.

In fact, reading Coulter's *¡Adios, America!*, I couldn't help but be reminded of a book written about a hundred years earlier with an eerily similar title: *The Passing of the Great Race* by Madison Grant. Called at the time the "Manifesto of Scientific Racism," *The Passing of the Great Race* said everything Coulter says, only deadlier.

Here's a small sampling of Mr. Grant's racial theories:

He advocates the supremacy of the Nordic (Aryan) race as the sole group responsible for the growth of human civilization.[*]

The desirable characteristics of a people—"family, life, loyalty, and truth"—are the exclusive products of the Nordic race.

The Nordic race is now (in 1916) in danger of committing "race suicide" by being outnumbered by a "defective strain."

---

[*] In his worldview, even Jesus was Nordic, which is why, he says, the Blond Savior was killed by the Jews, because he looked "un-Jewish."

And here's Madison Grant in his own words:

> On Nordic racial qualities: "The Nordics are ... a race of soldiers, sailors, adventurers, and explorers, but above all of rulers, organizers, and aristocrats ..."

> On New York City as the result of immigration: "New York is becoming a *cloaca gentium* [cesspool] which will produce many amazing racial hybrids and some ethnic horrors ... that will be beyond the powers of future anthropologists to unravel."

> "The man of the old stock [i.e., whites] is being literally driven off the streets of New York City by the swarms of Polish Jews."

And on the physical ideal of what he calls the White Person *Par Excellence*, his description is:

> ... wavy brown or blond hair and blue, gray or light brown eyes, fair skin, high, narrow, and straight nose ... and a long skull ...

Why, it's almost as if he's describing Ann Coulter on the cover of her book jacket.

Putting the final paragraph from each of their books side by side should seal the comparisons. Here's Ann Coulter:

> America needs to worry about Americans. How much is the price of guilt for having a successful society before we're entitled to say to the poor of the world *enough!* We gave at the office.

And here's Madison Grant:

> We Americans must realize that the altruistic ideals which
> have controlled our social development during the past cen-
> tury, and the maudlin sentimentalism that has made America
> "an asylum for the oppressed," are sweeping the nation to-
> ward a racial abyss. If the Melting Pot is allowed to boil with-
> out control . . . the type of American Colonial descent [i.e.,
> whites] will become as extinct as the Athenian of the age of
> Pericles.

The major differences between Grant and Coulter lie in their solutions for an America overrun by foreigners. Ann has two modest
proposals: close the borders to all further immigration so we Americans, as she says, can have some "me time." And second, deport the
11 million or so illegal Mexicans or get them somehow to deport
themselves. After all, if they got here by themselves, they should be
able to get back by themselves.

Madison Grant also had two solutions. But his were made of much
sterner stuff. First, he called for the establishment of city-run bureau-
cracies to segregate the "unfavorable races" into their own ghettos.*

And second, equally ambitious, was his advocation of eugenics—
the race-based practice of improving the genetic quality of the
human population either by sterilization or euthanasia of all
"undesirables."†

Now, the eugenics movement that began in America in the early
twentieth century was a big deal. The movement received funding
from the Rockefeller Foundation, the Harriman railroad fortune,
and the Kellogg's Corn Flakes people. A national Eugenics Record

---

* Makes you wonder how come Ms. Coulter didn't think of that.

† The one kind of birth control acceptable to fundamentalists.

Office, founded in 1911, collected masses of family "pedigrees" to separate the "fit" and "unfit." The Eugenic League, along with the American Breeders Association,* promoted the cause.

Here's an excerpt from their mission statement:

> Society must protect itself; as it claims to deprive the murderer of his life, so it may also annihilate the hideous serpent of hopelessly *vicious protoplasm*.† Here is where appropriate legislation will aid in Eugenics in creating a healthier and saner society in the future.

But eugenics did not exist solely in theory. Let me throw some horrifying numbers at you:

> In 1907, Indiana passed the first eugenics-based *compulsory* sterilization law in the world. Thirty states followed.

> Between 1907 and 1963 (yes, you read that right), more than 64,000 sterilizations were performed on men and women.

> In 1927, the Supreme Court *upheld* the sterilizations in the case *Buck v. Bell*, in which Oliver Wendell Holmes Jr. wrote that "public welfare" outweighed the interests of an individual. After the ruling, dozens of states added new sterilization statutes.

> By 1961, 61 percent of the total eugenic sterilizations were performed on women.

Which brings us back to Madison Grant—one of the most influential and powerful forces in the eugenics movement. He campaigned

---

* For people, not dogs.

† Emphasis mine.

for and helped pass Virginia's Racial Integrity Act of 1924 (designed to prevent interracial relationships), which required that a racial description of every person be recorded at birth. There were only two classifications: white and colored. It defined race by Grant's own "one-drop rule"*—the "cross between a white man and a Negro is a Negro . . . and the cross between any of the three European races and a Jew is a Jew."

Unlike Coulter, Madison Grant was not so politically correct in naming his true fear: the contamination that comes from the commingling of pure Nordic blood with that of the blood of inferior races.

To his credit, Grant *names* his fear and it is clearly a sexual one: The picture conjured up is a scene from D. W. Griffith's *The Birth of a Nation* where a mob of newly freed darkies comes lookin' to find 'em some blonde, virginal daughters of the Old South.

Coulter, on the other hand, hides behind her crime figures, too cowardly to even mention the real nightmare of all white supremacists: sexual relations with the "coloreds."

And I thought Ann Coulter had balls!

Despite Coulter's timidity, the two books do share some measure of importance. Obviously, *¡Adios, America!* formed a kind of "intellectual underpinning" to Trump's xenophobia, but even here she is but a pale comparison to the influence garnered by her predecessor.

The Passing of the Great Race became the first book in English to be translated by the Nazis when they came to power in 1933.† And later, it was none other than Adolf Hitler who wrote a personal note to Madison Grant, thanking him for writing the book, calling it "my Bible."

High praise indeed from the Führer.

And *that*, Ms. Coulter, is something to shoot for.

---

* Which defines as "colored" any person with one drop of Negro blood.

† During the Nuremberg Trials, Grant's book was introduced into evidence by a defense lawyer for the head of the Nazi T-4 Euthanasia Program, Dr. Karl Brandt, justifying policies not unique to the Nazis.

CHAPTER 15

The Shocking Truth About the Bill of Rights

I have not viewed the Bill of Rights in an important light.

—James Madison in a letter to Thomas Jefferson, 1788

Paper declarations of Rights are trifling things and no real security to liberty.

—Noah Webster in a letter to James Madison, 1789

When we think of the Constitution, we always think of the Bill of Rights. It is the Bill of Rights—guaranteeing our freedoms of speech, conscience, religion, and the press—that is the centerpiece of America's exceptionalism.

But the backstory of how the Bill of Rights originated, by whom and how, is not so familiar. At least it wasn't to me.

So it came as a shock to find out that the Bill of Rights was, in fact, a reluctant afterthought—a political and cynical ploy by the Federalists led by Washington, Hamilton, and Madison. This was a revelation that came while reading *The Bill of Rights* by Professor Carol Berkin, who summed it up this way: "Madison's Bill of Rights was . . . more a political strategy than a statement of America's most cherished values."

Let me put this in its historical context: Five days before the end of the Constitutional Convention, George Mason of Virginia proposed that a Bill of Rights be added to the Constitution. The delegates, almost to a man, soundly defeated the measure. They were tired. They wanted to go home. And the Constitution was already written. Besides, as Hamilton would later put it in *The Federalist*, a declaration of rights was mere "aphorisms ... which would sound much better in a treatise of ethics than in a constitution of government."

There may have been another unstated reason: the Framers did not entirely trust the "people" (only one foreclosure away from becoming a mob) and were leery about giving them too many freedoms.

Whatever the reasons, the Framers had made a serious mistake as the omission united the anti-Federalists and gave them the ammunition they needed to oppose a constitution they already mistrusted. To rectify their grievances, the anti-Federalists called for a second convention.

And here's where the politics of the story take shape. To prevent a second convention (which would undo everything) *and* to ensure ratification, the Federalists—with Madison in the lead—agreed to add a Bill of Rights. But it would be *their* Bill of Rights.

Written by them, *this* Bill of Rights would dose out just enough "freedoms" to appease the "people"; cut the anti-Federalists off from their base while taking credit for the bill themselves; and at the same time preserve the Constitution as *they* had written it.

Maybe you don't believe me. Maybe you think it's not possible that the Bill of Rights, our most sacred of documents, was really the result of such a calculated and Machiavellian plot. Trust me, I understand.

Which is why I have taken it upon myself to write the following three letters so you can read how it was all done from Madison himself.

The Letters of James Madison to an Unknown Friend in Which He Reveals the Shocking Truth About the Origination of the Bill of Rights

New York, May 8, 1789

Sir:

I write to you presently from our nation's temporary capital of New York City. I am happy to emphasize "temporary" as this city is more conducive to diversions of food, drink, and entertainment than it is to the serious business of government.

With each day, this city seems to open one new pleasure palace after another. Each more opulent and costly than the last. But as I am a dutiful member of our nation's first Congress, my days *and* nights have been spent either in Session at the Federal Building or at my lodging, preparing for the critical weeks ahead when my amendments to the Constitution are to be debated and voted upon.

Whilst it is usually within my temperament to refrain from frivolous amusements, I am now more than ever keeping to myself.

This is the result of not only concentrating on the arduous work ahead but a troubling concern for my dear, beloved mother, Nelly, who has taken ill from what nobody knows for certain. That, in addition to my own recent flare-up of an old condition—piles—has limited my movements if not my mind.

Were I at home in Montpelier this day, I would be sitting on a keg of ice to relieve my discomfort. Here, I'm reduced to a bedpan of lukewarm water.

Since we have not communicated in recent months, allow me to make you current regarding the aforementioned amendments or Bill of Rights, as they are more popularly called.

I do so in the utmost confidence that this letter will remain confidential—for should either the general public or the anti-

Federalists discover the true nature of my policies, it could very well doom not only my strategy but the very Republic itself.

As you know, since the Convention, there has been this outcry from many sides for a Bill of Rights to be amended to the Constitution as it now stands. Much of this incessant clamoring has come naturally from the anti-Federalists, claiming to speak on behalf of the people. Exactly who the people are, however, has as yet not been determined.

My position on this matter has been clear from the very beginning. A Bill of Rights can do little when harm is intended. Words on parchment—no matter their sincerity, no matter how rhetorically expressed—can neither preserve liberty nor insure justice if men in power choose otherwise.

This is not idle, hypothetical speculation. I know this from my own observation and experience.

For example: in Virginia, where Mr. Jefferson so brilliantly introduced his Religious Freedom Act, I have witnessed the persecution of local Baptists continue on an incessant and harrowing level.

And all the common laws in the land, including those of "due process," have not prevented the confiscation of Loyalist property, during which its home owners were run from their houses in the middle of the night by tyrannical mobs.

Nor has the Right of Freedom of the Press—long established in this country—provided sanctuary for a publisher daring to speak out against the policies of powerful adversaries.

No declared Freedom, no matter how codified, will keep one safe and secure in one's home or in one's person from those who mean no good. And mere parchment provides no barrier against tar and feathering.

As I said at the Convention, there was no need for any such amendments. Since the Constitution took no rights away, there was no necessity to enumerate them. To repeat an analogy: if the Constitution does not forbid one from burying the dead, why need an amendment that says you can?

Still, the ever-present chatter from the anti-Federalists about a Bill of Rights does not cease. And even though the Constitutions of many of their states have no such Rights themselves, their noise continues unabated.

No more so than Virginia, where Patrick Henry leads his campaign on behalf of the People, stoking their fears with his inflammatory, overblown, misbegotten oratory. (By the way, I have heard news that he recently fell from his horse, doing himself some damage. Pray write and tell me this is true.)

There is no man on Earth more responsible for my distrust of state legislators than Patrick Henry and his dark, persuasive skills in controlling the ignorant, the unprotected, and the unestablished.

This great Patrick Henry, who has not lifted his finger for his country since he signed the Declaration of Independence—who forced me from any chance for the Senate, sending me on horseback through the backwoods of Virginia seeking votes as a Congressman— this same Patrick Henry now has the temerity to claim he speaks for the People, not only of his State but for our Nation.

But Henry speaks only for himself and his interests: his 100,000-acre plantation, his land grabs in the West, and the untaxable monies from his tobacco productions.

This same Patrick Henry whose taste and character are best exemplified by that recent wedding gift to his daughter and her new husband: one male and one female slave. Like some starter set of silverware—made, no doubt, to stand beside the other gifts of punch bowls, bedding, and crockery.

The hypocrisy of Henry, George Mason, and the others—who know full well this Bill of Rights is but a smokescreen, a diversionary tactic to inflame the populace while disguising their real motives: a demand for a second Convention where they can stack the deck with their factions, rewrite the Constitution to their liking, and regain the power of taxation for themselves and their States.

Only the other day in Congress a resolution was introduced calling for such a Second Convention.

Which brings me to my present situation and one which, as I have mentioned, I trust you will preserve within the loyal confines of our old and valuable friendship.

I have devised a plan as simple as it will prove effective, a plan I then presented to President Washington, who readily agreed it must be put into practice at the earliest possible time:

It is my intention to assemble the amendments myself and then present them to Congress for their approval, thereby appeasing our detractors while safeguarding the vital elements of the Constitution as written; namely to wit: Article I, Section 8, which enumerates the powers of Congress, most especially the Power to Tax, raise a Standing Army, and make all Laws that are Necessary and Proper.

This plan, as I foresee it, will thus serve many purposes:

1. It will parry the anti-Federalists' argument that the new Government is not in favor of Rights for the People.
2. It will appropriate the issue of Rights once and for all, in our favor, thereby unifying the Nation behind the new Government.
3. It will, at the same time, insure that a strong Central Government, as presently organized under our Constitution, will go unscathed by any further attempts at restrictive limitations.

I will keep you informed as my plan goes forth. And now early to bed, praying that I may sleep through the night without being perpetually awakened by these infernal piles. I am Your Friend,

J. Madison Jr.

New York, June 4, 1789

Dear Sir,

My last dated from this place on the 8th of May informed you of my unpleasant situation regarding my piles. I write now to tell you that for the present they have happily subsided, to the point that I can now sit for extended periods of time which, as a Congressman, I can assure you is a vocational necessity.

With the exception of some occasional bowel discomfort (which I attribute to an overseasoned sausage), I am in unusually good health.

As for the amendments, they progress slowly as it seems my fellow Congressmen have taken up with more pressing business, such as how much in salary they will be allowed to pay themselves.

Before I proceed with news of the amendments, allow me to take time to repeat a joke told to me the other day over a bottle of Madeira by our Speaker of the House, Frederick Muhlenberg—generally an austere man but who, once in his cups, can prove to be surprisingly affable. This is the joke he told with a slight German accent which I will not try to imitate:

A lady goes into a butcher's market and says to the butcher, "I would like to buy a Long Island duck."

The butcher then proceeds to bring out a live duck.

The lady inserts two fingers up the duck's arse and says, "This is not a Long Island duck. This is a duck from Philadelphia."

The butcher takes back the duck and brings her a second duck.

Proceeding with the same inspection, she places two fingers into the duck's arse. "No," says the lady, "this duck is from Massachusetts. I told you I wanted a Long Island duck."

So the butcher again goes in the back and brings out a third duck. The lady then again inserts her fingers and proclaims: "Yes, this is a Long Island duck. Kill it, clean it, and I will buy it."

As the butcher is cleaning the duck, the lady decides to make conversation. "What's your name?" she asks the butcher.

"Thomas," he replies.

"Where are you from?" asks the lady.

Whereupon the butcher turns around, drops his breeches, points to his arse, and says: "Why don't you tell me?"

I assure you the joke set the table aroar with laughter.

Now, as to the amendments which I expect to submit to Congress at the first opportunity. They are as of today completed and, for your edification, let me explain the process upon which I arrived at them:

I began by assembling the over two hundred suggested amendments from the thirteen states, including, of all places, Rhode Island, as if they had something worthy to say about anything.

I then divided those into two piles (the very word sends shudders down my spine). One pile included all the amendments that would limit our present form of Government. Those I threw away.

The second pile contained the amendments granting various individual rights as well as liberties pertaining to legal justice. All of which I heartily approve.

From those I consolidated nine proposals, including forty-two distinct rights. To those I added a series of Amendments I wrote myself:

I increased the number of House seats—a token for those anti-Federalists fearing too elite a Congress.

I restricted financial self-dealing by members of Congress. Which I'm sure has no chance of making it through Ratification.

I reworded a clause I had tried (and failed) to incorporate into the Constitution whereby Congress could nullify the laws of the individual States.

I adjusted the Government's right to Eminent Domain so that property taken had to be justly compensated for.

I added an Amendment that the enumeration of any Rights herein should not be construed as negating those not named.

I also added a brief Preamble patterned somewhat after Mr. Jefferson's Declaration of Independence—and though difficult to improve on, I find mine to be almost as inspiring.

Finally, I placed each and every one of the proposals in the body of the Constitution as it now stands.

All in all, I believe these to be a suitable array of Amendments that should serve their purpose: to take the wind out of the sails of the anti-Federalists and prevent a Second Convention whilst doing the Nation no damage.

Now early to bed, with one question in my mind remaining: to sleep with the windows shut against the noise of the dissipation coming from the streets below *or* open in hopes that a calming breeze will leave me refreshed in the morning. If only the choice in American politics were so simple. I am yours affectly,

J. Madison Jr.

Philadelphia, October 10, 1789

My Dear Sir,

As you see, I'm writing this to you from Philadelphia, where I have been forced to stop on my way home to Montpelier in order to recuperate from a sudden attack of a bilious nature brought on, no doubt, by the long struggle in New York over the Amendments which entailed a minimum of sleep and a maximum of application.

I was so ill, only days ago, that I was compelled to call on that eminent but suspect physician Dr. Benjamin Rush. Fortunately, Dr. Rush had forgotten his bottle of leeches and so I was spared one of his infamous routines of bloodletting that I am certain have killed more men than cured. As I am now slowly regaining my health on my own, I will take this opportunity to recount the development of the Amendments (or Bill of Rights, as they are now being called) since last I wrote.

At that time, if I recall, the Amendments had not yet been received by the House. After a series of delays during which Congress thought its time better spent on such pressing business as the funding of lighthouses, the Amendments were at last received by a Select Committee. Making minor changes (not unexpected as we Federalists control overwhelming majorities in both Houses), the Committee then sent the proposals to the floor for a full debate.

The week of subsequent debates proved, however, to be most contentious. The sweltering heat of mid-August in New York only added to the foul mood. It had become so hot that Speaker Muhlenberg quipped that even "runaway slaves were walking."

The temperature and the general fatigue of the members (who were there since April) led to endless rounds of nitpicking and quarrels. Two duels, in fact, were narrowly averted last minute. It was Philadelphia all over again. Without the flies.

Some future historian would do well to consider just how much the desire to sleep in one's own bed contributed to the evolution of our young Nation.

Not surprisingly, Elbridge Gerry from Massachusetts—an old adversary from the Convention—proved to be my most vocal and determined opponent.

Looking like an out-of-sorts otter with a burr up his bum, Gerry played fast and loose with his supporters in the galleries, acting for all the world as the one true defender of the People's freedoms. The very People, of course, who during the Convention he had so steadfastly claimed had not the sense to be given the right to vote directly for their representatives. (Already I have heard rumors from his home state that he has been redrawing the lines of his Congressional Districts to favor his own faction.)

More dyspeptic than I remember, Gerry was down and up, up and down, out of his seat with one new objection after another. I can only suppose that fathering nine babies in nine years, as he has, will likely put a man on edge.

First, he demanded to see all two hundred of the various Amendments that I had received from the States.

Second, to the Amendment granting the People the right to petition the government "for a redress of grievances," he wished to add their right not only to "instruct" Congress but moreover that such instruction be considered binding. How he proposes that such a right could ever be properly executed he did not say.

Third, he strenuously objected to the clause (which I had added) providing a religious exemption for anyone asked to serve in the State Militia. As that particular proviso was generally disliked by Federalists as well, I felt no need to fight for it.

Next, he objected to the very idea of a government with a Standing Army. (Perhaps you have not heard his famous remark at the Convention in which he claimed that a Standing Army was like a standing penis—"excellent assurance of domestic tranquility, but a dangerous temptation to foreign adventure.") Well, if anyone should know about standing penises, it's Elbridge Gerry with his perpetually pregnant wife.

As always, Gerry's motions were defeated. As was Gerry's last-gasp attempt to negate Congress's power to tax.

I trust it is not uncharitable to note that Mr. Gerry speaks always with a most pronounced stutter. Whereby he not only speaks continuous mistruths, but also takes twice as long to do so.

After a few more days of debate, it soon became evident to Gerry and the other anti-Federalists that their arguments, motions, and objections, et cetera, had no chance for success. It was also dawning on my opponents that I had successfully usurped their issue of a People's Bill of Rights and was turning it against them. *Now* these same gentlemen, so once devoted to these Rights, sought to postpone these debates in favor of other legislation regarding the establishment of a Federal Judiciary. These attempts failed as well.

Any hope that they once might have had for a Second Convention melted like a snowball in the August New York heat.

As I had planned from the beginning, I successfully divided the anti-Federalists from their followers.

None other than Patrick Henry saw the situation for what it was, telling a friend (who then told me) that Henry had said, and I quote, "How wonderfully scrupulous have they [meaning me] been in stating Rights? The English language has been carefully culled to find words feeble in their Nature or doubtful in their meaning."

For once, Mr. Henry has gotten something right.

It was then on to the Senate, where certain changes—some substantive, some not—were implemented.

Much to my disappointment, the Senate Committee eliminated what I had always considered my most important Amendment: the Power of the Federal Government to prevent the States from threatening a citizen's freedom of conscience, speech, and press.

Without this clause, the States—regardless of any Bill of Rights—would retain the authority to write their own laws as they deemed fit: a serious flaw that would, I believe, haunt the new Republic until events may bring forth an Amendment (at some time in the future) to make things whole.

Whilst dismayed, I should not have been surprised by the Senate in this regard. They were, after all, dependent on the State Legislatures for their nomination to the Senate (as our present laws declare), and so it was always unlikely that they would do anything that might give these legislators offense.

I was also vexed with the Senate's decision to negate my attempt to place the Bill of Rights within the body of the Constitution, choosing instead to add it as a "supplement" (without my Preamble) at the end of the Constitution. By separating the Amendments from the body of the Constitution, the Senate has unfortunately contributed to what I am certain will be the difficulties and inherent ambiguities that must come with attempts at interpretation.

Otherwise I had prevailed. On September 14, the Senate sent its revised version of the Amendments back to the House, where they were resoundingly approved with only six dissenters—Elbridge Gerry, of course, being one.

President Washington, I might add, had been closely following the proceedings and was eminently satisfied with the results.

I think that anti-Government member from South Carolina, Thomas Tudor Tucker, best summed up my victory when he said:

"You will find our Amendments to the Constitution—as set forth by Mr. Madison and his cohorts—are calculated merely to amuse, or rather to deceive."

But the Republic has been saved. The People have the Bill of Rights, but the Government has the country.

As the Amendments now await Ratification from the States (the success of which I have no doubts), I am reminded of what Benjamin Franklin said after the Constitutional Convention when asked by a woman, "What kind of Government have you given us?" Mr. Franklin responded, "A Republic—if you can keep it." I now say the same. I have given the People their Bill of Rights. Let us see if they can keep it.

Now, early to bed, with the hope that I will awaken in the morning refreshed enough to begin my journey home. Adieu, I am, Dear Sir, Your sincere friend,

J. Madison Jr.

As Madison had predicted, the Bill of Rights, with little dissent and not much discussion, was soon passed. By then, nobody seemed to care about the Bill of Rights one way or the other, including the anti-Federalists *and* the American people. Even Thomas Jefferson, one of the Bill's staunchest defenders, seems to have lost interest.

Here is the historian Ray Raphael quoting Secretary of State Jefferson as he announced the passage of the Amendments this way in his official letter to the State Governors on March 1, 1792:

I have the honor to send you, herein enclosed, two copies, duly authenticated, of an Act concerning certain fisheries of the United States, and for the regulation and government of the fishermen employed therein; also of an Act to establish the Post office and Post roads within the United States; also the ratifications by three-fourths of the Legislatures of the Several States, of certain articles in addition to and amendment of the Constitution of the United States, proposed by Congress to the said Legislatures ... And of being with sentiments of the most perfect respect, your Excellency's Most obedient & most humble servant

There—as Mr. Raphael points out—embedded in a list of laws about fisheries, fishermen, and post office roads, is—can you believe it—our beloved Bill of Rights! Unlike the daylong celebrations of parades and fireworks that commemorated the signing of the Declaration of Independence (July 4, 1776) and the ratification of the Constitution (July 4, 1788), the passage of the Bill of Rights was met with complete indifference. The announcement did not even make the front pages of the newspapers but was buried instead among advertisements for "raw land," "cough syrups," and "half-off sales on preowned mulattoes."

March 1, 1792—the day the new nation got its long-awaited Bill of Rights. A day forgotten in American history.

It would take the Civil War, the Fourteenth Amendment, and two hundred years to make the Bill of Rights finally and truly relevant. But that's another story for another time.

CHAPTER 16

The Bill of Rights in the Real World

To invent a war means that you've become a wartime president, and you can suspend much if not all of the Bill of Rights.

—Gore Vidal

We're going to open up those libel laws. So when the *New York Times* writes a hit piece which is a total disgrace . . . we can sue them and win money instead of having no chance of winning because they're totally protected. . . . We're going to have people sue you like you've never got sued before.

—Donald Trump, candidate for president

Join me, will you, for a trip down memory lane as we review some of the worst examples in American history where the Bill of Rights turned out to be, regrettably, not worth the parchment it was written on.

It took only six years for the Bill of Rights to meet its first test. And fail. Miserably.

Alien and Sedition Acts (1798)

In 1798, Congress put into law four bills known as the Alien and Sedition Acts. In a nutshell: they made it harder for an immigrant (especially French and Irish) to become a citizen; allowed the President (John Adams) to imprison and deport noncitizens the government thought "dangerous"; and criminalized publishers and writers who criticized the federal government.

The laws were passed, of course, all in the name of national security. An old refrain sung as loud today as ever.

Here are a few examples where those "acts" clearly violated the First Amendment right of free speech:

Matthew Lyon, a Congressman from Vermont, was indicted for an essay he wrote accusing the Adams administration of "ridiculous pomp, foolish adulation, and selfish avarice." He was fined $1,000 and spent four months in jail.

James Callender wrote a book in which he called President Adams a "repulsive pedant, a gross hypocrite, and an unprincipled oppressor." He was fined $200 and given nine months in jail.

Luther Baldwin was fined $100 when, during a visit by John Adams to Newark, New Jersey, he yelled out that he hoped a random gunshot "had hit Adams in the ass."

None of these cases reached the Supreme Court, but a version of the Alien Enemies Act of 1798 remained on the books throughout World War I and was used by Franklin Roosevelt as the basis for interring Japanese Americans during World War II.

Black Codes (1789–1863)

From approximately 1789 to 1863, the slave states passed hundreds of laws known as Black Codes whereby slaves were forbidden to learn to read and write, testify against white people in court, or speak out against anyone (white).

Of course, as we know, slaves were not protected by the Bill of Rights since, as property, they were not regarded as either citizens or people.

I know what you're thinking. This was all before the Fourteenth Amendment. And as we know, Madison's Bill of Rights applied only to the federal government, not the states.

But *after* emancipation and *after* the Fourteenth Amendment, nothing really changed. In fact, the Black Codes became even more onerous: Southern states criminalized men who were out of work. Failure to pay certain special taxes constituted vagrancy, which meant jail sentences for many blacks. In eight states of the Old Confederacy, laws allowed convicts to be leased out for public and private work projects, thus providing free labor to white farmers and businessmen.

Black Codes also restricted African Americans from owning property, conducting business, or even traveling freely throughout their state.

All these laws were enforced by state and federal courts without even so much as a nod in the direction of the Bill of Rights and the Fourteenth Amendment.

Debs v. United States (1919)

In 1917 and 1918 respectively, Congress passed, and President Woodrow Wilson signed into law, the Espionage Act and the Sedition Act. Both were designed to keep people from speaking (or writing) against America's entry into World War I. One of the victims claimed by these Acts was Eugene Debs, onetime Socialist candidate for President.

Debs's protest against the war earned him the anger of Wilson, who called Debs a "traitor to his country." On June 16, 1918, Debs made a speech, part of which called for resistance to the military draft imposed by Wilson. Two weeks later, Debs was arrested and charged with ten counts of sedition under the new laws passed by Congress.

At his trial two months later (they can really give you a speedy trial when they want to), Debs was found guilty on all counts and sentenced to ten years in prison.

It's worth repeating here what Debs said at his sentencing:

> Your Honor, years ago I recognized my kinship with all living beings, and I made up my mind that I was not one bit better than the meanest on Earth. I said then, and I say now, that while there is a lower class, I am in it, and while there is a criminal element, I am of it, and while there is a soul in prison, I am not free . . .

Debs appealed his conviction to the Supreme Court on his First Amendment right to free speech, pointing out that his remarks contained only fleeting references to the draft and posed no present danger to the nation.

The Court ruled otherwise. The famous Oliver Wendell Holmes Jr. ruled that Debs's speech was not protected if even a small part of it was opposed to the war.

But as the Constitutional scholar Erwin Chemerinsky asks, "In democracy, shouldn't people be able to speak out against any government policy, including whether to go to war? In fact, isn't allowing free speech particularly important when the stakes are greatest, such as whether the nation will go to war?"

Debs served three years in jail (even running for President from there) and was pardoned, finally, by President Warren Harding. Suffering from ill health due to his stay in prison, Debs died five years later.

Today, few people remember Eugene Debs, but there isn't a law student or Supreme Court Justice who doesn't genuflect at the very mention of Holmes's name.

Buck v. Bell (1927)

For the first half of the twentieth century, the eugenics movement was in full stride. The pseudoscience of eugenics was aimed at protecting the human population, specifically the dominant, superior white race. The method most favored was forced sterilization.

To prevent them from breeding, the targets were primarily based on "class" and "race."

One of the foremost eugenicists of the era was Harry H. Laughlin, a PhD in cytology (the study of cells), who headed the Eugenics Record Office. He provided statistical testimony to Congress, much of it devoted to the "excessive insanity" among immigrants from Eastern Europe.

In 1922, Laughlin drafted his model law for compulsory sterilization. It targeted the following subjects: the feeble-minded, criminals, the insane, epileptics, the blind, alcoholics, deaf persons, deformed persons, and the indigent.

So persuasive was Laughlin that eighteen states passed laws based on his model. One state was Virginia, the state of Jefferson, Madison, and Washington.

The first person ordered sterilized in Virginia was Carrie Buck, then an eighteen-year-old patient at an institution called the Virginia State Colony for Epileptics and Feebleminded. An adopted child, Buck had been institutionalized on the grounds that she could read only "on the level of a sixth grader" (!) and was "incorrigible," having given birth to an illegitimate daughter named Vivian.*

Laughlin—who had never met or interviewed Buck—provided

---

* This was later proven to be the result of a rape by a relative of her adoptive mother.

the testimony arguing for her sterilization, calling her and Vivian members of the "shiftless, ignorant and worthless class of antisocial whites of the South."

Virginia won its case against Buck, which was then appealed to the Supreme Court.

Lawyers for Buck claimed she had been denied her Constitutional right of due process to procreate. They also argued that the Equal Protection Clause (the Fourteenth Amendment) was violated since not all similar kinds of people were being treated equally.

In an 8–1 decision, on May 2, 1927, the Court agreed that Carrie Buck and Vivian were "feeble-minded" and "promiscuous" and it was in the state's interests that she and her daughter be sterilized.

The ruling was written by the brilliant Oliver Wendell Holmes Jr., arguing that the interests of any one individual were outweighed by the "public welfare."

This is some of what he said:

It is better for all the world, if instead of waiting to execute degenerate offspring for crime, or to let them starve for their imbecility, society can prevent those who are manifestly unfit from continuing their kind. The principle that sustains compulsory vaccination is broad enough to cover cutting the Fallopian tubes . . .

The smartest guy in the room just compared the cutting of Carrie Buck's fallopian tubes with a smallpox vaccination.

Holmes then concluded his opinion with these words: "Three generations of imbeciles are enough."

Carrie Buck was operated on, as was her daughter, who later, it was noted, did very well in school before dying of measles five years later.

After the Supreme Court had validated compulsory sterilization, dozens of states added these laws to their books; those that already had them updated their old ones to match Virginia's. Sterilization became a common and widespread practice. And by the way, *Buck v. Bell* has not yet been completely overturned.

Harry H. Laughlin went on to receive an honorary degree from Heidelberg University in 1936 for his work on the "science of ethnic cleansing" (an event attended by the upper echelon of the Third Reich) and was scheduled to mark the anniversary of Hitler's 1934 purge of Jews from the Heidelberg faculty.

Korematsu v. United States (1944)

On February 19, 1942, President Roosevelt issued Executive Order 9066, authorizing that "all persons of Japanese ancestry report to designated assembly points." From there, Japanese Americans were forced into "relocation centers"—a euphemism for concentration camps. More than 100,000 Japanese Americans, mostly living on the West Coast, were given forty-eight hours to dispose of their homes and businesses. Bank accounts were forfeited. Jobs lost.

In discussing the internments, Professor Chemerinsky quotes William Manchester in his *The Glory and the Dream*: "Trucks took the internees to 15 assembly areas . . . among them the Rose Bowl and racetracks . . . [Their] families were housed in horse stalls . . . The average family of six or seven members was allowed an 'apartment measuring' 20' x 25'. None had a stove or running water."

One of those Japanese Americans was Fred Korematsu. Resisting internment, Korematsu went into hiding before being captured, arrested, and tried and convicted in a military court for violation of Executive Order 9066. He was given five years' probation and was taken by military police to the Central Utah War Relocation Center, where he was placed in a horse stall with one lightbulb. He remained in the detention center for the duration of the war, working eight hours a day at the camp for $12 a month.

In 1944, after a series of appeals, his case was heard before the Supreme Court. The Court ruled against him 6–2. Siding with the government, the Court ignored Korematsu's claims that his rights had been violated; that he had been denied due process solely because of his race; and that he had been denied *habeas corpus* and the right to a trial by jury.

In joining the Majority's decision, the renowned Justice Felix Frankfurter wrote:

> I find nothing in the Constitution which denies to Congress the power to enforce such a valid military order by making its violation an offense triable in the civil courts. To find that the Constitution does not forbid the military measures now complained of does not carry with it approval of that which Congress and the Executive did. That is their business, not ours.

Translation: What the government did was terribly wrong, but that's their business and not the Supreme Court's.

Later it was discovered that the government had falsified material claiming that Japanese Americans had been involved in espionage and thereby justifying massive incarceration.

Mr. Korematsu's conviction was never overturned. In a *New York Times* op-ed piece about her father, Karen Korematsu quoted President George H. W. Bush in 1991: "The internment of Americans of Japanese ancestry was a great injustice and it will never be repeated." Ms. Korematsu suggests otherwise, pointing to President Trump's recent Executive Orders banning Muslims and deporting Mexicans.

United States v. Stanley (1987)

In February 1958, James B. Stanley—a Master Sergeant in the US Army—volunteered to participate in what he was told was a program to test equipment against chemical warfare. However, while at the army's Aberdeen Proving Grounds in Maryland, Stanley was secretly given large doses of LSD as part of an army plan to study the effects of the drug on human subjects.

As a result, Stanley suffered from hallucinations, insomnia, and memory loss. As Stanley himself said, he would "awake from sleep at night and, without reason, violently beat my wife and children."

Eventually, he was discharged from the army, his wife divorced him, and he lost one job after another.

Stanley did not know he had been experimented on until 1975, when he received a letter from the army seeking his cooperation as part of a follow-up study.

Stanley filed a lawsuit against the military alleging negligence in the supervision and monitoring of the experimental program. The US Appeals Court upheld his claim.

But in 1987, the Supreme Court reversed the lower Court, in a 5–4 ruling, holding that the government could not be sued.

In writing for the Majority, Justice Antonin Scalia made no mention of Stanley's right to due process, nor did he comment on the horror of such medical experimentation on an involuntary serviceman.

Instead, the Court vacated the lower Court's ruling on the grounds of the government's "sovereign immunity."

Individual rights were violated; a subject's life was placed in jeopardy, and for no other purpose but information gathering on the effects of LSD. And yet the Court found no accountability—on anyone's part—necessary.

Stanley was not entitled to one red cent.

In her dissent, Justice Sandra Day O'Connor made the observation that the Nuremberg Military Tribunals required that "the voluntary consent of the human subject is absolutely essential ... to satisfy the moral, ethical, and legal concepts."

You would have thought that the United States would demand no less. But instead, Scalia and the Majority "invented" a Constitution that protects the guilty and ignores the innocent.

Bowers v. Hardwick (1986)

In August 1982, an Atlanta police officer named Keith Torick cited one Michael Hardwick for drinking in public. When Hardwick missed his court date because of a clerical error, Torick—tough cop that he was—obtained a warrant for Hardwick's arrest. In the meantime, unknown to Torick, Hardwick had paid his $50 fine.

Three weeks later, Torick showed up at Hardwick's apartment with a warrant for his arrest, even though that warrant was no longer valid. Hardwick's roommate asked Torick in and when asked where Hardwick was, the roommate pointed to a back bedroom. When Torick approached the open bedroom door, he saw Hardwick and a second man engaging in mutually consensual oral sex.

Hardwick,* naturally pissed at the intrusion, threatened to have Torick fired. In retaliation for Hardwick's "attitude problem," Torick arrested both men for violating Georgia's sodomy law, which carried a sentence from one to twenty years.

At the time, Georgia defined sodomy as "the carnal knowledge and connection against the order of nature by a man with a man or in the same unnatural manner with a man and a woman." In other words, Georgia's sodomy law included the prohibition of oral sex between a married couple. So, if my wife and I had happened to stay

---

* I suggest that those who feel the need to snicker at the name Hardwick do so now so we can get it out of the way and go on with the rest of the case.

overnight in Atlanta in 1982—and I got lucky—both of us could have ended up in the slammer for twenty years.

Anyway, after Hardwick's arrest, the local prosecutor, believing the law should not apply to consensual sex, dismissed the charges.

But Hardwick, looking to challenge Georgia's sodomy laws—with the help of the ACLU—brought a suit against Georgia's Attorney General, Michael Bowers. When the Court of Appeals dismissed the case on the grounds that Hardwick's constitutional rights had been violated, the State of Georgia appealed and the case went to the Supreme Court.

In a 5–4 ruling, the Supreme Court upheld Georgia's sodomy law. Writing the Majority opinion, Justice Byron White framed the legal question this way: Does the Constitution confer "a fundamental right to engage in homosexual sodomy?"

Now, where exactly did Justice White expect to find proof that the Framers endorsed homosexual sodomy? In Madison's notes on the Convention? In *The Federalist?* In the debates on Ratification? In the Constitution itself?

Or maybe in some anti-Federalist pamphlet* demanding a clause be included in the Bill of Rights in favor of "oral sex between consenting males"?

It takes no Constitutional scholar or Supreme Court Justice to figure out that the Framers were not interested in sex, at least as far as the Constitution was concerned. Simply put: there is no "sex"—one way or the other—in the Constitution. The Constitution is as sexless as Donald Trump's marriage.

But by making the case about homosexual behavior, Justice White had predetermined the result.

The answer would have been much different had the question been "What business was it of the State of Georgia to invade the privacy of one of its citizens without probable cause?"

---

* Written under the pseudonym "Caligula."

On this issue of "sexual" privacy, the Court had two major precedents it could have considered.

The first was *Griswold v. Connecticut* (1965), in which the Court ruled (7–2) that the Connecticut law prohibiting the use of contraception was unconstitutional on the grounds that it violated the right to "marital privacy." As the Majority argued, it was a privacy protected by the "due process" clause of the Fourteenth Amendment.

The second relevant precedent should have been *Stanley v. Georgia* (1969). In that case, Mr. Stanley, a sports bookie, had been arrested when police, looking for evidence of his bookmaking, found instead three reels of pornographic movies—"obscene matter" under Georgia's statutes. Stanley was tried and convicted. When the case reached the Supreme Court, the Court ruled by a vote of 9–0 that the private possession of pornographic material was protected by the First Amendment.

The Court held that the Constitution protects an individual's right to receive "information" regardless of its social worth as long as that type of "expression" causes no significant public harm. They also said that the state had no right to deprive Mr. Stanley of his right to pursue his own "happiness."*

But instead of recognizing those precedents (of an implied "sexual" privacy), the Court in *Bowers v. Hardwick* obsessed on the homosexual nature of the case. Shocked like cloistered monks, the Court could not imagine that human beings might dare express their desire for one another in a physical manner. Here is some of what Chief Justice Warren Burger wrote while concurring with the Majority:

> I . . . underscore my view that, in Constitutional terms, there
> is no such thing as a fundamental right to commit homosexual sodomy.

---

* A reference, I guess, to the Declaration of Independence.

The proscriptions against sodomy have very "ancient roots." Decisions of individuals relating to homosexual conduct have been subject to state intervention throughout the history of Western civilization.

Condemnation of those practices is firmly rooted in Judeo-Christian moral and ethical standards.

Homosexual sodomy was a capital crime under Roman law.*

During the English Reformation ... the first English statute criminalizing sodomy was passed.†

Blackstone‡ described "the infamous *crime against nature*" as ... a heinous act, the "very mention of which is a disgrace to human nature" and "a crime not fit to be named ..."

And "to hold that the act of homosexual sodomy is somehow protected ... would be to cast aside a millennia of moral teaching."

In a nutshell: What Justice Burger and the Majority were saying is that since the history of Western civilization condemns homosexual sodomy, well, by gum, so do we. And not a thought to the possibility that the Church might have been wrong about some things over the last couple of centuries—like when they burned Giordano Bruno alive for the heresy of not believing the Earth was the center of the universe.

The Court also called attention to the fact that more than twenty

---

* Roman law? The Supreme Court quotes the laws of the Roman Empire—that bastion of civil liberties? Why not bring back crucifixion?

† That would be from Henry VIII—beheader of wives.

‡ William Blackstone, English jurist and Right-Wing politician, circa 1778.

other states besides Georgia had antisodomy laws—all laws punishing the offender with twenty years in prison. So—they couldn't *all* be wrong, could they?

These laws, incidentally, when you look closer, punish various and assorted combinations of oral and anal sex between homosexual couples, unmarried heterosexual couples, and married heterosexual couples.

The Court did not consider the heterosexual prohibitions, choosing to condemn only homosexual conduct. As they stated: it would be "facetious" to think that sodomy is in any way a part of our nation's history and tradition.

Of course, no one was arguing that "sodomy" was part of a great American tradition—like guacamole dip on Super Bowl Sunday. Hardwick (and his lawyers) merely said that what he did in the privacy of his own home, if it did no public harm, was nobody's friggin' business but his own.

All of which leads me to ask why did Georgia, and those other states, stop at sodomy? Why not include—in their Biblically inspired statutes—prohibitions against other forbidden practices such as masturbation?*

After all, Onan (if we remember Genesis 38:8–10) is looked on with Divine Displeasure when he "spills his seed upon the ground."

Or consider the "nocturnal emissions" that were such a serious bugaboo for Saint Augustine.

And while we're headed down this "slippery slope"—so to speak—why not laws against unusual and uncommon sexual positions such as "doggy style"† or, as I like to call it, "the canine arrangement"?

---

* I'm talking self-masturbation, which I assume is also consensual.

† Another custom not protected by the Constitution.

The *Bowers v. Hardwick* case got me thinking about the origin of that word *sodomy*. (I mean, in a good, old-fashioned, heterosexual way.) So I dug up my Bible and turned to Chapter 19 in Genesis to find out just what happened back then in that infamous city of Sodom, population unknown.

Here's the story: Apparently even God Himself did not know what was going on down there, so He sent two Angels, disguised as ordinary men, to check things out. When they arrived at the gates to the city, they were met by a man named Lot—brother to Abraham, the first Jew—who lived in Sodom with his wife, two daughters, and their husbands.

Lot invited the men to stay overnight at his house. But the men had no sooner settled in for the night when the house was surrounded by "the men of Sodom, both old and young, from every quarter" of the city. Outside Lot's house, these men yelled at Lot to bring out the two visitors. (News traveled fast in Sodom.) "Bring out the visitors," shouted the men of Sodom. "Bring them out to us that we may know them *carnally*." (Italics, the Bible.)

Whether this was a typical display of welcome in Sodom is not quite clear, but it does give one a general sense of that city's, as the Bible calls it, "depravity."

To protect his guests, Lot called back, telling the gathered men that he would send out his daughters instead, who he claimed "have not known a man." Was Lot lying about their virginity since they were both married? Who knows? But when the men failed to respond to Lot's offer, he added this inducement: "Let me bring them out and do to them as you wish." But the men, plainly not interested in the two daughters, began to break down Lot's door. Here, the two Angels revealed themselves to Lot and struck the men from Sodom blind.

After the Sodomites stumbled from Lot's house, the Angels informed Lot that he must take his family and leave Sodom immediately because "the Lord has sent us to destroy it." And oh, by the way, they added: "Don't look back as you go."

In short order: Lot and his family headed for the mountains, and the Lord destroyed Sodom and its sister city Gomorrah with "fire and brimstone."*

Unfortunately, Lot's wife looked back and was turned into a pillar of salt. Otherwise, the journey was uneventful.

So what have we learned about the Sodomites? Well, for one thing, they certainly weren't interested in consensual sex with women or men. No. The Sodomites, in fact, were *rapists!* And *that* is why God destroyed them and their city.

Which leads me to this question: Has everyone misunderstood the story of the Sodomites, from the early Church fathers to Henry VIII to Blackstone right up to our present-day Supreme Court? Has no one read the story? Because the Bible makes it absolutely clear: Sodomites were not men who loved other men. They were men who forcibly possessed others against their will.

Again, if you didn't get it the first time: Sodomites were rapists! They were not gay men who hooked up after a night of sweaty dancing and tequila shots.

In 2003, *Bowers v. Hardwick* was overturned in *Lawrence v. Texas*, which struck down Texas's sodomy laws and by extension all those other states by a 6–3 vote. Explicitly overruling *Bowers*, the Court held that intimate, consensual sex between *anybody* is a liberty protected by the Fourteenth Amendment.

What a relief.

Kelo v. City of New London (2005)

In 1998, the pharmaceutical giant Pfizer announced plans to build a $350 million research facility adjacent to the neighborhood of Fort

---

* We're never told what they were doing in Gomorrah to deserve such a terrible fate. Most people suspect something "sexual." But given Jehovah's temper, it could just as easily have been mixing milk with meat.

Trumbull in New London, Connecticut. The Fort Trumbull area consisted of lower- and middle-class, century-old homes, some with river views. A private real estate developer with ties to Pfizer then proposed plans to build office buildings, condos, and a hotel on the nearby land. To implement their plan, the developers needed to purchase the properties belonging to ninety Fort Trumbull families.

In 2000, the New London City Council—in league with the developers—authorized the use of "eminent domain" to "take" the homes of those who had not yet agreed to sell. Those who had already sold their homes had done so reluctantly out of fear that their properties would eventually be condemned.

Before continuing with the rest of the story, a word first about eminent domain. *Eminent domain* means that since it is the government and/or state and/or city that really owns your land, they can, if they choose, "take it" from you for the flimsiest of reasons.

The practice of eminent domain came over to the Colonies from Britain as part of English Common Law. But because land was so abundant, it had never become a major issue. Nonetheless, to check the power of the federal government, Madison included this in the Bill of Rights: ". . . nor shall private property be taken for public use without just compensation."*

It was Madison himself who added the words "public use" and "without just compensation," specifically to protect property owners (and, of course, the Framers were all property owners) from unreasonable, unfair seizures of their land.

Despite Madison's Fifth Amendment, the Supreme Court has *never* decided a case (since 1905) *against* the government when it took property under the authority of eminent domain. The Supreme Court even approved the transfer of "nonblighted" areas to private developers, expanding the meaning of "public use" to "public benefit."

That these few cases got to the Supreme Court is in itself sur-

---

* Also known as the "taking" clause.

prising. Because what most of us don't know is that once a state institutes an act of eminent domain against you and doesn't make what you consider to be a reasonable offer for your property, your only recourse is then for *you* to sue the state for "just compensation." And since eminent domain is used almost exclusively by the rich and powerful against the ordinary citizen, it is an expensive and (as it turns out) futile legal process to pursue. Most people simply take what they are offered.

In the New London case, one person who decided to fight the system was Susette Kelo, who had resisted selling her house to the commercial developers. Unable to find an attorney to take her case, let alone afford one if she did, Ms. Kelo was eventually represented by the Institute for Justice, a libertarian law firm concerned with the Court's expanding definition of "public use" in the Fifth Amendment. Here was a case, after all, in which "condemned property" was clearly being taken not for public use but for private profits.

However, on June 23, 2005, the Supreme Court ruled against Ms. Kelo by a 5–4 vote in favor of the city of New London. The Majority—a mix of "moderate" and "liberal" justices—did not establish any new law. They simply reinforced the old precedents. While the "taking" was not expressly for "public use," the rejuvenation of the area would serve a "public purpose," they agreed, by increasing the city's tax revenue when lower-middle-class home owners were forced out to make way for wealthier residents.

In her strong dissent, Justice Sandra Day O'Connor wrote: "As for the victims, the government now has license to transfer property from those with fewer resources to those with more."

The well-publicized decision by the Majority was met by a shit storm of public outrage: angry indignation across all spectrums of political ideologies. And for good reason: miscalculating the consequences of their decision, the Court had sided *against* a middle-class woman who loved her house in *favor* of a wealthy land developer and Pfizer.

Remember who we're talking about here—Pfizer,* which makes around $3 billion a year selling drugs that can be bought in Mexico, India, Belgium, and Canada for a third of what we pay here. Like Viagra at $50 a pop, and just try looking for a copay. Then as an inducement, they have the nerve to suggest you *might* get an erection lasting for over four hours. Take it from me: no such luck.

Then there's Lyrica. A drug developed for epileptics that now can be taken for anything from insomnia to restless leg syndrome. At $400 a bottle at Walgreens with a discount card ($850 for the liquid). And with more side effects than divorce.

And Pfizer's other hot item: Ibrance, which is used to treat breast cancer. Only problem is it costs $11,191.10 (Kmart and CVS, slightly less) for a one-month supply of twenty-one capsules.

A few years after the Supreme Court's decision, Pfizer moved out of New London, taking its imaginary research facility with them along with 1,500 real jobs. The land where Ms. Kelo's house once stood has become a dump for storm debris and, as of this writing, is a large, vacant lot. Part of the empty acres waiting to be scooped up one day by the Kushner family at a bargain price.

Shelby County v. Holder (2013)

In 1965, Congress passed the historic Voting Rights Act in an effort to end racial discrimination in voting throughout the country. The bill, passed in the Senate (77–19) and House (328–74) and signed by President Lyndon Johnson, is considered the most effective and significant piece of legislature ever enacted to protect black voters.

Since then, the Act has been amended five times to expand and protect the rights of minority voters, especially in the South where

---

* According to a *New York Times* story, there are more than 140 lobbyists in Washington on the payroll of giant pharmaceutical companies.

Jim Crow laws never really died out. Two of the major provisions of
the bill—its heart and soul—were Sections 4 and 5, which required
certain states with the worst records of systemic discrimination to
obtain a "preclearance" from the Justice Department (and its Attorney General) before legislating any changes to their voting laws.

The states in question were Alabama, Alaska, Arizona, Georgia, Louisiana, Mississippi, South Carolina, Texas, and Virginia in
their entirety plus parts of California, Florida, Michigan, New York,
and North Carolina. This "preclearance" was upheld by the Supreme
Court as constitutional on four occasions: 1966, 1973, 1980, and 1999.

In 2006, Congress updated its data, documenting the continued
discriminatory practices against minority voters, and voted 98–0 in
the Senate—with only 33 "no"s in the House—to extend the Voting
Rights Act for another twenty-five years. The law was then signed
by President George W. Bush.

In 2011, Shelby County of Alabama sued the US Attorney General Eric Holder, seeking a judgment that Sections 4 and 5 of the
Voting Rights Act were unconstitutional. The District Court upheld the provisions as did the Court of Appeals, accepting Congress's conclusions that the "preclearance" formula was still necessary
to protect minority voters and was therefore constitutional.

The case then went to the Supreme Court, which in a 5–4 ruling
held that the substance of the Voting Rights Act—the preclearance
part of Section 4—was unconstitutional. In other words, the Court
ruled that those states on the Attorney General's list of the worst of-
fenders no longer needed approval to change their voting laws.

In declaring the Voting Rights Act (and Section 4) to be unconstitutional, Chief Justice Roberts made two main arguments. Let
me sum them up for you.

The first was that the law applies to only nine states (and additional counties) and that treating one state differently from another
is, well, unconstitutional. How he doesn't say. The Voting Rights Act
discriminates against those states for past offenses and is in conflict

with the principle of "equal sovereignty of the states"! Which is also apparently unconstitutional. How he doesn't say.

Another thing: the goddamn Civil War was fought and won so that some states (namely the Confederacy) *would* be treated "differently." That's why Congress wrote the Fourteenth and Fifteenth Amendments. And for the benefit of the Chief Justice, let me quote the Fifteenth:

> Section 1. The right of citizens of the United States to vote shall not be denied or abridged by the United States or by any State on account of race, color, or previous condition of servitude.

> Section 2. The Congress shall have power to enforce this article by appropriate legislation.

So there it is, in black and white, for all to read—and I repeat: "*Congress shall have power to enforce this article . . .*"

Yet, Chief Justice Roberts and his band of four say that Congress does *not* have that right. (Talk about your activist judges.) Tell me then how in hell is Congress acting "unconstitutionally" by enforcing the Fifteenth Amendment? Again, Chief Justice Roberts does not stay for an answer.

But wait. There's more. The Chief Justice has a third argument to back up the other two. Here he is, in his own words:

> Our country has changed, and while any racial discrimination in voting is too much, Congress must ensure that the legislation it passes to remedy that problem speaks to current conditions.

Consequently, there is no longer evidence of "widespread" and "flagrant" discrimination!

Justice Clarence Thomas seconds that blabber this way:

Blatantly discriminatory evasions of Federal decrees are
rare . . .

There you have it: Jim Crow is dead, its obituary written by the
Supreme Court, a vestige of American history now as obsolete as a
doctor's house call and as irrelevant as Newt Gingrich.

However, within *hours* of the decision, Texas and Mississippi
passed new voter ID laws. And they were not the only ones. Here is
a partial list of states that jumped at the chance to reinstitute their
favorite election laws:

ARIZONA
Prior to *Shelby*, the Department of Justice had blocked twenty-two
voting changes. After *Shelby*, Arizona initiated new documentary
proof of citizenship to create a "dual" registration system. (A similar system tried by Mississippi in 1995 was blocked by the DOJ
as racially discriminatory.) Arizona also cut its polling places by
70 percent from 200 to 60, and always in minority communities.

VIRGINIA
Prior to *Shelby*, the DOJ had blocked fifteen discriminatory attempts by Virginia to change its voting laws. After *Shelby*, starting
that year (2013), Virginia adopted restrictions on community voter
registration drives and changed its existing ID laws. They eliminated all nonphoto ID, such as paychecks, utility bills, Social Security checks, and even prior voter registration cards. After the new
photo ID laws went into effect, 200,000 voters—mostly black and
Latino—were promptly removed from the rolls.

GEORGIA
Prior to *Shelby*, Georgia had tried to implement twenty discriminatory changes in its voting laws. Four days after the decision, coun-

ties throughout Georgia moved their election days from November to July, targeting black voters. (North Carolina did the same thing in 1898.) Election boards reduced the number of African American voters by redistricting. Voting was made harder for minorities by cutting early voting, closing polling places (mostly in black neighborhoods), and in a few cases moving polling places to police stations.

What is the opposite of "prescient"? Perversely naïve? Because that is what the Supreme Court turned out to be when they decided *Shelby County v. Holder*.

What's next for the Supreme Court to get wrong? I suspect they'll have trouble with those transgender bathroom laws coming out of Texas and North Carolina. You know the ones I mean—where the state demands that men who have become women must go into the *men's* bathrooms in their makeup, dresses, and high heels and piss standing up over the toilet.

Here's one such (imaginary) case along those lines. How, I wonder, will the Court rule on it?

Spencer v. North Carolina

The Case: Woodrow W. Spencer is a transgender long-haul trucker for Walmart. He was formerly known as Wilhelmina W. Wilson, but at the age of twenty-five, realizing he was really a man trapped in a woman's body, he began a series of surgeries and hormonal treatments that transformed her into a man with a well-trimmed beard and moustache.

While driving a truck containing Christmas tree lights and ornaments from Passaic, New Jersey, to Jackson, Mississippi, he pulls into a truck stop in Asheville, North Carolina. After a sandwich and a cup of coffee, Mr. Spencer goes to use the men's room and finds beside the door a notice informing *all* patrons that it is illegal to use a bathroom that does not conform to the gender of one's birth certificate. To obey the law, Mr. Spencer enters the ladies' room, only to be met by various women in stages of undress who immediately scream obscenities at him. Mr. Spencer quickly retreats.

Mr. Spencer crosses the highway to a remote area and relieves himself, whereupon he's discovered by a county sheriff who charges him with public urination and issues him a summons for that misdemeanor.

Upset at this development, Mr. Spencer tears up the ticket and throws the pieces in the air. As he tries to return to his truck, Mr. Spencer is handcuffed, thrown into the back of the police car, and charged with resisting arrest, public indecency, and destruction of a county document (i.e., the summons).

Mr. Spencer spends one night in jail and is sentenced to six months' probation plus a $1,000 fine. The injuries suffered during his arrest (to lower back and rib cage) cause him to incur hospital bills that are not covered under Walmart's health insurance. Furthermore, the incident leads to his termination as a truck driver for that company.

Mr. Spencer sues the city of Asheville for damages, resulting from his wrongful arrest, as well as the state of North Carolina, claiming that his rights have been violated under the Fourteenth Amendment. Joining that second claim (filed in an amicus brief)—that the bathroom laws of North Carolina are unconstitutional—is the Walt Whitman chapter of the Log Cabin Republicans.

The Questions: (1) Does Mr. Spencer have a legitimate claim against the Asheville Police Department for injuries suffered during his arrest? And (2) Does the state of North Carolina's "bathroom law" abridge Spencer's privileges and immunities, guaranteed him under the Fourteenth Amendment, which says that all citizens of the United States shall not be deprived of liberty without due process "nor deny to any person within its jurisdiction the equal protection of the laws"?

Good luck.

CHAPTER 17

The Chapter of Leftovers: Part II

One of James Madison's rejected proposals during the Constitutional Convention was that the salary of congressmen be tied to the price of wheat.

One of Benjamin Franklin's least-famous inventions was one he came up with during the hot summer of 1787: a chair with a foot pedal connected to an overhead fan.

Before the President entered office, he had to take the following oath: "I do solemnly swear (or affirm) that I will faithfully execute the Office of President of the United States and will to the best of my ability preserve, protect, and defend the Constitution of the United States." Before any elected official in Pennsylvania could take office in 1787, he had to swear to the following: "I do believe in one God, the Creator and Governor of the Universe, the Rewarder of Good and the Punisher of the Wicked. And I do acknowledge the Scriptures of the Old and New Testament to be given by Divine Inspiration."

Of the three thousand copies of the Constitution that were first printed in Philadelphia in 1787, one thousand five hundred were in German.

In a letter written to James Madison at the time he was compiling the Bill of Rights, Thomas Jefferson floated the idea that all debts should be forgiven after nineteen years.

The following is George Washington's bill for the Constitutional Convention wrap party at the City Tavern in
Philadelphia:

To 55 Gentlemans Dinners & Fruit

-Rellishes, Olives etc.	20	12	6
-54 Bottles of Madera	20	5	
-60 of Claret ditto	21		
-8 ditto of Old Stock	3	6	8
-22 Bottles of Porter ditto	2	15	
-8 of Cyder ditto	16		
-12 ditto Beer	12		
-7 Large Bow[e]ls of Punch	4	4	
-Segars Spermacity candles, etc.	2	5	
To Decantors Wine Glass[e]s & Tumblers	1	2	6
Broken etc.			
To 16 Servants and Musicians Dinners	2		
-16 Bottles of Claret	5	12	
-5 ditto Madera	1	17	6
-7 Bo[u]ls of Punch	2	16	
	£89	4	2*

* In today's money, the party cost around $18,000. Including the cost of broken
dishes and tumblers.

CHAPTER 18

The Emperor Has No Robes:

Justice Antonin Scalia and Citizens United

Judges who accepted bribes are to be punished by losing all knowledge of divine law.

—Rabbi Shlomo (b. 1040–1105)

The following quote is from the *National Review*—one among the many tributes paid to Justice Scalia after his death: "... so consistent, so powerful and so penetrating in their devotion to the rule of law are Scalia's judicial opinions that one may take one or two almost at random and catch a glimpse of the great patterns of his jurisprudence ..."

That same issue contains, coincidentally, a two-page ad offering a 2016 postelection Caribbean cruise (sponsored by the magazine) hosted by its contributors and editorial staff, along with various Right-Wing, unemployed politicians.*

The cruise features these attractions:

- two fun-filled night-owl seminars
- a late-night smoker

---

* It was on a similar cruise to Alaska in 2007 that William Kristol, neocon intellectual, discovered Sarah Palin.

- three revelrous poolside cocktail receptions and intimate dining on at least two occasions with a guest speaker or editor

I mention this fun-filled cruise because it is the last place on Earth that Scalia would have found himself. Scalia, as it turns out, was given to more exclusive, less plebian entertainments. Like the hunting trip he was on when he died unexpectedly on February 12, 2016.

According to Jeffrey Toobin of the *New Yorker*, this was no ordinary hunting trip. The hunt—for quail, duck, and other birds—took place on the 30,000-acre Texas resort owned by John Poindexter, a Republican industrialist who recently had a case before the Supreme Court.

Scalia was flown to the secluded ranch on the private plane of his good friend C. Allen Foster,* a prominent Washington lawyer whose clients have included the Republican Party (in redistricting cases) and Blackwater, the paramilitary organization that supplied "contractors" for the Bush-Cheney-Rumsfeld wars in Iraq and Afghanistan.

The thirty-odd attendees at the ranch, including Scalia, belonged to a secret hunting fraternity called the International Order of St. Hubertus.†

Their motto is *Deum Diligite Animalia Diligentes*, which loosely translates to "We honor God by killing His creatures."‡

Members of this fraternity wear "dark green robes emblazoned with a large cross." Their officers hold such titles as Grand Master and Knight Grand Officer.

---

* In his biographical essay for the Princeton class of '63, Foster brags of killing more than 150,000 birds of various species. He also wrote: "It won't surprise anyone that I still rail against liberals, the academic kleptocracy, and feminazis."

† St. Hubertus is the patron saint of hunting and fishing. No connection to the word, which means arrogance resulting from excessive pride.

‡ *My* translation. But then, I was never very good at Latin.

Its current leader and Supreme Grand Master is His Royal Highness, the Archduke of Austria.

All of which might explain the mystery surrounding Scalia's death. Some on the Right suspected he was assassinated. Perhaps a professional hit man from the Occupy Wall Street movement?

What other secret organizations Scalia belonged to we will never know, but publicly he was an admitted Right-Wing, ultraconservative Roman Catholic ideologue.

A sample of Scalia's theology can be found, in his own words, in this interview with the reporter Jennifer Senior:

> My God! Are you so out of touch with most of America, most of which believes in the Devil? I mean, Jesus Christ believed in the Devil! It's in the Gospels! You travel in circles that are so, so removed from mainstream America that you are appalled that anybody would believe in the Devil! Most of mankind has believed in the Devil, for all of history. Many more intelligent people than you or me have believed in the Devil.

Celebrated on the Right for his "penetrating" and "powerful" reasoning, Scalia was especially clever when denouncing homosexuality. Here are just a few examples:

> If we protect gays, why not child molesters?

> The Texas statute [banning homosexual acts] undeniably seeks to further the belief of its citizens that certain forms of sexual behavior are "immoral and unacceptable"—the same interest furthered by criminal laws against fornication, bigamy, adultery, adult incest, bestiality, and obscenity.

> Men and women, heterosexuals and homosexuals, are all subject to [Texas's] prohibition of deviate sexual intercourse with someone of the same sex.

His words practically sing off the page. About women's rights, Scalia claimed that:

> ... women's equality is ... one of the "smug assurances" of our time.

Scalia's cultivated vision of the Constitution made him unquestionably one of the great minds of the thirteenth century.

Scalia called his method of interpreting the Constitution Originalism. He defined it this way: "I consult the writings of some men who happened to be delegates to the Constitutional Convention—Hamilton and Madison's writings in *The Federalist*, for example. I do so, however, not because they were Framers and therefore their intent is authoritative and must be law, but rather because their writings, like those of other intelligent and informed people of the time, display how the text of the Constitution was originally understood."

It's a neat trick Scalia had: locking into rules he can hide behind so that his every decision seemed untainted by his partisan prejudices.

To see exactly how he did this, let's consider the famous case of *Citizens United v. The Federal Election Commission* (2010), in which the Supreme Court, by a 5–4 decision, ruled that billionaire donors can legally give unlimited and anonymous amounts of money to political candidates under the protection of "free speech."

On behalf of the government, the Solicitor General cited Supreme Court precedents to show that "corporate political speech can be banned [by the government] in order to prevent corruption or its appearance."

Scalia disagreed, saying that because big donors can write massive checks to political campaigns, there is no more risk of corruption than there would be from "limited" donations by individuals.

To paraphrase Scalia's ruling: $50 million from the Koch brothers has the same "influence" as $250 from Joe Schmuck.

My question is, who exactly of the "intelligent and informed people of the time" did Scalia read to support his claim that massive amounts of money are not a corruptive force in the democratic process?

Certainly, he couldn't have read any of the following:

I hope we shall . . . crush in its birth the aristocracy of our monied corporations which dare already to challenge our government to a trial of strength, and to bid defiance to the laws of our country. —Thomas Jefferson

If we do not provide against corruption, our government will soon be at an end. —George Mason, delegate from Virginia

Look at Britain . . . see the bribery and corruption defiling the fairest fabric that ever human nature reared. —Patrick Henry

One of the weak sides of republics . . . is that they afford too easy an inlet to foreign corruption. —Alexander Hamilton

There are two passions which have a powerful influence on the affairs of men. These are ambition and avarice: the love of power, and the love of money . . . But when united in view of the same object, they have in many minds the most violent effects . . . —Benjamin Franklin

The stockjobbers will become the pretorian band of the Government, at once its tool and its tyrant; bribed by its largesses and overawing it, by clamours and combinations. —James Madison

... the danger may be ... the rich will strive to establish their dominion and enslave the rest. —Gouverneur Morris, delegate from Pennsylvania

And these fears were from rich guys!

And let us not forget this other little fact: Jefferson, Madison, and Hamilton all agreed to move the nation's capital from New York to remote lands in Virginia to keep the big-money boys away from those doing the country's business.

So I have to ask again: What exactly did Scalia read? Did he read these "intelligent and informed people of the time," then forget about them? Or did he just choose to ignore what they wrote as an inconvenient fact in order to align himself with those hunting buddies he so loved to kill little birds with?

Scalia has to be the 1 percent's favorite judge since Pontius Pilate.

CHAPTER 19

Scarier Than Scalia:

Introducing Justice Clarence Thomas

Who put pubic hair on my Coke?

—Clarence Thomas as quoted by Anita Hill,
testifying before the Judiciary Committee, 1991

In 2011, the liberal advocacy group Common Cause reported that between 2003 and 2007, Justice Thomas failed to report his wife's earnings of around $700,000 from the Heritage Foundation, a Republican think tank. (A serious, if not criminal, omission on his financial disclosure form.) Thomas described the failure as "inadvertent."

Justice Thomas also failed to fully report his involvement at a secret "political strategy" and fund-raising seminar organized by the Koch brothers at an exclusive resort near Palm Springs in 2008. Talk about your "activist judges."

Thomas's wife, Virginia, currently heads her own Republican consulting firm, describing herself as an "ambassador to the Tea Party."

I mention Thomas's wife as a possible explanation for the Justice's consistently Right-Wing Supreme Court decisions: the man doesn't want to sleep on the couch.

Justice Thomas provides two other theories guiding his interpretations of the Constitution. The first is his belief in "natural law."

Thomas first mentioned his faith in natural law during his confirmation hearings. Unfortunately, the Senate Judiciary Committee grilled him more on his pornography collection.*

In a nutshell, natural law holds that there is a divine legal code underlying the Constitution and that all laws must yield to a "Higher Authority"—namely, God.

An early example of how natural law was used can be found in *Bradwell v. Illinois* (1873), a Supreme Court case in which Myra Bradwell had been denied admission to the Illinois State Bar because she was a woman. The Supreme Court *upheld* the lower Court's ruling, its Chief Justice stating:

> . . . that God designed the sexes to occupy different spheres of action, and that it belonged to men to make, apply and execute the laws, was regarded as an almost axiomatic truth.

Which goes to show how stupid you can be when you're sure you know what God is up to.

To understand natural law, you have to go back to the mid-thirteenth century and the theologian Saint Thomas Aquinas. For Aquinas, divine or natural law is designed from God's eternal laws as it is revealed to Man through the scriptures: the Old and New Testaments.

For the record, Aquinas also believed that heretics should be punished by death, along with such other felonies as forgery and fraud. Aquinas, who justified slavery (it's in the Bible), was also reported to be able to levitate while praying.

Once you know that Aquinas is Justice Thomas's point man for the Constitution, you have no trouble figuring out how Thomas would rule on *Roe v. Wade* should he ever get a whack at it.

Since God once commanded Adam and Eve to "Be fruitful, and multiply," anything less should be seen as a violation of God's natu-

---

* A far less dangerous fixation.

ral law. Justice Thomas even referred to the right of married couples to use birth control as an "invention."

Amazing, isn't it, how God and Republicans think so much alike.

Thomas (who once studied for the priesthood) is no different than Scalia in believing the government should carry the sword as "minister of God to execute wrath upon the evildoers." And that the Ten Commandments are "a symbol of the fact that government derives its authority from God."

Justice Thomas, it seems, cannot distinguish between democracy, which requires debate and dissent, and religion, which needs only faith in ultimate authority. And in every case where Thomas chooses religion, democracy suffers.

Who knew we would get so sick of hearing from a judge who opens his mouth only once every ten years?

When Justice Thomas is not talking to God, he is wrapping himself in the Declaration of Independence.

The Declaration of Independence remains the Right Wing's last refuge to prove that America was founded by God's Hand and Special Blessing. To do so, they quote Jefferson's inspiring words:

> We hold these truths to be self-evident, that all men are created equal, that they are endowed by their Creator with certain unalienable Rights, that among these are Life, Liberty, and the Pursuit of Happiness . . .

By giving rights this divine origin, the Declaration elevates them to God-given and therefore they cannot be revoked or denied by anyone, including the King of England.*

The Declaration, remember, was the Founders' justification for

---

* Even Scalia said that Constitutional appeals to the Declaration of Independence are irrelevant.

revolution. And because foreign nations could not get involved in a *civil* war, the Declaration of Independence was written so that the new country (already at war with England) could borrow money as an independent nation.

But the Founders and Framers never applied the language of the Declaration when writing the Constitution. There is no appeal to God or God-given law. In fact, the Constitution says plainly that the Constitution and the laws and treaties "in pursuance thereof . . . shall be the Supreme Law of the land."

No matter. When Justice Thomas can't claim Leviticus as precedent, he calls on the Declaration of Independence to justify his subjective, preconceived opinions.

For example, take the Supreme Court's (*Obergefell v. Hodges*, 2015) decision stating that the Constitution guarantees the right to same-sex marriage. In his homophobic dissent, Thomas claims that since God gives man his dignity (per the Declaration of Independence), it cannot be taken away by the government. He supports that argument with most peculiar logic. Here is Justice Thomas in his own words:

> When the Framers proclaimed in the Declaration of Independence that "all men are created equal" and "endowed by their Creator with certain unalienable Rights," they referred to a vision of mankind in which all humans are created in the image of God and therefore of inherent worth. That vision is the foundation upon which the Nation was built. The corollary of that principle is that human dignity cannot be taken away by the government. *Slaves did not lose their dignity any more than they lost their humanity** [emphasis mine] because the government allowed them to be enslaved. The government cannot bestow dignity, and it cannot take it away.

---

* If a man in a *white* robe said that, they'd call it hate speech.

According to the Book of Thomas, therefore, the slave who saw his family auctioned off to the highest bidder suffered no loss of dignity. Perhaps Thomas did not read Thomas Jefferson on the subject:

> The whole commerce between master and slave is a perpetual exercise [of] . . . the most unremitting despotism on the one part, and degrading submissions on the other.

And Jefferson knew a thing or two about slavery.

So in this same bizarre way, Thomas is saying that since the government does not grant homosexuals benefits (like marriage), gays do not lose dignity by not getting them. Why? Because all dignity is *given only by God!*

Thomas also suggested, in the same dissent, that gays have been given enough liberties already. The right to travel is one. For example: "They have been able to travel freely around the country."*

Justice Thomas seems to think that just because gays have the right to spend a nude weekend in Palm Springs at the Bearfoot Inn (where clothes are optional), sip frozen daiquiris poolside, and splash each other with sunblock, that is all the freedom they need, and any aspiration to government-sponsored monogamy is strictly off-limits. Certainly, if God wanted homosexuals to marry, Clarence Thomas would have been the first to know.

Had Justice Thomas been a Federal judge back in Virginia in 1967, he would have sentenced himself and his white wife to two years in prison for miscegenation.

---

* Yes, Thomas actually said that.

CHAPTER 20

What in Hell Is a
Strict Constructionist?

President Trump is going to keep his promise and he's going
to nominate a strict constructionist to the Supreme Court.

—Vice President Mike Pence

*The following is a transcript of a lecture I never gave to a joint conference
of Yale and Harvard law professors:*

Every Right-Wing conservative ideologue identifies himself as a
strict constructionist. And there hasn't been a Republican candidate
for President since Nixon who hasn't promised to appoint one of
them to the Supreme Court.

So what in hell is a strict constructionist?

That's the subject of today's lecture.

First off, I think conservatives love anything that has the word
strict in it. It suggests, for example, some Old Testament virtue as
written in Proverbs: "Spare the rod and spoil the child." (And if that
isn't in the Bible, it should be.) Strict, of course, is appealing because
it means "closely enforced," "following the rules," and *rigid*. But not
in the *best* sense of that word.

A strict constructionist can be defined as one who interprets the
Constitution by determining what the original text is as written by
the Framers. The key word here is *text*. Plain and simple—clean as
a whistle—the Constitution says what it means and means what it

says, and it is as precise a legal document as my three-year contract with DIRECTV.

Since progress is only a distraction, the SC* guys are not interested in the social evolution of America. If it ain't in the Constitution, it ain't constitutional.

When a strict constructionist pictures the Constitutional Convention, he sees a version of that oil painting that now hangs in the Capitol: a stately George Washington on his pedestal looking out at the delegates. Some standing, some seated—all classically posed—attired in their cutaway coats, breeches so snug you'd have to lie down to take them off, and long, white stockings, calves rakishly exposed. As if at any moment one of them was about to rise and utter the sacred words that would define our nation for centuries to come.

For the SCs to view the Framers in any other way would be sacrilegious. It would undermine the essence of their argument—that is, the Framers were divinely inspired; that Independence Hall was hallowed ground, and that the Constitution itself is like one of those foot bones of Saint Peter buried deep under the Vatican—a relic to be worshiped.

I see a somewhat different picture: It's a hot August afternoon. The air in the room is stale, stuffy, and smoke-filled. (If the delegates from Virginia and the Carolinas didn't smoke cigars or chew and spit tobacco, I'll eat my Sandy Koufax–signed baseball card.) The windows are closed against the huge black flies Philadelphia was famous for. The room is half-empty. Many delegates have already left the Convention for home. Of those remaining, some have gone right back to bed after a breakfast of bangers, mash, warm beer, and salted fish. Those in the room sit sprawled, coats off, ruffled shirts loose, breeches open at the waistlines. Wigs askew. Now and then an occasional belch.

---

* Pardon the abbreviation.

So there you have it. Two very different pictures of our Framers at work. One that sees the Framers as infallible, like so many collected Popes. And mine: the Framers as all too human.

And the Constitution they put together? I see it as a living, breathing document. To be cherished, yes; but flawed, inconsistent, and less than perfect—like the men who wrote it.

Let me give you four examples of why I'm saying the Constitution is less than perfect:

First: The Amendments

Within seven years of its signing, it took twelve Amendments to correct what was originally drafted, including how to elect the President: the second election after Washington ended in a tie between Thomas Jefferson and Aaron Burr—a tie that then took thirty-seven consecutive votes in Congress to break.

Second: The Constitution, as written, is undemocratic

The cornerstone of American democracy is "one man, one vote," yet that phrase never appears in the Constitution.* In fact, the Framers—suspicious of the common man—did everything to make sure there was no *direct* vote for President, for the Senate, or the Judiciary.

---

* Nor does the word *democracy*.

Third: Slavery

There's no way around this: the Framers endorsed slavery. They counted every slave as three-fifths of a person for the purposes of representation. They also extended the slave trade for twenty years.

By calling for an import tax on all new slaves from Africa, they officially reduced "these persons of servitude" to property. In doing so, the Framers unwittingly set the stage for the bloody Civil War less than a hundred years later.

To that point, let me quote one of the delegates, Elbridge Gerry, saying the same thing in 1787 in a letter he wrote to his wife:

> I am exceedingly distressed at the proceedings of the Convention . . . I am almost sure they will, if not altered materially, lay the foundation of a civil war . . .

Then there was that little thing called the Fugitive Slave Clause in Article IV, Section 2, whereby runaway slaves had to be "delivered up" to their rightful masters. Further evidence that the slave-owning states drove a hard bargain.

Fourth: The Bill of Rights

By refusing to add a bill of rights, the Framers (out of indifference or exhaustion) made a serious miscalculation, opening the door for the anti-Federalists to demand serious changes before Ratification.

So there you have it: four good reasons why the Constitution—as originally constructed—is less than the perfect document the SCs think it is.

[Pause here dramatically for a long sip of water]

The strict constructionist also believes that the Constitution was written with a clear, concise unity of opinion. Any close look at how the Convention actually operated tells a different story.

To explain what I mean, here's a quick snapshot of the Framers at work:

Of the original seventy-three delegates named to the Convention, eighteen never showed up.

Of the fifty-five who did, only thirty-nine were there at the end to sign.

Three of those thirty-nine—George Mason, Elbridge Gerry, and Edmund Randolph—refused to sign.

During the Convention, Alexander Hamilton left in mid-July and came back only for the last week.

Rhode Island was never heard from. New Hampshire didn't arrive until July 23. One delegate, William Few of Georgia, checked in on May 27 and signed the Constitution on September 17. But there is no record of him ever attending one session.

Luther Martin, a notorious drunk (from Maryland), arrived two months late, and when he got there, he still didn't know what was going on. He thought they were rewriting the Articles of Confederation.

Dr. James McClurg of Virginia arrived late on May 25 and left on July 21. And not a peep from him in between.

The sixty-six-year-old Roger Sherman was in and out of the Convention, leaving sporadically to go home to Connecticut to check on the whereabouts of his much younger wife.

William Samuel Johnson—running out of cash—was absent for days looking for cheaper lodgings.

Pierce Butler of South Carolina was on the lam for months, fearing for his life after being challenged to a duel by a long-time creditor.

And the list goes on, proving, I think, that the Constitutional Convention was—as my first wife described our marriage—one hot mess.

The reason the delegates could come and go at will was because the rules of the Convention stated that each state had the right to decide how many delegates were needed to be present for any vote. A single vote was all that was required from Connecticut and Maryland. New Hampshire, North and South Carolina, and Georgia needed two. New York didn't care since its delegates left early anyway. Massachusetts, New Jersey, Delaware, and Virginia required only three.

So rather than a *unified* Convention, what we ended up with is this: *it only took ten delegates out of the fifty-five to pass any resolution!**

In fact, the final draft of the Constitution, including the Preamble, was written by one man, Gouverneur Morris of Pennsylvania, who headed the Committee of Style. He rearranged words, changed punctuation, ignored Articles already agreed to, and added some of his own no one had expected.

The final days of the Convention were a whirlwind of last-minute, even reluctant decisions as the delegates rushed to return to their plantations, lucrative law practices, and neglected wives.

After three exhausting months of a Philadelphia summer, cramped boardinghouse rooms, and swarming black flies, the dele-

---

* That's by my calculation, but I'm not very good at math.

gates had had enough. They were running out of money* and clean underwear.

The Constitution would not even have been signed if it hadn't been for a last-ditch plea by Benjamin Franklin, urging that "for the sake of our posterity, we shall act heartily and unanimously." His motion was carefully worded so that even those delegates who didn't like the Constitution could still put their names on it.

And there was a lot not to like. But let the men who worked on it speak for themselves:

> The plan, should it be adopted, will neither effectually answer its national object nor prevent the local mischiefs which everywhere excite disgusts. —James Madison to Thomas Jefferson

> [The Constitution] was done by bargain and compromise. Yet notwithstanding its *imperfections*,† on the adoption of it depends . . . whether we shall become a respectable nation. —Nicholas Gilman, New Hampshire

> There are features so odious in the Constitution as it now stands that I doubt whether I shall agree to it. —Edmund Randolph, Virginia

> And this from George Washington: "I wish the Constitution which is offered had been more perfect, but I sincerely believe it is the best that could be obtained at this time."

* For example, on September 5, one delegate (Nathaniel Gorham from New Hampshire) had to borrow thirty pounds from the financier Robert Morris for his trip home.

† My emphasis.

And to quote Alexander Hamilton in *The Federalist No. 85*: "I never expect to see a perfect work from an imperfect man."

Hardly the ringing endorsement the SC guys are looking for: the Constitution as sacred text, written in stone, from which no jurist dare dissent.

No amount of evidence matters. The strict constructionist persists in claiming that the text and only the text is the way to go.

But did the Framers really believe that in those terse 4,400 words* they had answered every question as to how to organize and operate a government, not just for their time but for every generation thereafter? The SC boys say yes. James Madison says no:

> In framing a system which we wish to last for ages, we should not lose sight of the change which ages will produce.

[Another dramatic pause, then:]

Not everything can be in the text, as the SCs would claim. Much has happened over the last 230 years that we take for granted but the Framers never gave a thought to. Certain subjects, for example— women.

That's right. The Framers forgot all about women. They spent more time discussing the Emoluments Clause than they did the rights of their wives, mothers, and daughters.

Instead of "We the People," the Preamble should read, "We the Men ..."

So if the Framers forgot women, could there be possibly something else they omitted or just plain got wrong? You tell me.

---

* And written in less than one hundred days.

But the strict constructionists say—again and again—it's all there in the words. And I say: the words are only half of it.

[*Pause for applause*]

And now I'll be happy to take some questions.

Question: You denigrate strict constructionists while forgetting to mention that both James Madison and Thomas Jefferson considered themselves strict constructionists.

Answer: Madison and Jefferson—like all strict constructionists—believed in it when it suited their purpose. Let me give you an example from Madison. In 1790—three years after the Constitution was signed—Alexander Hamilton, as Secretary of the Treasury, wanted to create a federal bank that would serve as a government lender and a depository for federal funds.

James Madison opposed the idea on the grounds that it was unconstitutional, since there was nothing in the Constitution that gave Congress the right to form a federally owned and operated bank. Which was a lot less self-serving an argument than opposing it because Madison, a representative of a rural Virginia district, feared that such a bank would make New York (and not Virginia) the financial capital of the new nation.

Hamilton's answer was pretty much what a "living" (as opposed to "dead") interpreter would make today: Article I, Section 8 granted Congress "implied powers."

That is: if Congress has the right "to lay and collect taxes, borrow money on the credit of the United States, regulate commerce, and raise and support a standing army," it had to have its own bank to do so.

What was Madison thinking? That George Washington was going to take the money home at night?

Eventually, the Supreme Court (and, more important, George Washington) sided with Hamilton. And I would say that history has proven Hamilton right. It's pretty hard to imagine a country without its own bank.*

This conflict over the bank between Madison and Hamilton should prove a point: Madison and Hamilton were roomies† during the Constitutional Convention. They consulted regularly on its progress. Together, they wrote the bulk of *The Federalist*, defending the Constitution. Yet within two years, even *they* could not agree on what it meant. How, then, do the SCs expect to know centuries later what the Constitution really "says" when the men who wrote it did not?

Now here's the interesting part: when Madison became President, he discovered during the War of 1812 that the country needed a bank, so, no longer a strict constructionist, he got one.

Same thing with Thomas Jefferson—another so-called strict constructionist. Nothing in the Constitution allowed him to purchase the Louisiana Territory. Realizing that it was too good a deal to pass up, Jefferson circumvented the Constitution, claiming he had the power under Article II, Section 2, giving the executive the "power . . . to make treaties." Obviously, the Louisiana Purchase was not a treaty, but when it suited Jefferson to interpret the Constitution broadly, he did so.

And while we're on the subject of double standards, let me give you a more recent example. The right-to-lifers— all strict constructionists—claim that the newly conceived human embryo has the same guarantees as any citizen under the Constitution, including those granted by the Fourteenth

---

* We need a bank just to bail out all the other banks.

† Both stayed at the same boardinghouse in Philadelphia.

Amendment, like due process and, no doubt, the right to own a gun.

Next question.

Question: On one hand, you acknowledge our Framers' genius, while on the other, you delight in showing how inconsistent they were.

Answer: Exactly right. I am as inconsistent as they were: slave owners with a passion for liberty. Religiously tolerant yet racially bigoted. Visionaries while at the same time practical men of the world. Patriots devoted to good government while motivated by their own self-interests.

Question: I'm not sure that you really answered your own question, "What the hell is a strict constructionist?"

Answer: Then let me give it another try. As the examples from Madison and Jefferson show, the strict constructionist doesn't really care about the text unless he can own it. And since there is no way in hell to interpret the Constitution *solely* by the text, the term strict constructionist is only a political trademark, a brand name—a secret handshake, as it were, between members of the same club that says "I too am against immigration, welfare safety nets, and a woman's right to choose."

Like the Mandrill of New Guinea, exposing his purple buttocks to all the other primates in the jungle, the strict constructionist is simply showing us his true colors.

[*Exit to standing ovation*]

CHAPTER 21

Anonymous Letter to Certain Members of the Supreme Court

No matter whether th' Constitution follows th' flag or not, th' Supreme Court follows th' election returns.

—Finley Peter Dunne, American humorist (1867–1936)

I write to you as a friend of the Court. I sympathize with you. I feel your plight.

Of all the jobs in our three branches of government, yours is the toughest because your job is to interpret the Constitution. A Constitution that was cobbled together by many hands (to form a more perfect union) out of political expediency, compromise, and self-interest—a Constitution elusive, complex, contradictory, and even at times, God help us, unconstitutional.

No wonder you're in over your heads. And I mean that in the nicest way.

I blame the Constitution. Look what you're up against: a dense, 4,400-word document of laws written in the eighteenth century that you believe were meant to govern this nation for all time.

Then there's the language. That pesky Commerce Clause. The broad generalities of the Preamble: "...to insure Domestic Tranquility...promote the general Welfare and secure the Blessings of Liberty." And all those mysteries lurking beneath Congress's power to make "all laws which shall be necessary and proper."

And let's not forget those Latinate constructions, the obscure gerunds and dangling participles. Why, to misread even one semicolon and—oops—there goes another black defendant on to death row in Oklahoma.

And if the Constitution proper is no piece of cake, it sure doesn't get easier with the Bill of Rights.

I mean, what the hell is "due process"? How fast is a "speedy trial"? And what's "excessive" when it says "excessive bail shall not be required"?

It's enough to make your heads spin.

But it's not like you weren't warned—and by your favorite Framer, James Madison. Who said—as I'm sure you remember—that when Congress inserted the Bill of Rights at the end of the Constitution and *not*, as he intended, in the body of the Constitution itself, there'd be hell to pay. As he put it in a letter to Alexander White, fellow Congressman from Virginia, by adding the ten Amendments to the Constitution as an additional supplement, "it is already apparent I think that *some ambiguities* [my emphasis] will be produced by this change, as the question will often arise and sometimes be not easily solved, how far the original text is or is not necessarily superseded, by the supplemental act."

I repeat: "Some ambiguities will be produced."

Of course, as Supreme Court Justices, you cannot admit to any "ambiguities." Every day you must get up, slip into your black robes, and go to work pretending you know exactly what you're talking about.

I understand your problem. Believe me. The nation's fate is in your hands, and the last thing you can do is look confused. *Not* to look confused has to be one of the first things you're taught in law school, right after how to open and manage an escrow account.

Now, I know that there is not one of you who has ever awakened in a cold sweat from a deep sleep, screaming: "Holy shit! This Constitution is a bitch." But nonetheless, I can't help but notice a sense of your own self-doubt.

How else to explain all those gizmos, gimmicks, and "tricks of the trade" you call "methodologies" for interpreting the Constitution? You know what I'm talking about: those "tools" you've come up with to explain your decisions. You've got your strict constructionists. You've got your "Originalism." You've got your "Original Intent." And the hot one at the moment—"the Framers' Intent."

That last tool is, I believe, where you have to figure out what the Framers were thinking when they wrote the Constitution. So I look forward to your opinions regarding those transgender bathroom laws in which transgenders have to use the bathroom corresponding to the sex on their birth certificates. Considering that the Framers didn't have bathrooms, powdered their hair, and dressed up in what looked like women's clothing—that case will not be so easy.

I've even heard tell that one of you (who will remain nameless) is so enamored with the Framers' Intent, he sends his clerks scurrying to the library looking for eighteenth-century dictionaries so he can look up the words *keep, bear,* and *arms* when deciding cases regarding the Second Amendment. And isn't it curious how these definitions always line up *exactly* with the mission statement from the NRA?

(By the way, these clever little devices of yours can't help but remind me of those decoder rings I got as a boy for a Wheaties boxtop: turn the dial and a secret message will appear!)

When any of the above "tools" don't quite work, you've still got plenty more where they came from. You've got your "Let's find out what everyone was thinking *before* the Constitution was written." "Let's find out what everyone was thinking *when* the Constitution was written." "Let's find out what everyone was thinking one hundred years *after* the Constitution was written." There's also your precedent, historical context, common law, and natural law. You guys have more choices than the Bachelorette.*

One of you (who will remain nameless, but Chief Justice Roberts knows who he is) uses a somewhat different method. He describes

---

* And let's not forget your other devices: federalism, structuralism, "Fair Reading," and that good old standby, creeping Catholicism.

his process as much like that of an umpire, crouching behind the plate, merely calling balls and strikes as opposing lawyers hurl their arguments at him.

At first, this sounds like disingenuous drivel. Then, after thinking about it, the metaphor made perfect sense: the Supreme Court and baseball are much alike. Nine players on a team. Nine Supreme Court Justices. All in uniform. All sitting on a bench. Players work their way up to the majors from lower leagues. Justices from lower courts. The one distinction, however, between umpires and Supreme Court Justices is their impartiality. An umpire doesn't care who wins. But in the case of *Citizens United* (where corporations became people), was there ever any doubt that Umpire Roberts would dare rule against the very people who gave him his job?

Which brings me to my main point: Since you guys switch your "tools" as the occasion arises, it might appear (as it does to me) that what you're really doing is deciding the outcome first and then picking your reasons to justify it.

How else can you explain what seem like random, often unsubstantiated, and idiosyncratic rulings?

Let me provide some examples. And while they may be from your predecessors, nothing—as we shall see—has changed:

In 2005, the Supreme Court decided by a 5–4 vote that the display of the Ten Commandments on the grounds of the *Texas* state capitol did not violate the separation of church and state and was, in fact, constitutional.

However, on the same day—June 27, 2005—within the hour of that last ruling, the very same Court decided (also by 5–4) that the display of the Ten Commandments at the *Kentucky* state courthouse *violated* the First Amendment's requirement of separation between church and state and was, indeed, *unconstitutional*. Same Court. Same day. Same Constitution.

A similar puzzlement can be found in an earlier Court's ruling that involved the Jevovah's Witnesses. In this 1940 case—*Minersville School District v. Gobitis*—the Jehovah's Witnesses challenged the right of a public school to force its students to salute the American flag. In his Majority opinion, the so-called great Justice Felix Frankfurter ruled against the Jehovah's Witnesses, holding that "the flag is the symbol of the nation's power, the emblem of freedom in its truest best sense."

Apparently, Judge Frankfurter missed the irony in his description of the flag as an "emblem of freedom" while at the same time compelling elementary students to salute it or face expulsion.

But then, only three years later the Supreme Court changed its mind, and in *West Virginia State Board of Education v. Barnette* (an almost identical case) ruled in favor of the Jehovah's Witnesses, stating that their refusal to salute the flag was because of their sincerely held religious beliefs. And *not*, as the Court had previously decided, out of a lack of patriotism.

Same case. Same Jehovah's Witnesses. Same Constitution.

To press my case further, I draw your attention to the "free speech" case of *McIntyre v. Ohio Elections Commission* (1995). I like this case because I believe it demonstrates the Court's bewildering and tortured logic in trying to justify already-held opinions.

In a nutshell: taxpayer Margaret McIntyre distributed leaflets protesting a proposed tax outside a school board meeting. She was fined $100 on the grounds that the pamphlets were unsigned and therefore anonymous, which was against the law in Ohio.

Ms. McIntyre appealed the fine all the way to the Supreme Court, then headed by Chief Justice William Rehnquist. By a 6–2 vote, the Court declared that the Ohio law was unconstitutional. Anonymous free speech (or a leaflet in this case) is protected under the First Amendment. So the Court, it would seem, got it right. But the story does not end there. At least not for me. Because when we examine *how* it was decided, this case becomes, well, curious.

The majority of Justices (Sandra Day O'Connor, Anthony Kennedy, David Souter, Ruth Bader Ginsburg, and Stephen Breyer) made the argument that since great works of literature had been published anonymously, *not* to protect such material would be detrimental to mankind. As examples, they list the great writers who published anonymously: Voltaire, George Eliot, Mark Twain, and Shakespeare.

One problem: none of them *ever* published anonymously.

The Victorian novelist George Eliot was really Mary Anne Evans. She chose a man's name for a variety of reasons (one was sexism). But after the publication of her first novel, George/Mary Anne quickly revealed her identity. After that, everyone in England (at least) knew that George Eliot was actually Mary Anne Evans.

Voltaire's real name was François-Marie Arouet. In 1718, after being released from prison, he took the name Voltaire, reversing the syllables of his family's hometown. And he took the name because, as explained to one and all, he was unhappy with his real name, which sounded too much like that of an inferior poet of the day.

Nothing he ever wrote under the name Voltaire was published anonymously. Voltaire was his *nom de plume!* For Chrissakes.

Early in his career, Samuel Clemens began writing under the name of Mark Twain, as every schoolchild knows. Clemens *never* wrote anonymously! Everyone in America—everyone in the world—knew that Mark Twain and Samuel Clemens were the same person.

As for Shakespeare: there are those conspiracy theorists who claim that Shakespeare's plays were really written by the Earl of Oxford, Lord Bacon, or even Queen Elizabeth. In which case, *they* would have been writing anonymously. But Shakespeare—the one from Stratford-upon-Avon—the one with the earring—*that* Shakespeare—the real Shakespeare—never used any other name.

In 1623, the title of his collected plays was *William Shakespeare's Comedies, Histories, and Tragedies.* And there was even a picture of the man on the cover!

That the majority of the Supreme Court seems to have understood none of this makes me wonder what else they know nothing about.

Now, back to *McIntyre v. Ohio*: Justice Clarence Thomas agreed with the outcome of the Majority but strongly took issue with the means of getting there. So he wrote his own opinion. Chastising the Majority for its failure to consult American history, Thomas argued that he could not join their opinion because "It deviates from our settled approach to interpreting the Constitution and because it imposes its modern theories concerning expression upon the Constitutional text."

As a member of the Original Intent Club, Thomas wanted to know whether the Framers believed in anonymous speech sufficiently enough to "deserve the protection of the Bill of Rights."

Since the subject of "anonymous pamphlets" never came up during the Congressional or Ratification debates, Thomas has to go *backward* to the Revolutionary Era to find what he's looking for.

And there he discovers political tracts written under the anonymous names of Cato, Brutus, etc. He also comes up with one of the most famous cases in the history of American "free speech": the trial of the publisher John Peter Zenger, a true patriot, who in 1734 was arrested for refusing to divulge the names of anonymous writers (all British subjects) critical of the English occupation.

In this, at least, as an Originalist, Thomas is consistent. But what about the revered Justice Antonin Scalia, the foremost Originalist of our time? Surely, he'd have to agree with Thomas.

But Scalia, as you already know, dissented, holding that Ms. McIntyre had no constitutional right to hand out her anonymous pamphlets. Along with Chief Justice Rehnquist, Scalia sided with Ohio.

To everyone's surprise, Scalia abandoned his good buddy Thomas. More important, he abandoned the Founders and didn't even consider the Framers. Instead, he made this argument: laws forbidding anonymous speech (or written material) existed in forty-nine states. To overturn them would be—in Scalia's eyes—to go against the "widespread and long-accepted practices of the American people."

This from the Justice who a few years earlier concurred with the Majority in *Texas v. Johnson* (1989), which stated that the First Amendment protected Mr. Johnson's right to burn the American flag!—*even though all fifty states had laws against doing so.*

And what an odd time, in a First Amendment case, for this self-proclaimed Originalist, this Right-Wing defender of American liberties, to be more worried about overturning a state law of Ohio than protecting the free speech of one of its citizens.

Justice Scalia would later claim (in *Citizens United v. Federal Election Commission*) that the right to spend vast amounts of *anonymous* money to win an election was guaranteed under the First Amendment. But Ms. McIntyre—with her antitax pamphlets—was not entitled to the same rights. And what could be more American than that: protesting what she thought was an unfair tax?

Summing up: we have the Majority who ignored the Framers and instead believed that the "value" of the anonymous writings by such giants as Mark Twain, Voltaire, and Shakespeare makes such material, like Ms. McIntyre's, protected by the First Amendment.

Then we have Justice Thomas, who sees Ms. McIntyre's rights protected because the Framers (remembering Zenger, Cato, and Brutus) would have agreed.

And then there's Justice Scalia (and Justice Rehnquist), who considered the Framers and the Founders irrelevant, arguing that anonymous speech is unconstitutional because that has been the "long-accepted practice of the American people."

I am only sorry I was not there in your offices the day you discussed *McIntyre v. Ohio.* You know, that room you go to when talking about a case, right before you send your clerks off to write your opinions for you.

I would've said something like this:

To Justice Clarence Thomas: Why in the world would you have to rely on *pre*-Constitutional history when the only argument you needed was *The Federalist*, written *anonymously* (to defend the Constitution) by two of its more important Framers—Alexander Hamilton and James Madison—under the pseudonym of Publicus?!* What more proof of the "Framers' Intent" than Madison, who practically put the Bill of Rights together by himself? And it's not as if Hamilton and Madison stopped writing anonymous tracts after *The Federalist*. In 1793, Hamilton wrote a series of magazine essays under the name of Pacificus that were in turn answered by Madison (no longer an ally) under the name Helvidius. Did you really think our beloved Founders had acted unconstitutionally?

To Justice Scalia: How could you—the Grand Poobah of Originalism—so conveniently ignore the most famous anonymous tract in American history? I'm talking about *Common Sense*, written in January 1776 by Founding Father Thomas Paine under the pseudonym "an Englishman" and described by Christopher Hitchens, among others, as the "catalyst that altered the course of history."

The pamphlet—like nothing that had been written before or since, for that matter—sold more than 150,000† copies in the first month. Paine's treatise inspired the Declaration of Independence, which followed it by a few months. George Washington ordered it to be read aloud to his despairing troops before the Battle of Trenton. If ever there was precedent for protected, anonymous speech, it is Paine's *Common Sense*, a rousing, poetical call to arms on behalf of freedom, liberty, and the inalienable rights of man.

According to George Washington, there would have been no

---

* Yeah, I know. I forgot John Jay.

† While some historians are skeptical about this figure, it still sold a helluva lot of copies.

American Revolution without Paine's anonymous tract. Yet it seems to have escaped your memory.[*]

You who parse every word of our Founding Fathers like an Etruscan priest reading the entrails of a sacrificial animal? You—the Be-All and End-All of that divination known as Originalism? What happened to Originalism when you chose Ohio over Ms. McIntyre? Just one more "tool" to discard when it suited you?

And to the Majority: Why would you mistakenly call on the "values" of Shakespeare, Voltaire, and Mark Twain to make your case when there is the Bible. Yes, incredibly—you forgot the Bible! That sacred yet anonymous text believed in and worshiped by billions across the world for centuries.

I'm not just talking about the Old Testament and the anonymity of Genesis, Proverbs, Psalms, and Ecclesiastes. I'm also talking about the New Testament and the Four Gospels—written by unknown writers who made it clear that theirs was the Gospel *according* to Matthew, Mark, Luke, and John.

Perhaps you might want to consider that anonymous Book when deciding future cases. For example:

When ruling on the constitutionality of capital punishment:
"Let any one of you who is without sin be the first to throw a stone."

In cases of separation between church and state:
"Render therefore unto Caesar the things which are Caesar's and unto God the things that are God's."

In cases of unlimited campaign contributions by global corporations:

---

[*] You also forgot (or never knew) that Abraham Lincoln, as a politician in Illinois, wrote anonymous editorials denouncing his opponents.

"It is easier for a camel to go through the eye of a needle than for someone who is rich to enter the Kingdom of God."

In cases regarding universal health care:
"It is not the healthy who need a doctor but the sick."

Then as a general note, I would remind all of you:
"Blessed are the merciful for they will be shown mercy."

Next time you go hunting for your citations, try Jesus. You could do worse. And have.

—Thespian

CHAPTER 22

The Chapter of Leftovers: Part III

In 1789, George Washington's first inaugural address was written by James Madison. As a member of Congress, Madison then wrote that body's response to the inaugural. When Washington replied, he had Madison write the reply to the reply. Congress's next reply to Washington's reply was also written by Madison.

Here is Thomas Jefferson's divinely inspired Declaration of Independence:

> We hold these truths to be self-evident, that all men are created equal, that they are endowed by their Creator with certain unalienable Rights, that among these are Life, Liberty and the pursuit of Happiness ... (July 4, 1776).

Which sounds like a rewrite of George Mason's draft of the Virginia Declaration of Rights, composed a month earlier on June 12, 1776:

> That all men are by nature equally free and independent, and have certain inherent rights, of which ... they cannot, by any compact, derive or divest their posterity; namely, the enjoyment of life and liberty, with the means of acquiring and possessing property, and pursuing and obtaining happiness and safety ...

In 1789, as the first president of the United States, George Washington "hired" fourteen servants and seven slaves from Mount Vernon to tend to his and Martha's personal needs at his residence in Philadelphia.

Thomas Jefferson designed his plantation home, Monticello, to have spectacular views from every window. But the slave quarters could not be seen from any one of them.

Thirty-nine men signed the Constitution. One—George Washington—was the presiding officer. Of the thirty-eight remaining delegates, nineteen were from free states and nineteen from slave states.*

During the debates over representation between the large and small states, Benjamin Franklin suggested, as one solution, that Pennsylvania slice off portions of its land and give them to Delaware and New Jersey.

Slaves were obviously prohibited from owning guns. They were also prohibited from owning dogs, which were seen as potential weapons.

George Washington's last gesture right before he died was to check his pulse.

---

* Or what were to become "free" and "slave" states. In 1787, slavery was legal in all of them.

CHAPTER 23

The Second Amendment: Guns and the NRA

Guns don't kill people. People kill people.

—Slogan of the NRA

Bats don't hit home runs. People hit home runs.
But if you take away the bats, you can't hit a home run.

—Anonymous

A gun kills many men before it's done.

—Stephen Sondheim, *Assassins*

There are 300 million guns in the United States. And I own two of them. I bought my first gun, a Glock 15, after I received a death threat through the mail. The year was 1979, and I had just spoken out in favor of the Sandinistas, a socialist revolutionary party about to overthrow the despotic Somoza regime that had been running and ruining Nicaragua since the thirties.

The anonymous author of that threat promised that he (I assume it was a he) would shoot off my genitalia. Since the letter came from Little Rock, Arkansas, I figured he would not be seeing me anytime soon as I had no immediate plans to be anywhere near Little Rock, and I guessed by his handwriting that the gentleman did not have the bus fare to get to Toluca Lake.

Still, there's nothing like a misspelled death threat written in Crayola to catch a man's attention. So, to protect myself and my family, I did the reasonable thing and bought myself a gun. Because I had young children, I kept it in a locked box, separate from its ammunition. Since it would have taken ten minutes at least to load and fire, should the need arise, I felt much safer knowing there was a signed Hank Aaron baseball bat under my bed.

A few years later, I bought a Beretta Px4 for no good reason except I liked its look and the heft of it in my hand.

I mention all this because I am not against guns and the good people who own them. I am one of them. I do have an opinion, however, about the gun culture we now live in and the senseless, never-ending bloody deaths it's brought us.

Maybe you haven't read the numbers:

Between the years 1968 and 2011, deaths from gunfire totaled 1.4 million Americans. The total number of deaths in every military conflict from the Revolutionary War of 1776 to Iraq comes to 1.2 million.

Sixty percent of the 30,000-plus gun deaths a year in this country are suicides.

Every day, ninety-three Americans are killed by guns.

In the last decade, there have been more than 300,000 deaths from guns, while in the same period terrorists killed 31 people.

Cases of road rage involving a firearm more than doubled from 247 in 2014 to 620 in 2016.

America's gun homicide rate is 25 times more than that of any other developed nation.

Between 2004 and 2013, 207 children from the ages of one to sixteen were killed by guns.

Then there's this: IPV—intimate partner violence. Close to ten women each week are shot to death by their husbands, boyfriends, or former dating partners.

Not a pretty picture. And I have not even included those special categories like the number of police who killed unarmed black men by firing warning shots through their hearts.

Not to mention the grim and terrible fact that after every gun massacre in this country like Sandy Hook, Fort Hood, or the Pulse nightclub, gun sales go up and regulations go down.

It's a bloody trail that leads right back to the Second Amendment. Not the Second Amendment itself, of course, but the Right Wing's interpretation of it: an unfettered license for every American to own, carry, collect, trade, and eventually shoot a gun. As if that were our Founders' fondest wish.

Here's that tricky Second Amendment as written in the Bill of Rights:

A well-regulated Militia, being necessary to the security of a free State, the right of the people to keep and bear Arms, shall not be infringed.

Arguably not the clearest amendment in the Constitution. And that's the problem with it: while stating the need for a "well-regulated Militia," does it at the same time *also* guarantee the individual citizen the *personal* right to "keep and bear arms"?

I say *no* and here are my reasons. If the Framers really wanted everyone to have a gun, why didn't they come right out and say so?

One word and one semicolon would have made that absolutely clear.
To wit:*

> A well-regulated Militia, being necessary to the security of a
> free State, shall not be infringed; nor the right of the people
> to keep and bear Arms.

But the Framers didn't write it that way. They did not combine
those *two* rights in one clause. Nor did they use the word *person*,
as if referring to individuals, as they did in the Fifth Amendment,
which states "No person shall be held to answer for a capital ...
crime ...," etc.

Instead, the only two subjects in the Second Amendment are *col-
lective* nouns: "state Militia" and "people." Where, then, can anyone
find an *individual* right to own a weapon except as part of a "well-
regulated Militia"?

So much for my textual analysis. Now let's consider the Second
Amendment in its historical context.

The Second Amendment was one of nineteen original Amendments, suggested by the thirteen State Legislatures, that were com-
piled (and rewritten) by James Madison and presented to Congress
in 1791 as part of the Bill of Rights. And most important, this is how
James Madison first wrote it:

> The right of the people to keep and bear arms shall not be
> infringed, a well-armed and well-regulated militia being the
> best security of a free country; **but no person religiously
> scrupulous of bearing arms shall be compelled to render
> military service in person.**

---

* I can't believe I'm actually using that phrase.

Madison's intent could not be more obvious: the Second Amendment refers *only* to state militias. If not, why include that exemption for what we now call conscientious objectors?

When Madison's amendment was rewritten by a joint committee from the House and Senate,* the "religious" exemption was lopped off as too cumbersome in language and too complex to enforce. Thus, the amendment as it now stands.

But Madison's Original Intent remains and is there hiding in plain sight for any Supreme Court Justice who takes the pains to look for it.

The gun crowd and their apparatchiks ignore, as well, the very reason the Second Amendment got into the Constitution in the first place: to calm the anti-Federalists'† fears of the establishment of a standing army. The Second Amendment is, in fact, Madison's (and the Federalists') response to those who felt threatened that the strong central government, as proposed in the new Constitution, might disarm the state militias. And to miss that connection is to . . . well, miss everything.

As written, the Second Amendment follows closely in meaning and in language previous state and national Constitutions—all of which *explicitly* refer to militias and not individuals.

The Articles of Confederation—the US plan that preceded the ratification of the Constitution—put it this way:

> . . . every State shall always keep up a well-regulated and disciplined Militia, sufficiently armed and accoutered, and shall provide and consistently have ready for use in Public stores, a

---

* Which gives the lie to those who claim the Second Amendment was written by the Founders and Framers instead of a handful of anonymous congressmen.

† Most notably Patrick Henry of Virginia, Elbridge Gerry of Massachusetts, and Thomas Jefferson.

due number of field pieces and tents, and a proper quantity of arms, ammunition and camp equipage.[*]

Of all the thirteen state Constitutions, only one—Pennsylvania's—granted the right of an individual to own a gun. It's worth reading in its entirety:

> That the people have a right to bear arms for the defence of themselves and their own state, or the United States, or for the purpose of killing game; and no law shall be passed for disarming the people or any of them, unless for crimes committed, or real danger of public injury from individuals; and as standing armies in the time of peace are dangerous to liberty, they ought not to be kept up: and that the military shall be kept under strict subordination to and be governed by the civil powers.

Pennsylvania—the outlier—proved the exception because of the demands of its western settlers who feared Indian attacks almost as much as they despised the pacifist Quakers back east who hated guns. But even here it's worth noting the built-in regulations that allowed disarmament in cases of "real danger of public injury from individuals." Again, as always, our American forefathers limited any and all freedoms when they clashed with public safety.

Let there be no confusion: individual gun rights were *not* discussed, debated, voted on, or even mentioned at the Constitutional Convention, the Congressional debates of 1791, or in *The Federalist*. Like women, guns may have been part of American life, but as far as a man's right to own one of them—the Constitution is silent.

And here's the evidence:

---

[*] Article VI.

Jefferson—writing to Madison from Paris about the Bill of Rights—only talks about the State's "protection against Standing Armies."

In a search of the Library of Congress database containing the official records of *all* debates in the United States at that time, thirty uses of the phrase "to bear arms" were found. And in every single one of those uses, the phrase has an *unambiguous military meaning*.

In a national archives search of the database of *all* the writings of Washington, Adams, Franklin, Hamilton, and Madison, the term "bear arms" produces 153 mentions—*all* in a military context.

Let me put my argument another way: the Constitution was written, a new nation conceived, and a more perfect union formed *because* the Founders were afraid of guns—and the wrong hands they might fall into. Not just slaves. Not just Indians. But angry white men.

What I'm saying is: *This country was founded on gun control.*

Stay with me now as I make that point: In 1787, the year of the Constitutional Convention, a man in rural Massachusetts named Daniel Shays led a protest of 1,500 outraged citizens—mostly farmers and ex–Revolutionary War veterans—against high taxes, foreclosures, and bankruptcy proceedings. They were marching toward the armory in Springfield when the state militia squashed the rebellion.

It was what some with a better vocabulary than mine would call a *seminal* event in American history, and it scared the livin' bejesus out of the Founders, George Washington in particular. Writing to his friend General Henry Knox, Washington said this:

If three years since any person had told me that at this day, I should see such a formidable rebellion against the laws . . . of our own making . . . I should have thought him a bedlamite, a fit subject for a madhouse." Adding that if the government "shrinks or is unable to enforce its laws . . . , anarchy and confusion must prevail."

To Washington and the other Founders, the rebellion proved the failure of the Articles of Confederation and the urgent need for a new and strong central government.

You can almost hear their cries of distress: "My God, what would have happened had that mob broken into the armory and gotten their hands on the guns stored there?"

It was that dread over Shays's Rebellion and the anarchy it represented that kept the Framers literally glued to their Windsor chairs during the hot summer of 1787.

And yet today, despite the evidence, the gun lobby has the *chutzpah* to claim that the Second Amendment belongs to them and them alone. How un-American.

Why don't they just write our country a new Bill of Rights and be done with it?

Congress shall make no law establishing any religion—unless it's Christianity.

Church and state are to be separated except when it comes to tax deductions, especially on the second homes of evangelical ministers.

The right of the people to be secure in their own persons and houses shall not be violated, except when those persons are having sex or visiting their doctors.

There shall be no abridgement of freedom of speech except when making people say "Merry Christmas" instead of "Happy Holidays."

> Cruel and unusual punishment shall not be inflicted except
> by the electric chair or lethal injection.

On Valentine's Day, 1929, seven mobsters were mowed down in a Chicago warehouse. The weapons used were two sawed-off shotguns and two Thompson submachine guns. It became famously known as the St. Valentine's Day Massacre. It sparked a national outrage that caused—eventually—Congress to pass the first of several National Firearms Acts that limited the sale and transfer of weapons associated with criminal behavior.

Let me point out that in 2012, when twenty elementary schoolchildren and their teacher were massacred in Newtown, Connecticut, by a deranged young man with a Bushmaster XM15-e2s, that also sparked national outrage—and caused Congress to send its *thoughts and prayers* to the victims' families.

The Firearms Acts of 1934 and 1938 were not the country's first attempts at gun control. And here from the historian Saul Cornell are a few examples from the Constitutional era:*

- It was illegal in Boston (1787) to keep a loaded gun in your house.
- Major cities—Philadelphia, New York, and Boston—prohibited the firing of guns within the city limits.
- All states prohibited people considered "dangerous" from owning a weapon.
- A Boston statute (1786) called for the safe storage of gunpowder within the city limits and allowed for the town's fire wardens to confiscate weapons for violating that law.

All of these restrictions—seeking to balance gun ownership with the demands for public safety—went unchallenged until 1939 when Jack Miller claimed that his right to own a sawed-off shot-

---

* All you Originalists out there pay attention.

gun was protected by the Second Amendment. The case went to the Supreme Court, which ruled in *United States v. Miller* that the 1934 and 1938 National Firearms Acts were constitutional by an 8–1 margin. Writing for the Majority, Justice James C. McReynolds noted:

> The Court cannot take judicial notice that a shotgun having a barrel less than 18 inches long has today any reasonable relation to the ... efficiency of a well-regulated militia.

For the next seven decades, state and federal courts—following the Miller decision—held that the Second Amendment must be interpreted and applied with the view of maintaining a militia.

But all that was to change when the gun manufacturers poured money into their front organizations: the NRA, the ultraconservative think tanks, and their chosen Constitutional law professors.

The slow but lethal attack on the Second Amendment had begun, culminating in the Roberts Court's decision in *District of Columbia v. Heller* (2008), where by a vote of 5–4 the DC law that banned handguns in the nation's capital was overturned.

The Majority decision was written by Justice Antonin Scalia— the midwife at the birth of Originalism. Worshiped before and after his death like some Holy Memento, Scalia—with his sidekick Justice Clarence Thomas*—claimed that the only way to interpret the Constitution was to discover the Original Intent of the Framers and the original meaning of the text.

One can almost picture Scalia and Thomas in their powdered wigs, tight velvet breeches, and white ruffled shirts scampering around in the 1787 theme park in their minds, in search of a public hanging.

---

* The Huck and Jim of American jurisprudence.

In *District of Columbia v. Heller*, Scalia ignores two hundred years of precedent, historical context, the Framers' Intent, *and* the DC laws of its elected officials to focus solely on the *text* of the Second Amendment. He arbitrarily divides the Amendment into two parts: what he calls the prefatory clause—"A well-regulated Militia, being necessary to the security of the free State"—and what he calls the operative clause: "the right of the people to keep and bear Arms, shall not be infringed." And like a kosher butcher who chops off the head of a chicken and throws it in the garbage, Scalia asks the world to see only the operative clause—alone and naked—so it now reads:

> "... the right of the people to keep and bear arms, shall not be infringed."

As pointed out by Michael Waldman,* this truncated portion of the Second Amendment just happens to be the exact same words inscribed on the wall of the NRA headquarters lobby! Coincidence? Or proof that the Roberts Court has become a card-carrying member—in good standing—of the National Rifle Association?

The NRA is a $400-million-a-year, tax-free enterprise funded not just by the dues of its members but by the millions from gun and ammunition manufacturers.

And that is as simple a reason there is as to why the NRA wants everyone to own a gun. Or ten. And if you can't get a gun from a federally licensed gun dealer because of those pesky background checks, there's the internet, mail order, and the ever-present gun shows. There, *everyone*—to the NRA's profit—can buy a gun.

---

* President of the Brennan Center for Justice at NYU School of Law and author of *The Second Amendment*.

- If you have a tattoo of a swastika on the back of your shaved head—you can buy a gun.
- If your last known address was Raqqa and your Arabic middle name means "death to the infidels"—you can buy a gun.
- If you're wearing a T-shirt with Timothy McVeigh's face on it—you can buy a gun.
- If you're a teenager with a Kim Jong-un haircut, high on elephant tranquilizers—you can buy a gun.
- If you walk in wearing a suicide vest—you can buy a gun.
- If you're a hunter who once mistook your wife for a duck—you can buy a gun.

If the NRA could find a way to teach dogs how to shoot, they'd sell your dog a gun. And why not? If a dog can be taught to sit up, beg, and "speak," how hard can it be to get a paw to squeeze a trigger?

And, of course, they'd tell you why it makes perfect sense: Wouldn't you feel safer at night knowing there was an armed dog in your house? And wouldn't it be fun to go hunting with a dog who not only retrieved your pheasant but shot it first?

And remember, they'd tell you, the only thing that can stop a bad guy with a gun is a Schnauzer with a gun.

While the dog market may be only a dream in the NRA's utopian future, children are not. Children, the NRA has come to realize, are an untapped resource worth billions. Which is why they promote their cute, feathery mascot Eddie Eagle and his Tree House Wing Squad, featured in NRA videos, singalongs, and coloring books.

And if that doesn't get the little ones begging their parents for that lightweight rifle called the Cricket—an air gun designed for children under ten that shoots real bullets and comes in hot pink for girls—what will?

And if Eddie Eagle doesn't hook the youngsters, the NRA has a variety of youth programs that offer a wide range of kid-friendly activities. I can only guess such activities include:

- Nature hikes where plants and animals are viewed through the lens of high-powered sniper scopes.
- Orientation in the latest "stand-your-sandbox" laws.
- Lessons in how to assemble model kits into life-sized Howitzers.

And then as the sun goes down, NRA counselors toast marshmallows around a campfire, telling the kids scary stories about that time—not so long ago—when Congress *almost* passed a ban on assault rifles.

The propaganda arm of the NRA is not as playful as the children's division as it encourages reams of law review essays, magazine articles, and books written by professors of criminology, law, and economics.

One professor, no doubt beloved by the NRA, is John Lott Jr., PhD, whose résumé includes the John M. Olin Fellow at the University of Chicago Law School. Called by *Newsweek* "the gun crowd's guru," Mr. Lott has written at least two books that must be on all NRA members' top ten list: *More Guns, Less Crime* and *The War on Guns.**

Praise for *The War on Guns* comes from Newt Gingrich, Ted Cruz, Mark Levin, and the Honorable Andrew P. Napolitano. The Honorable Napolitano, as I write this, has been suspended from Fox News (as a legal analyst) for *not* harassing female coworkers.

Mr. Lott specializes in arcane data that is as murky as his prose—every other sentence reading like a misprint. To paraphrase Christopher Hitchens in describing a similar nitwit: Mr. Lott will forever be a "footnote in the history of piffle."

Here is a sample of Mr. Lott's preposterous and irrelevant pseudoscientific conclusions:

---

* Both books published by a subsidiary of the Salem Media Group, owners of more than one hundred Christian radio stations.

- Cars kill more people than guns.
- Children are more likely to drown in bathtubs than be shot to death.
- Switzerland has more mass gun massacres than the United States.
- Stand-your-ground laws save black lives.
- Every year, 2.5 million people successfully defend themselves against violence by the use of personal firearms.

That last statistic comes from the criminologists Gary Kleck and Marc Gertz, who came up with it after making five thousand random telephone calls around the country. It was also presented as fact by the plaintiff Dick Heller before the Supreme Court.

Should we be surprised that the distinguished John M. Olin Professor of Economics is so absurdly biased in favor of the gun lobby? Not really. The John M. Olin family is the owner of the nation's largest manufacturer of ammunitions, having made its first great fortune during World War I selling its bullets to all comers in that gruesome conflict.

The total military dead in World War I came to around 11 million. How many of those Mr. John M. Olin can take credit for personally is hard to say.

So, where do things stand today since the gibberish of Justice Scalia in *Heller* that "we start therefore with a strong presumption that the Second Amendment right is exercised individually and belongs to all Americans"?

A brief but gory picture:

- Revenue from the US gun industry totals more than a billion dollars a year.
- US gun makers turn out over 6 million guns a year.
- The Freedom Group—a gun consortium—sells over 1.8 million

weapons a year and 3.1 billion rounds of ammunition. Its Bushmaster XM15-e2s* alone brought in a cool $240 million.

Meanwhile:

- The Dickey law that blocks the federal government from investigating the public health effects of firearms-inflicted violence is still on the books.
- So is the law that uniquely protects gun manufacturers from product-liability lawsuits.

And the laws keep coming:

- President Trump signed an executive order that puts guns in the hands of the mentally disabled.
- In Florida, the state legislature perfects its stand-your-ground laws.†
- In Missouri, new laws will allow gun owners to carry concealed weapons in public without a permit, criminal background check, or firearms training. Missouri now joins ten other states with similar laws.
- In South Carolina, less than two years after nine church members were shot to death during Bible study, a bill is ready to be signed as of this writing by the Governor that permits citizens to carry guns openly or concealed—without a state weapons permit.
- Still in the works: national reciprocity laws that would allow gun owners from one state—say, Mississippi—to carry their assault rifles on the streets of—say, New York.‡

---

* The same Bushmaster used in the Sandy Hook massacre.

† Which is a little like the French Revolutionaries perfecting the guillotine.

‡ Assuring them, no doubt, a place at the front of the line at Shake Shack.

• Meanwhile, the gun used by George Zimmerman to kill Trayvon Martin recently sold on the internet for $200,000.

Guns first came to these shores with the Pilgrims, who also brought a taste for witch hunts and a general lack of clear thinking. Since then, guns have become an American fact of life, a long, venerated tradition. Without guns, how would slave owners put down slave revolts? Without guns, how would the Indians have been driven from their lands? Without guns, how would Mexicans have been dispatched from Texas and California?

Guns will always be with us.

What's at issue is whether the Second Amendment can be read as a *fundamental* and *absolute* right (as the NRA claims) that can neither be limited nor regulated.

There are two sides to that issue: On one side we have the Founders. For example, James Madison, who, as a member of the Virginia legislature, introduced a bill for the "Preservation of Deer" that penalized persons

. . . who shall bear a gun out of his enclosed ground *unless* whilst performing military duty.

Then there's the other side: the NRA and its fellow travelers of Republican legislators, Right-Wing pundits, and Originalists on the Supreme Court—all bloodied but unbowed.

The question then is: Whose side are you on?

The answer is a matter of life or death.

CHAPTER 24

In Conclusion

These are the times that try men's souls. The summer
soldier and the sunshine patriot will, in this crisis, shrink
from the service of their country; but he that stands it
now, deserves the love and thanks of man and woman.
Tyranny, like hell, is not easily conquered; yet we have this
conclusion with us, that the harder the conflict, the more
glorious the triumph.

> —Thomas Paine, *Common Sense*,
> Philadelphia, February 14, 1776

The earth belongs ... to the living: that the dead have
neither power nor rights over it.

> —Thomas Jefferson,
> a letter to James Madison, September 6, 1789

As I write this, the television is on and there with the President
stand the current members of the House of Representatives, con-
gratulating one another on passing a health care bill that eliminates
health care.

Their self-satisfied smirks of satisfaction remind me of another
news day when another President with a similar arrogant, unctuous
smile swaggered across an aircraft carrier under a banner that read
"Mission Accomplished."

I think back to that last day of the Convention in Philadelphia—

September 17, 1787—when the Framers signed the Constitution. The mood—a mix of uncertainty and concern—was not as jubilant.

Wise men who knew only too well what they did not know were sharply aware that their Constitution was less than perfect. They were not so superior to believe that they had solved and settled, once and for all, the governing of a new nation. Their ambivalence can best be summed up by Benjamin Franklin's less-than-enthusiastic endorsement: "I am not sure I shall never approve it [the Constitution] . . . I am not sure that it is not the best."

They knew they had made mistakes: slavery, for one, troubled them, but not enough to end its perpetuation. And they never considered themselves soothsayers. They could not even predict political parties (only two years away) that one day would collect enough "factions" into a majority that controlled both houses of Congress, the Presidency, and the Supreme Court. A form of tyranny that would threaten the core of their political faith: a robust system of checks and balances.

But, then, how could they ever know that? For all their genius, they were—to state the obvious—very much men of their time: When black families were sold at auction. When men in debt were sent to prison. When children as young as seven were forced to work long hours in mills and factories. And when women had no rights under the law, either to vote or to own property.

All the more curious then that the Right-Wing syndicate turns to the Constitution as Holy Writ and the men who wrote it as infallible as the Apostles.

Jefferson had warned us of this when he wrote:

Laws and institutions must go hand in hand with the progress of the human mind . . . each generation has a right to choose for itself the form of government it believes most promotive of its own happiness . . . Some men look at constitutions with *sanctimonious reverence* [my emphasis] and deem them like the Ark of the Covenant, too sacred to be touched.

Unfortunately, his words have fallen on deaf minds. And ironic, isn't it, that the Framers who despised "hereditary succession" have now themselves become rulers—in absentia—of our own destiny?

Meanwhile, the Right—its Originalists, politicians, and pundits—continues its attack on the Constitution with a fierce evangelism that infects their every interpretation. The Constitution has become, in their hands, a weapon in the service of the self-righteous:

- When they read the First Amendment, they see *their* right to threaten journalists and late-night comedians. *Their* right to let corporations spend billions to further their own political ends. *Their* right for churches to contribute tax-free dollars to Republican candidates.
- When they read the Second Amendment, they see *their* right to sell guns to anyone with the bucks to buy them.
- When they read the Fifteenth Amendment, they see *their* right to disenfranchise blacks and Latinos.

This is America at its worst.

It's time now to redeem the America the Founders wanted for us:

- A government that rules by reason, tempered with compassion and advanced by science;
- That guarantees free speech in the public square;
- That respects and grants liberties to all;
- That drives big money from politics;
- That separates church and state;
- That promotes sane and civil discourse;

- That protects the most vulnerable of its citizens;
- That ensures a society of the "haves" *and* the "haves";
- That its elected officials share a civic virtue, disinterested in their own advancements;
- Whose criminal justice system is more "justice" than "criminal."

It's time for a new age of Enlightenment.

And speaking of Enlightenment—let me quote once again from Thomas Jefferson:

> The care of human life and happiness and not their destruction, is the first and only legitimate object of good government.

A curtain line if I ever heard one.

Appendix

The Constitution of the United States:
A Transcription

We the People of the United States, in Order to form a more perfect Union, establish Justice, insure domestic Tranquility, provide for the common defence, promote the general Welfare, and secure the Blessings of Liberty to ourselves and our Posterity, do ordain and establish this Constitution for the United States of America.

Article. I.

SECTION. 1.

All legislative Powers herein granted shall be vested in a Congress of the United States, which shall consist of a Senate and House of Representatives.

SECTION. 2.

The House of Representatives shall be composed of Members chosen every second Year by the People of the several States, and the Electors in each State shall have the Qualifications requisite for Electors of the most numerous Branch of the State Legislature.

No Person shall be a Representative who shall not have attained to the Age of twenty five Years, and been seven Years a Citizen of the United States, and who shall not, when elected, be an Inhabitant of that State in which he shall be chosen.

Representatives and direct Taxes shall be apportioned among the several States which may be included within this Union, according to their respective Numbers, which shall be determined by adding to the whole

Number of free Persons, including those bound to Service for a Term of Years, and excluding Indians not taxed, three fifths of all other Persons. The actual Enumeration shall be made within three Years after the first Meeting of the Congress of the United States, and within every subsequent Term of ten Years, in such Manner as they shall by Law direct. The Number of Representatives shall not exceed one for every thirty Thousand, but each State shall have at Least one Representative; and until such enumeration shall be made, the State of New Hampshire shall be entitled to chuse three, Massachusetts eight, Rhode-Island and Providence Plantations one, Connecticut five, New-York six, New Jersey four, Pennsylvania eight, Delaware one, Maryland six, Virginia ten, North Carolina five, South Carolina five, and Georgia three.

When vacancies happen in the Representation from any State, the Executive Authority thereof shall issue Writs of Election to fill such Vacancies.

The House of Representatives shall chuse their Speaker and other Officers; and shall have the sole Power of Impeachment.

SECTION. 3.

The Senate of the United States shall be composed of two Senators from each State, chosen by the Legislature thereof, for six Years; and each Senator shall have one Vote.

Immediately after they shall be assembled in Consequence of the first Election, they shall be divided as equally as may be into three Classes. The Seats of the Senators of the first Class shall be vacated at the Expiration of the second Year, of the second Class at the Expiration of the fourth Year, and of the third Class at the Expiration of the sixth Year, so that one third may be chosen every second Year; and if Vacancies happen by Resignation, or otherwise, during the Recess of the Legislature of any State, the Executive thereof may make temporary Appointments until the next Meeting of the Legislature, which shall then fill such Vacancies.

No Person shall be a Senator who shall not have attained to the Age of thirty Years, and been nine Years a Citizen of the United States, and who shall not, when elected, be an Inhabitant of that State for which he shall be chosen.

The Vice President of the United States shall be President of the Senate, but shall have no Vote, unless they be equally divided.

The Senate shall chuse their other Officers, and also a President pro tempore, in the Absence of the Vice President, or when he shall exercise the Office of President of the United States.

The Senate shall have the sole Power to try all Impeachments. When sitting for that Purpose, they shall be on Oath or Affirmation. When the President of the United States is tried, the Chief Justice shall preside: And no Person shall be convicted without the Concurrence of two thirds of the Members present.

Judgment in Cases of Impeachment shall not extend further than to removal from Office, and disqualification to hold and enjoy any Office of honor, Trust or Profit under the United States: but the Party convicted shall nevertheless be liable and subject to Indictment, Trial, Judgment and Punishment, according to Law.

SECTION. 4.

The Times, Places and Manner of holding Elections for Senators and Representatives, shall be prescribed in each State by the Legislature thereof; but the Congress may at any time by Law make or alter such Regulations, except as to the Places of chusing Senators.

The Congress shall assemble at least once in every Year, and such Meeting shall be on the first Monday in December, unless they shall by Law appoint a different Day.

SECTION. 5.

Each House shall be the Judge of the Elections, Returns and Qualifications of its own Members, and a Majority of each shall constitute a Quorum to do Business; but a smaller Number may adjourn from day to day, and may be authorized to compel the Attendance of absent Members, in such Manner, and under such Penalties as each House may provide.

Each House may determine the Rules of its Proceedings, punish its Members for disorderly Behaviour, and, with the Concurrence of two thirds, expel a Member.

Each House shall keep a Journal of its Proceedings, and from time to time publish the same, excepting such Parts as may in their Judgment require Secrecy; and the Yeas and Nays of the Members of either House on any question shall, at the Desire of one fifth of those Present, be entered on the Journal.

Neither House, during the Session of Congress, shall, without the Consent of the other, adjourn for more than three days, nor to any other Place than that in which the two Houses shall be sitting.

SECTION. 6.

The Senators and Representatives shall receive a Compensation for their Services, to be ascertained by Law, and paid out of the Treasury of the United States. They shall in all Cases, except Treason, Felony and Breach of the Peace, be privileged from Arrest during their Attendance at the Session of their respective Houses, and in going to and returning from the same; and for any Speech or Debate in either House, they shall not be questioned in any other Place.

No Senator or Representative shall, during the Time for which he was elected, be appointed to any civil Office under the Authority of the United States, which shall have been created, or the Emoluments whereof shall have been encreased during such time; and no Person holding any Office under the United States, shall be a Member of either House during his Continuance in Office.

SECTION. 7.

All Bills for raising Revenue shall originate in the House of Representatives; but the Senate may propose or concur with amendments as on other Bills. Every Bill which shall have passed the House of Representatives and the Senate, shall, before it become a law, be presented to the President of the United States: If he approve he shall sign it, but if not he shall return it, with his Objections to that House in which it shall have originated, who shall enter the Objections at large on their Journal, and proceed to reconsider it. If after such Reconsideration two thirds of that House shall agree to pass the Bill, it shall be sent, together with the Objections, to the other House, by which it shall likewise be reconsidered, and if approved by two thirds of that House, it shall become a Law. But in all such Cases the Votes of both Houses shall be determined by Yeas and Nays, and the Names of the Persons voting for and against the Bill shall be entered on the Journal of each House respectively. If any Bill shall not be returned by the President within ten Days (Sundays excepted) after it shall have been presented to him, the Same shall be a Law, in like Manner as if he had signed it, unless the Congress by their Adjournment prevent its Return, in which Case it shall not be a Law.

Every Order, Resolution, or Vote to which the Concurrence of the Senate and House of Representatives may be necessary (except on a question of Adjournment) shall be presented to the President of the United States; and before the Same shall take Effect, shall be approved by him, or being disapproved by him, shall be repassed by two thirds of the Senate and House of Representatives, according to the Rules and Limitations prescribed in the Case of a Bill.

SECTION. 8.

The Congress shall have Power To lay and collect Taxes, Duties, Imposts and Excises, to pay the Debts and provide for the common Defence and general Welfare of the United States; but all Duties, Imposts and Excises shall be uniform throughout the United States;

To borrow Money on the credit of the United States;

To regulate Commerce with foreign Nations, and among the several States, and with the Indian Tribes;

To establish an uniform Rule of Naturalization, and uniform Laws on the subject of Bankruptcies throughout the United States;

To coin Money, regulate the Value thereof, and of foreign Coin, and fix the Standard of Weights and Measures;

To provide for the Punishment of counterfeiting the Securities and current Coin of the United States;

To establish Post Offices and post Roads;

To promote the Progress of Science and useful Arts, by securing for limited Times to Authors and Inventors the exclusive Right to their respective Writings and Discoveries;

To constitute Tribunals inferior to the supreme Court;

To define and punish Piracies and Felonies committed on the high Seas, and Offences against the Law of Nations;

To declare War, grant Letters of Marque and Reprisal, and make Rules concerning Captures on Land and Water;

To raise and support Armies, but no Appropriation of Money to that Use shall be for a longer Term than two Years;

To provide and maintain a Navy;

To make Rules for the Government and Regulation of the land and naval Forces;

To provide for calling forth the Militia to execute the Laws of the Union, suppress Insurrections and repeal Invasions;

To provide for organizing, arming, and disciplining, the Militia, and for governing such Part of them as may be employed in the Service of the United States, reserving to the States respectively, the Appointment of the Officers, and the Authority of training the Militia according to the discipline prescribed by Congress;

To exercise exclusive Legislation in all Cases whatsoever, over such District (not exceeding ten Miles square) as may, by Cession of Particular States, and the Acceptance of Congress, become the Seat of the Government of the United States, and to exercise like Authority over all Places purchased by the Consent of the Legislature of the State in which the Same shall be, for the Erection of Forts, Magazines, Arsenals, dock-Yards, and other needful Buildings;—And

To make all Laws which shall be necessary and proper for carrying into Execution the foregoing Powers, and all other Powers vested by this Constitution in the Government of the United States, or in any Department or Officer thereof.

SECTION. 9.

The Migration or Importation of such Persons as any of the States now existing shall think proper to admit, shall not be prohibited by the Congress prior to the Year one thousand eight hundred and eight, but a Tax or duty may be imposed on such Importation, not exceeding ten dollars for each Person.

The Privilege of the Writ of Habeas Corpus shall not be suspended, unless when in Cases or Rebellion or Invasion the public Safety may require it.

No Bill of Attainder or ex post facto Law shall be passed.

No Capitation, or other direct, Tax shall be laid, unless in Proportion to the Census of Enumeration herein before directed to be taken.

No Tax or Duty shall be laid on Articles exported from any State.

No Preference shall be given by any Regulation of Commerce or Revenue to the Ports of one State over those of another: nor shall Vessels bound to, or from, one State, be obliged to enter, clear, or pay Duties in another.

No Money shall be drawn from the Treasury, but in Consequence of Appropriations made by Law; and a regular Statement and Account of the Receipts and Expenditures of all public Money shall be published from time to time.

No Title of Nobility shall be granted by the United States: And no Person holding any Office of Profit or Trust under them, shall, without the Consent of the Congress, accept of any present, Emolument, Office, or Title, of any kind whatever, from any King, Prince, or foreign State.

SECTION. 10.

No State shall enter into any Treaty, Alliance, or Confederation; grant Letters of Marque and Reprisal; coin Money; emit Bills of Credit; make any Thing but gold and silver Coin a Tender in Payment of Debts; pass any Bill of Attainder, ex post facto Law, or Law impairing the Obligation of Contracts, or grant any Title of Nobility.

No State shall, without the Consent of the Congress, lay any Imposts or Duties on Imports or Exports, except what may be absolutely necessary for executing its inspection Laws: and the net Produce of all Duties and Imposts, laid by any State on Imports or Exports, shall be for the Use of the Treasury of the United States; and all such Laws shall be subject to the Revision and Controul of the Congress.

No State shall, without the Consent of Congress, lay any Duty of Tonnage, keep Troops, or Ships of War in time of Peace, enter into any Agreement or Compact with another State, or with a foreign Power, or engage in War, unless actually invaded, or in such imminent Danger as will not admit of delay.

Article. II.

SECTION. 1.

The executive Power shall be vested in a President of the United States of America. He shall hold his Office during the Term of four Years, and, together with the Vice President, chosen for the same Term, be elected, as follows:

Each State shall appoint, in such Manner as the Legislature thereof may direct, a Number of Electors, equal to the whole Number of Senators and Representatives to which the State may be entitled in the Congress: but no Senator or Representative, or Person holding an Office of Trust or Profit under the United States, shall be appointed an Elector.

The Electors shall meet in their respective States, and vote by Ballot for two Persons, of whom one at least shall not be an Inhabitant of the same State with themselves. And they shall make a List of all the Persons voted for, and of the Number of Votes for each; which List they shall sign and certify, and transmit sealed to the Seat of the Government of the United States, directed to the President of the Senate. The President of the Senate shall, in the Presence of the Senate and House of Representatives, open all the Certificates, and the Votes shall then be counted. The Person having the greatest Number of Votes shall be the President, if such Number be a Majority of the whole Number of Electors appointed; and if there be more than one who have such Majority, and have an equal Number of Votes, then the House of Representatives shall immediately chuse by Ballot one of them for President; and if no Person have a Majority, then from the five highest on the List the said House shall in like Manner chuse the President. But in chusing the President, the Votes shall be taken by States, the Representatives from each State having one Vote; a quorum for this Purpose shall consist of a Member or Members from two thirds of the States, and a Majority of all the States shall be necessary to a Choice. In every Case, after the Choice of the President, the Person having the greatest Number of Votes of the Electors shall be the Vice President. But if there should remain two or more who have equal Votes, the Senate shall chuse from them by Ballot the Vice President.

The Congress may determine the Time of chusing the Electors, and the Day on which they shall give their Votes; which Day shall be the same throughout the United States.

No Person except a natural born Citizen, or a Citizen of the United States, at the time of the Adoption of this Constitution, shall be eligible to the Office of President; neither shall any person be eligible to that Office who shall not have attained to the Age of thirty five Years, and been fourteen Years a Resident within the United States.

In Case of the Removal of the President from Office, or of his Death, Resignation, or Inability to discharge the Powers and Duties of the said Office, the Same shall devolve on the Vice President, and the Congress may by Law provide for the Case of Removal, Death, Resignation or Inability, both of the President and Vice President, declaring what Officer shall then act as President, and such Officer shall act accordingly, until the Disability be removed, or a President shall be elected.

The President shall, at stated Times, receive for his Services, a Compensation, which shall neither be increased nor diminished during the Period for which he shall have been elected, and he shall not receive within that Period any other Emolument from the United States, or any of them.

Before he enter on the Execution of his Office, he shall take the following Oath or Affirmation:—"I do solemnly swear (or affirm) that I will faithfully execute the Office of President of the United States, and will to the best of my Ability, preserve, protect and defend the Constitution of the United States."

SECTION. 2.

The President shall be Commander in Chief of the Army and Navy of the United States, and of the Militia of the several States, when called into the actual Service of the United States; he may require the Opinion, in writing, of the principal Officer in each of the executive Departments, upon any Subject relating to the Duties of their respective Offices, and he shall have Power to Grant Reprieves and Pardons for Offences against the United States, except in Cases of Impeachment.

He shall have Power, by and with the Advice and Consent of the Senate, to make Treaties, provided two thirds of the Senators present concur; and he shall nominate, and by and with the Advice and Consent of the Senate, shall appoint Ambassadors, other public Ministers and Consuls, Judges of the supreme Court, and all other Officers of the United States, whose Appointments are not herein otherwise provided for, and which shall be established by Law: but the Congress may by Law vest the Appointment of such inferior Officers, as they think proper, in the President alone, in the Courts of Law, or in the Heads of Departments.

The President shall have Power to fill up all Vacancies that may happen during the Recess of the Senate, by granting Commissions which shall expire at the End of their next Session.

SECTION. 3.

He shall from time to time give to the Congress Information of the State of the Union, and recommend to their Consideration such Measures as he shall judge necessary and expedient; he may, on extraordinary Occasions, convene both Houses, or either of them, and in Case of Disagreement between them, with Respect to the Time of Adjournment, he may adjourn them to such Time as he shall think proper; he shall receive Ambassadors and other public Ministers; he shall take Care that the Laws be faithfully executed, and shall Commission all the Officers of the United States.

SECTION. 4.

The President, Vice President and all Civil Officers of the United States, shall be removed from Office on Impeachment for, and Conviction of, Treason, Bribery, or other high Crimes and Misdemeanors.

Article. III.

SECTION. 1.

The judicial Power of the United States, shall be vested in one supreme Court, and in such inferior Courts as the Congress may from time to time ordain and establish. The Judges, both of the supreme and inferior Courts, shall hold their Offices during good Behaviour, and shall, at stated Times, receive for their Services, a Compensation, which shall not be diminished during their Continuance in Office.

SECTION. 2.

The judicial Power shall extend to all Cases, in Law and Equity, arising under this Constitution, the Laws of the United States, and Treaties made, or which shall be made, under their Authority;—to all Cases affecting Ambassadors, other public ministers and Consuls;—to all Cases of admiralty and maritime Jurisdiction;—to Controversies to which the United States shall be a Party;—to Controversies between two or more States;—between a State and Citizens of another State;—between Citizens of different States;—between Citizens of the same State claiming Lands under Grants of different States, and between a State, or the Citizens thereof, and foreign States, Citizens or Subjects.

In all Cases affecting Ambassadors, other public Ministers and Consuls, and those in which a State shall be Party, the supreme Court shall have original Jurisdiction. In all the other Cases before mentioned, the supreme Court shall have appellate Jurisdiction, both as to Law and Fact, with such Exceptions, and under such Regulations as the Congress shall make.

The Trial of all Crimes, except in Cases of Impeachment, shall be by Jury; and such Trial shall be held in the State where the said Crimes shall have been committed; but when not committed within any State, the

Trial shall be at such Place or Places as the Congress may by Law have directed.

SECTION. 3.

Treason against the United States, shall consist only in levying War against them, or in adhering to their Enemies, giving them Aid and Comfort. No Person shall be convicted of Treason unless on the Testimony of two Witnesses to the same overt Act, or on Confession in open Court.

The Congress shall have Power to declare the Punishment of Treason, but no Attainder of Treason shall work Corruption of Blood, or Forfeiture except during the Life of the Person attainted.

Article. IV.

SECTION. 1.

Full Faith and Credit shall be given in each State to the public Acts, Records, and judicial Proceedings of every other State. And the Congress may by general Laws prescribe the Manner in which such Acts, Records and Proceedings shall be proved, and the Effect thereof.

SECTION. 2.

The Citizens of each State shall be entitled to all Privileges and Immunities of Citizens in the several States.

A Person charged in any State with Treason, Felony, or other Crime, who shall flee from Justice, and be found in another State, shall on Demand of the executive Authority of the State from which he fled, be delivered up, to be removed to the State having Jurisdiction of the Crime.

No Person held to Service or Labour in one State, under the Laws thereof, escaping into another, shall, in Consequence of any Law or Regulation therein, be discharged from such Service or Labour, but shall be delivered up on Claim of the Party to whom such Service or Labour may be due.

SECTION. 3.

New States may be admitted by the Congress into this Union; but no new State shall be formed or erected within the Jurisdiction of any other State; nor any State be formed by the Junction of two or more States, or Parts of States, without the Consent of the Legislatures of the States concerned as well as of the Congress.

The Congress shall have Power to dispose of and make all needful Rules and Regulations respecting the Territory or other Property belonging to the United States; and nothing in this Constitution shall be so construed as to Prejudice any Claims of the United States, or of any particular State.

SECTION. 4.

The United States shall guarantee to every State in this Union a Republican Form of Government, and shall protect each of them against Invasion; and on Application of the Legislature, or of the Executive (when the Legislature cannot be convened), against domestic Violence.

Article. V.

The Congress, whenever two thirds of both Houses shall deem it necessary, shall propose Amendments to this Constitution, or, on the Application of the Legislatures of two thirds of the several States, shall call a Convention for proposing Amendments, which, in either Case, shall be valid to all Intents and Purposes, as Part of this Constitution, when ratified by the Legislatures of three fourths of the several States, or by Conventions in three fourths thereof, as the one or the other Mode of Ratification may be proposed by the Congress; Provided that no Amendment which may be made prior to the Year One thousand eight hundred and eight shall in any Manner affect the first and fourth Clauses in the Ninth Section of the first Article; and that no State, without its Consent, shall be deprived of its equal Suffrage in the Senate.

Article. VI.

All Debts contracted and Engagements entered into, before the Adoption of this Constitution, shall be as valid against the United States under this Constitution, as under the Confederation.

This Constitution, and the Laws of the United States which shall be made in Pursuance thereof; and all Treaties made, or which shall be made, under the Authority of the United States, shall be the supreme Law of the Land; and the Judges in every State shall be bound thereby, any Thing in the Constitution or Laws of any state to the Contrary notwithstanding.

The Senators and Representatives before mentioned, and the Members of the several State Legislatures, and all executive and judicial Officers, both of the United States and of the several States, shall be bound by Oath or Affirmation, to support this Constitution; but no religious Test shall ever be required as a Qualification to any Office or public Trust under the United States.

Article. VII.

The Ratification of the Conventions of nine States, shall be sufficient for the Establishment of this Constitution between the States so ratifying the same.

The Word, "the," being interlined between the seventh and eighth Lines of the first Page, The Word "Thirty" being partly written on an Erazure in the fifteenth Line of the first Page, The Words "is tried" being interlined between the thirty second and thirty third Lines of the first Page and the Word "the" being interlined between the forty third and forty fourth Lines of the second Page.

Attest William Jackson Secretary

done in Convention by the Unanimous Consent of the States present the Seventeenth Day of September in the Year of our Lord one thousand seven hundred and Eighty seven and of the Independence of the United States of America the Twelfth. In witness whereof We have hereunto subscribed our Names,

G°. Washington
Presidt and deputy from Virginia

DELAWARE
Geo: Read
Gunning Bedford jun
John Dickinson
Richard Bassett
Jaco: Broom

MARYLAND
James McHenry
Dan of St Thos. Jenifer
Danl. Carroll

VIRGINIA
John Blair
James Madison Jr.

NORTH CAROLINA
Wm. Blount
Richd. Dobbs Spaight
Hu Williamson

SOUTH CAROLINA
J. Rutledge
Charles Cotesworth Pinckney
Charles Pinckney
Pierce Butler

GEORGIA
William Few
Abr Baldwin

NEW HAMPSHIRE
John Langdon
Nicholas Gilman

MASSACHUSETTS
Nathaniel Gorham
Rufus King

CONNECTICUT
Wm. Saml. Johnson
Roger Sherman

NEW YORK
Alexander Hamilton

NEW JERSEY
Wil: Livingston
David Brearley
Wm. Paterson
Jona: Dayton

PENNSYLVANIA
B Franklin
Thomas Mifflin
Robt. Morris
Geo. Clymer
Thos. FitzSimons
Jared Ingersoll
James Wilson
Gouv Morris

The US Bill of Rights
(Constitutional Amendments 1–10)
Amendment I

Congress shall make no law respecting an establishment of religion, or prohibiting the free exercise thereof; or abridging the freedom of speech, or of the press; or the right of the people peaceably to assemble, and to petition the Government for a redress of grievances.

Amendment II

A well regulated Militia, being necessary to the security of a free State, the right of the people to keep and bear Arms, shall not be infringed.

Amendment III

No Soldier shall, in time of peace be quartered in any house, without the consent of the Owner, nor in time of war, but in a manner to be prescribed by law.

Amendment IV

The right of the people to be secure in their persons, houses, papers, and effects, against unreasonable searches and seizures, shall not be violated, and no Warrants shall issue, but upon probable cause, supported by Oath or affirmation, and particularly describing the place to be searched, and the persons or things to be seized.

Amendment V

No person shall be held to answer for a capital, or otherwise infamous crime, unless on a presentment or indictment of a Grand Jury, except in cases arising in the land or naval forces, or in the Militia, when in actual service in time of War or public danger; nor shall any person be subject for the same offence to be twice put in jeopardy of life or limb; nor shall be compelled in any criminal case to be a witness against himself, nor be deprived of life, liberty, or property, without due process of law; nor shall private property be taken for public use, without just compensation.

Amendment VI

In all criminal prosecutions, the accused shall enjoy the right to a speedy and public trial, by an impartial jury of the State and district wherein the crime shall have been committed, which district shall have been previously ascertained by law, and to be informed of the nature and cause of the accusation; to be confronted with the witnesses against him; to have compulsory process for obtaining witnesses in his favor, and to have the Assistance of Counsel for his defence.

Amendment VII

In Suits at common law, where the value in controversy shall exceed twenty dollars, the right of trial by jury shall be preserved, and no fact tried by a jury, shall be otherwise re-examined in any Court of the United States, than according to the rules of the common law.

Amendment VIII

Excessive bail shall not be required, nor excessive fines imposed, nor cruel and unusual punishments inflicted.

Amendment IX

The enumeration in the Constitution, of certain rights, shall not be construed to deny or disparage others retained by the people.

Amendment X

The powers not delegated to the United States by the Constitution, nor prohibited by it to the States, are reserved to the States respectively, or to the people.

Amendments 11–27

Amendment XI

Note: Article III, section 2, of the Constitution was modified by amendment II.

The Judicial power of the United States shall not be construed to extend to any suit in law or equity, commenced or prosecuted against one of the

United States by Citizens of another State, or by Citizens or Subjects of any Foreign State.

Amendment XII

Note: A portion of Article II, section 1 of the Constitution was superseded by the 12th amendment.

The Electors shall meet in their respective states and vote by ballot for President and Vice-President, one of whom, at least, shall not be an inhabitant of the same state with themselves; they shall name in their ballots the person voted for as President, and in distinct ballots the person voted for as Vice-President, and they shall make distinct lists of all persons voted for as President, and of all persons voted for as Vice-President, and of the number of votes for each, which lists they shall sign and certify, and transmit sealed to the seat of the government of the United States, directed to the President of the Senate;—the President of the Senate shall, in the presence of the Senate and House of Representatives, open all the certificates and the votes shall then be counted;—The person having the greatest number of votes for President, shall be the President, if such number be a majority of the whole number of Electors appointed; and if no person have such majority, then from the persons having the highest numbers not exceeding three on the list of those voted for as President, the House of Representatives shall choose immediately, by ballot, the President. But in choosing the President, the votes shall be taken by states, the representation from each state having one vote; a quorum for this purpose shall consist of a member or members from two-thirds of the states, and a majority of all the states shall be necessary to a choice. [And if the House of Representatives shall not choose a President whenever the right of choice shall devolve upon them, before the fourth day of March next following, then the Vice-President shall act as President, as in case of the death or other constitutional disability of the President.—]* The person having the greatest number of votes as Vice-President, shall be the Vice-President, if such number be a majority of the whole number of Electors appointed, and if no person have a majority, then from the two highest numbers on the list, the Sen-

* Superseded by Section 3 of the 20th amendment.

ate shall choose the Vice-President; a quorum for the purpose shall consist of two-thirds of the whole number of Senators, and a majority of the whole number shall be necessary to a choice. But no person constitutionally ineligible to the office of President shall be eligible to that of Vice-President of the United States.

Amendment XIII

Note: A portion of Article IV, Section 2, of the Constitution was superseded by the 13th Amendment.

SECTION 1.

Neither slavery nor involuntary servitude, except as a punishment for crime whereof the party shall have been duly convicted, shall exist within the United States, or any place subject to their jurisdiction.

SECTION 2.

Congress shall have power to enforce this article by appropriate legislation.

Amendment XIV

Note: Article I, section 2, of the Constitution was modified by section 2 of the 14th amendment.

SECTION 1.

All persons born or naturalized in the United States, and subject to the jurisdiction thereof, are citizens of the United States and of the State wherein they reside. No State shall make or enforce any law which shall abridge the privileges or immunities of citizens of the United States; nor shall any State deprive any person of life, liberty, or property, without due process of law; nor deny to any person within its jurisdiction the equal protection of the laws.

SECTION 2.

Representatives shall be apportioned among the several States according to their respective numbers, counting the whole number of persons in each State, excluding Indians not taxed. But when the right to vote at any election for the choice of electors for President and Vice-President of the United States, Representatives in Congress, the Executive and Judicial officers of a State, or the members of the Legislature thereof, is denied to any of the male inhabitants of such State, being twenty-one years of age,* and citizens of the United States, or in any way abridged, except for participation in rebellion, or other crime, the basis of representation therein shall be reduced in the proportion which the number of such male citizens shall bear to the whole number of male citizens twenty-one years of age in such State.

SECTION 3.

No person shall be a Senator or Representative in Congress, or elector of President and Vice-President, or hold any office, civil or military, under the United States, or under any State, who, having previously taken an oath, as a member of Congress, or as an officer of the United States, or as a member of any State legislature, or as an executive or judicial officer of any State, to support the Constitution of the United States, shall have engaged in insurrection or rebellion against the same, or given aid or comfort to the enemies thereof. But Congress may by a vote of two-thirds of each House, remove such disability.

SECTION 4.

The validity of the public debt of the United States, authorized by law, including debts incurred for payment of pensions and bounties for services in suppressing insurrection or rebellion, shall not be questioned. But neither the United States nor any State shall assume or pay any debt or obligation incurred in aid of insurrection or rebellion against the United States, or any claim for the loss or emancipation of any slave; but all such debts, obligations and claims shall be held illegal and void.

---

* Changed by section 1 of the 26th amendment.

SECTION 5.

The Congress shall have the power to enforce, by appropriate legislation, the provisions of this article.

Amendment XV

SECTION 1.

The right of citizens of the United States to vote shall not be denied or abridged by the United States or by any State on account of race, color, or previous condition of servitude—

SECTION 2.

The Congress shall have the power to enforce this article by appropriate legislation.

Amendment XVI

Note: Article I, section 9, of the Constitution was modified by amendment 16.

The Congress shall have power to lay and collect taxes on incomes, from whatever source derived, without apportionment among the several States, and without regard to any census or enumeration.

Amendment XVII

Note: Article I, section 3, of the Constitution was modified by the 17th amendment.

The Senate of the United States shall be composed of two Senators from each State, elected by the people thereof, for six years; and each Senator shall have one vote. The electors in each State shall have the qualifications requisite for electors of the most numerous branch of the State legislatures.

When vacancies happen in the representation of any State in the Senate, the executive authority of such State shall issue writs of election to fill such vacancies: Provided, That the legislature of any State may empower the executive thereof to make temporary appointments until the people fill the vacancies by election as the legislature may direct.

This amendment shall not be so construed as to affect the election or term of any Senator chosen before it becomes valid as part of the Constitution.

Amendment XVIII

Repealed by amendment 21.

SECTION 1.

After one year from the ratification of this article the manufacture, sale, or transportation of intoxicating liquors within, the importation thereof into, or the exportation thereof from the United States and all territory subject to the jurisdiction thereof for beverage purposes is hereby prohibited.

SECTION 2.

The Congress and the several States shall have concurrent power to enforce this article by appropriate legislation.

SECTION 3.

This article shall be inoperative unless it shall have been ratified as an amendment to the Constitution by the legislatures of the several States, as provided in the Constitution, within seven years from the date of the submission hereof to the States by the Congress.

Amendment XIX

The right of citizens of the United States to vote shall not be denied or abridged by the United States or by any State on account of sex.

Congress shall have power to enforce this article by appropriate legislation.

Amendment XX

Note: Article I, section 4, of the Constitution was modified by section 2 of this amendment. In addition, a portion of the 12th amendment was superseded by section 3.

SECTION 1.

The terms of the President and the Vice President shall end at noon on the 20th day of January, and the terms of Senators and Representatives at noon on the 3d day of January, of the years in which such terms would have ended if this article had not been ratified; and the terms of their successors shall then begin.

SECTION 2.

The Congress shall assemble at least once in every year, and such meeting shall begin at noon on the 3d day of January, unless they shall by law appoint a different day.

SECTION 3.

If, at the time fixed for the beginning of the term of the President, the President elect shall have died, the Vice President elect shall become President. If a President shall not have been chosen before the time fixed for the beginning of his term, or if the President elect shall have failed to qualify, then the Vice President elect shall act as President until a President shall have qualified; and the Congress may by law provide for the case wherein neither a President elect nor a Vice President shall have qualified, declaring who shall then act as President, or the manner in which one who is to act shall be selected, and such person shall act accordingly until a President or Vice President shall have qualified.

SECTION 4.

The Congress may by law provide for the case of the death of any of the persons from whom the House of Representatives may choose a President whenever the right of choice shall have devolved upon them, and for the case of the death of any of the persons from whom the Senate may choose a Vice President whenever the right of choice shall have devolved upon them.

SECTION 5.

Sections 1 and 2 shall take effect on the 15th day of October following the ratification of this article.

SECTION 6.

This article shall be inoperative unless it shall have been ratified as an amendment to the Constitution by the legislatures of three-fourths of the several States within seven years from the date of its submission.

Amendment XXI

SECTION 1.

The eighteenth article of amendment to the Constitution of the United States is hereby repealed.

SECTION 2.

The transportation or importation into any State, Territory, or possession of the United States for delivery or use therein of intoxicating liquors, in violation of the laws thereof, is hereby prohibited.

SECTION 3.

This article shall be inoperative unless it shall have been ratified as an amendment to the Constitution by conventions in the several States, as provided in the Constitution, within seven years from the date of the submission hereof to the States by the Congress.

Amendment XXII

SECTION 1.

No person shall be elected to the office of the President more than twice, and no person who has held the office of President, or acted as President, for more than two years of a term to which some other person was elected President shall be elected to the office of President more than once. But this Article shall not apply to any person holding the office of President when this Article was proposed by Congress, and shall not prevent any person who may be holding the office of President, or acting as President, during the term within which this Article becomes operative from holding the office of President or acting as President during the remainder of such term.

SECTION 2.

This article shall be inoperative unless it shall have been ratified as an amendment to the Constitution by the legislatures of three-fourths of the several States within seven years from the date of its submission to the States by the Congress.

Amendment XXIII

SECTION 1.

The District constituting the seat of Government of the United States shall appoint in such manner as Congress may direct:

A number of electors of President and Vice President equal to the whole number of Senators and Representatives in Congress to which the District would be entitled if it were a State, but in no event more than the least populous State; they shall be in addition to those appointed by the States, but they shall be considered, for the purposes of the election of President and Vice President, to be electors appointed by a State; and they shall meet in the District and perform such duties as provided by the twelfth article of amendment.

SECTION 2.

The Congress shall have power to enforce this article by appropriate legislation.

Amendment XXIV

SECTION 1.

The right of citizens of the United States to vote in any primary or other election for President or Vice President, for electors for President or Vice President, or for Senator or Representative in Congress, shall not be denied or abridged by the United States or any State by reason of failure to pay poll tax or other tax.

SECTION 2.

The Congress shall have power to enforce this article by appropriate legislation.

Amendment XXV

Note: Article II, section 1, of the Constitution was affected by the 25th amendment.

SECTION 1.

In case of the removal of the President from office or of his death or resignation, the Vice President shall become President.

SECTION 2.

Whenever there is a vacancy in the office of the Vice President, the President shall nominate a Vice President who shall take office upon confirmation by a majority vote of both Houses of Congress.

SECTION 3.

Whenever the President transmits to the President pro tempore of the Senate and the Speaker of the House of Representatives his written declaration that he is unable to discharge the powers and duties of his office, and until he transmits to them a written declaration to the contrary, such powers and duties shall be discharged by the Vice President as Acting President.

SECTION 4.

Whenever the Vice President and a majority of either the principal officers of the executive departments or of such other body as Congress may by law provide, transmit to the President pro tempore of the Senate and the Speaker of the House of Representatives their written declaration that the President is unable to discharge the powers and duties of his office, the Vice President shall immediately assume the powers and duties of the office as Acting President.

.Thereafter, when the President transmits to the President pro tempore of the Senate and the Speaker of the House of Representatives his written declaration that no inability exists, he shall resume the powers and duties of his office unless the Vice President and a majority of either the principal officers of the executive department or of such other body as Congress may by law provide, transmit within four days to the President pro tempore of the Senate and the Speaker of the House of Representatives their written declaration that the President is unable to discharge the powers and duties of his office. Thereupon Congress shall decide the issue, assembling within forty-eight hours for that purpose if not in session. If the Congress, within twenty-one days after receipt of the latter written declaration, or, if Congress is not in session, within twenty-one days after Congress is required to assemble, determines by two-thirds vote of both Houses that the President is unable to discharge the powers and duties of his office, the Vice President shall continue to discharge the same as Acting President; otherwise, the President shall resume the powers and duties of his office.

Amendment XXVI

Note: Amendment 14, section 2, of the Constitution was modified by section 1 of the 26th amendment.

SECTION 1.

The right of citizens of the United States, who are eighteen years of age or older, to vote shall not be denied or abridged by the United States or by any State on account of age.

SECTION 2.

The Congress shall have power to enforce this article by appropriate legislation.

Amendment XXVII

No law, varying the compensation for the services of the Senators and Representatives, shall take effect, until an election of representatives shall have intervened.

Notes

Chapter 1: Introduction: Why I Wrote This Book

1 *"but the tyrant, stand forth!"*: Thomas Paine, *Common Sense* (New York: Peter Eckler Publishing Co., 1918), 37.

2 *"I, as a constitutional conservative, as a believer in Jesus Christ . . . readily embrace [Donald Trump's agenda]"*: Michele Bachmann, speech to Values Voter Summit, Washington, DC, September 9, 2016.

2 *"If standing for liberty and standing for the Constitution make you a wacko bird, then you can count me a very proud wacko bird"*: Ted Cruz, keynote address at the Conservative Political Action Conference, National Harbor, MD, March 16, 2013.

2 *"a Constitution that allows that Judeo-Christian belief to be the foundation of our lives"*: Sarah Palin, *The O'Reilly Factor*, Fox News, May 6, 2010.

3 *"It is my number one duty as a human being—to earn an experiment in self-government every day by spotlighting cockroaches who violate their oath to the US Constitution and wipe their ass with the US Constitution"*: Ted Nugent, All Access Interview, July 14, 2014.

Chapter 2: The Founders and Framers: Who Were Those Guys?

7 *"a superabundance of secretions, which he could not find Whores enough to draw off"*: John Adams, letter to Benjamin Rush, November 11, 1806.

7 *"He means well . . . but sometimes and in somethings, is absolutely out of his senses"*: Benjamin Franklin, letter to Robert Livingston, July 22, 1783.

7 *"his country"*: Jefferson to Madison, March 17, 1796. Quoted by Joseph J. Ellis, *Founding Brothers* (New York: Vintage Books, 2000), 139.

7 *"The Life of Dr. Franklin was a scene of continual dissipation"*: John Adams, *Diary of John Adams*, May 27, 1778.

7 *"Jefferson . . . would soon be revealed as a voluptuary and an intriguing in-*

Notes

cendiary": as cited by David McCullough in *John Adams* (New York: Simon & Schuster, 2001), 436.

7 *"The Convention is really an assembly of demigods"*: Thomas Jefferson, letter to John Adams, August 30, 1787.

10 *"smart dress is essential. When not attended to, the soldier is exposed to ridicule and humiliation"*: Alexander Hamilton, letter to James McHenry, May 18, 1799.

10 *"The jackets ought to be made of some of the stuffs of which sailors' jackets are usually made"*: Ron Chernow, *Alexander Hamilton* (New York: Penguin Press, 2004), 473.

11 *"There was a deep fondness of friendship [between the two men] which approached the tenderness of feminine attachment"*: Ibid., 95.

11 For more on the Maria Reynolds story, see ibid.

12 *"We forgot"*: Ibid., 235.

12 *"It ought to be regarded as the work of many heads and many hands"*: James Madison, letter to William Cogswell, March 10, 1834.

14 *"A Likely negro woman to be sold. Enquire at the Widow Read's"*: Alan Craig Houston, *Benjamin Franklin and the Politics of Improvement* (New Haven: Yale University Press, 2008), 299.

14 *"the least regard such an inconsiderable nothing as a man"*: Benjamin Franklin and Jared Sparks, *The Works of Benjamin Franklin* (T. MacCoun, 1882), 2. This paper bears the date of November 20, 1728, when the author was twenty-two years old. It purports to be the First Part, but the continuation has never been published.

15 *"intrigues with low women that fell in my way"*: Benjamin Franklin, *The Autobiography of Benjamin Franklin* (Applewood Books, 2008 [reprint]), 103.

15 *"with great satisfaction"*: John Adams, Inaugural Address of John Adams, March 4, 1797.

15 *"advice and consent"*: US Constitution, Article II, Section 2.

15 *"in a constitution, can never be preserved without a strong executive"*: David McCullough, *John Adams* (New York: Simon & Schuster, 2001), 375.

16 *"that guilt should be punished"*: Ibid., 68.

16 *"manner most agreeable to the dictates of his own conscience"*: Kent Greenawalt, *Religion and the Constitution, Vol. 1: Free Exercise and Fairness* (Princeton, NJ: Princeton University Press, 2006), 18.

16 *"put to sleep for a time"*: John Adams, letter to James Warren, July 7, 1777.

17 *"into the hands of the husbands"*: Abigail Adams, letter to John Adams, March 31, 1776. Since this letter was written eleven years before the Constitution, Abigail was obviously referring to the Articles of Confederation.

18 *"preached to man into mystery and jargon"*: Thomas Jefferson, letter to Horatio G. Spafford, March 17, 1814.

Chapter 3: Snapshots of Life in Philadelphia, 1787

Sources

Life in Early Philadelphia, ed. Billy G. Smith.

Early Philadelphia, Horace Mather Lippincott.

Framers' Coup, Michael J. Klarman.

James Madison, Lynne Cheney.

Benjamin Franklin: A Biography, Walter Isaacson.

Chapter 4: Heckling the Right Wing: Their Top Ten Talking Points and My Top Ten Comebacks

Stuff I made up myself.

Chapter 5: God and the Constitution, Part I: Epistle to the Christian Right

For this chapter, I am deeply indebted to the brilliant Isaac Kramnick and R. Laurence Moore for their book *Godless Constitution: The Case Against Religious Correctness*.

27 *"Christianity and that is the truth that makes men free"*: Pat Buchanan, September 1993 speech to the Christian Coalition, *ADL Report*, 1994.

27 *"This is a country built on Judeo-Christian values"*: Ted Cruz, speech after Iowa caucus, February 1, 2016.

28 *"do ordain and establish this Constitution for the United States of . . ."*: US Constitution, Preamble.

28 *"protect and defend the Constitution of the United States . . ."*: US Presidential Oath.

28 *"as a qualification to any office or public Trust under the United States"*: US Constitution, Article VI, Clause 3.

29 For more on God in the Constitution: See Isaac Kramnick and R. Laurence Moore, *The Godless Constitution: The Case Against Religious Correctness* (New York: W. W. Norton & Company, Inc., 1997), 35–39.

29 *"a day of judgement, or a future state of rewards and punishments . . ."*: Herbert J. Storing, *The Complete Anti-Federalist, Vol. 1* (Chicago: University of Chicago Press, 2008), 207.

29 *"or at least in God"*: Michael J. Klarman, *The Framers' Coup* (New York: Oxford University Press, 2016), 392.

30 *"he hath also rejected thee"*: Isaac Kramnick and R. Laurence Moore, *The Godless Constitution*, 35–36.

30 *"men are ordained of, and mediately derived from God . . ."*: Ibid., 37.

31 *"after it shall have been presented to him, the same shall be a law . . ."*: US Constitution, Article I, Section 7.

31 *"We have hereunto subscribed our names"*: US Constitution, Article VII.

31 *"Establishment of this Constitution between the States so ratifying the same"*: US Constitution, Article VII.

33 *"no other proof that he was a believer"*: Bishop William White, as quoted by B. Wilson, *Memoir of the Life of the Right Rev. William White* (Philadelphia: C. H. Kay & Co, 1839), 193.

33 *"Sir, Washington was a Deist"*: James Abercrombie as quoted in Kim A. Mayyasi, *Call to Virtue: Republics of Character from Rome to 1776* (Minneapolis: Hillcrest Publishing Group, 2016), 233.

34 *"belief in the Xn religion"*: Thomas Jefferson, *The Anas*, February 1, 1800, as published in *The Works of Thomas Jefferson in Twelve Volumes*, Vol. 1, Federal Edition, Paul Leicester Ford, ed. (New York: G. P. Putnam's Sons, 1904), 352–353.

35 *"I should have more dependence in works than in faith"*: Benjamin Franklin, letter to John Franklin, May 1745.

35 *"will be treated with Justice in another life respecting its Conduct in this . . ."*: Benjamin Franklin, letter to Ezra Stiles, March 9, 1790.

35 *"present Dissenters in England, some Doubts as to His divinity . . ."*: Benjamin Franklin, letter to Ezra Stiles, March 9, 1790.

35 *"to retain in them the practice of virtue till it becomes habitual"*: Benjamin Franklin, *The Select Works of Benjamin Franklin*, letter from Benjamin Franklin to Thomas Paine, Epes Sargent, ed. (Boston: Phillips, Sampson and Co., 1853), 488.

36 *"tolerance, individual merit, civic virtue, good deeds, and rationality"*: Wal-

ter Isaacson, *Benjamin Franklin: An American Life* (New York: Simon & Schuster, 2004), 109.

36 *"in all Combinations of human society"*: Newt Gingrich with Callista Gingrich, *Rediscovering God in America* (Tennessee: Thomas Nelson, 2009), xxi.

37 *"charm and bewitch the simple and ignorant"*: John Fea, *Was America Founded as a Christian Nation?* (Louisville: Westminster John Knox Press, 2011), 195.

37 *"and Pillage hundreds and thousands of their fellow creatures"*: Ibid.

37 *"not to be fathomed by our narrow understandings"*: Ibid., 198.

38 *"the duty which we owe to our Creator"*: Joshua Charles, *Liberty's Secrets* (Washington, DC: WND Books, 2015). (Glenn Beck's coauthor on *The Original Argument*.)

38 *"diabolical Hells of Persecution"*: Kramnick and Moore, *The Godless Constitution: The Case Against Religious Correctness*, 103.

38 For Madison's views on government involvement in religion, see ibid., 103 and 106.

39 *"Thou shalt have no other God before Me"*: Exodus 20:3.

39 *"and the Pursuit of Happiness"*: US Declaration of Independence.

39 *"authority rests then on the harmonizing sentiments of the day"*: Thomas Jefferson, letter to Richard Henry Lee, May 8, 1825.

39 *"confirmed infidel"*: Mark A. Beliles and Jerry Newcombe, *Doubting Thomas: The Religious Life and Legacy of Thomas Jefferson* (New York: Morgan James Publishing, 2015), 53.

40 *"now devoted to the worship of the Most High"*: Alf J. Mapp Jr., *Thomas Jefferson: Passionate Pilgrim* (Lanham: Rowman & Littlefield Publishers, Inc., 2009), 93.

40 *"man may be trusted with the formation of his own opinions"*: M. Andrew Holowchak, *Thomas Jefferson: Moralist* (Jefferson: McFarland & Company, Inc., 1858), 181–182.

41 *"or no god. It neither picks my pocket nor breaks my leg"*: Alf J. Mapp Jr., *The Faiths of Our Fathers: What America's Founders Really Believed* (Lanham: Rowman & Littlefield Publishers, Inc., 2005), 8.

41 *"support roguery and error all over the earth"*: Susan Jacoby, *Freethinkers: A History of American Secularism* (New York: Henry Holt and Company, LLC, 2005), 45.

Chapter 6: God and the Constitution, Part II:
Epistle to the Mormons

43 *"whose builder and maker is God"*: Joseph Smith, *Joseph Smith's Teachings: A Classified Arrangement of the Doctrinal Sermons and Writings of the Great Latter-day Prophet* (Salt Lake City: *The Deseret News, 1913*), *124*.

43 *"They are both sacred scriptures"*: Glenn Beck, Speech at MorningStar Fellowship Church in Fort Mill, South Carolina, February 11, 2016.

45 *"and concubines he shall have none"*: the Church of Jesus Christ of Latter-day Saints, Book of Mormon, 1840.

46 *"Solomon having many wives and concubines . . ."*: Andrew H. Hedges, Alex D. Smith, and Brent M. Rogers, *Journals, Vol. 3: May 1843–June 1844* (Church Historian Press, November 30, 2015).

46 *"that may bear the souls of men"*: the Church of Jesus Christ of Latter-day Saints, *The Doctrine and Covenants*, 1921.

47 *"the shedding of blood"*: Ibid.

47 *"be maintained for the rights and protection of all flesh . . ."*: Dallin H. Oaks, *The Divinely Inspired Constitution*, The Church of Jesus Christ of Latter-day Saints, 1992, https://www.lds.org/ensign/1992/02/the-divinely-inspired-constitution?lang=eng.

47 *"its establishment that cannot be explained in any other way"*: Gordon B. Hinckley, Weber State University commencement speech, August 1999.

48 *"carrieth it unto the hearts of the children of men"*: Book of Mormon, the Church of Jesus Christ of Latter-day Saints, 1840.

49 *"by which he is called is The Word of God"*: Holy Bible, English Standard Version, Revelation 19:11.

49 *"Rider on the White Horse"*: Dana Milbank, "Mormon Prophecy Behind Glenn Beck's Message," *Huffington Post*, October 5, 2010; George Cobabe, "The White Horse Prophecy," Foundation for Apologetic Information and Research, https://www.fairmormon.org/wp-content/uploads/2011/12/cobabe-whitehorse.pdf.

50 *"conduct the affairs of men in righteousness"*: Joseph Smith, *Times and Seasons*, vol. 5 no. 8, April 15, 1844.

51 *"upon some Indian Nations in North Carolina"*: *The Catholic Church in the United States of America* (New York: Catholic Editing Company, 1914), 240.

51 *"God was pleased to make ready a place prepared as an asylum for our early*

settlers": National Humanities Center, *Becoming American: The British Atlantic Colonies, 1690–1763*, http://nationalhumanitiescenter.org/pds/be comingamer/growth/text7/indianlands.pdf.

51 *"all efforts to extinguish black slavery are idle . . ."*: Larry R. Morrison, "The Religious Defense of American Slavery Before 1830," *Journal of Religious Thought* 37, no. 2 (Fall 80/Winter 81): 16–29, 18.

51 *"You helped this happen"*: Jerry Falwell, *The 700 Club*, September 13, 2001.

51 For more on this subject, see Al Franken, *Lies and the Lying Liars Who Tell Them* (New York: Penguin Group, 2003).

52 *"the incoherences of our own nightly dreams . . ."*: Thomas Jefferson, *The Writings of Thomas Jefferson*, volume 16 (Washington, DC: Thomas Jefferson Memorial Association of the United States, 1904), 100–101.

Chapter 7: The Writing of the Constitution: Notes from the Constitutional Convention as Recorded by Billey, Slave to James Madison, May 6 to September 17, 1787

53 *"much of the difficulty would be removed"*: James Madison, speech at Virginia Convention, December 2, 1829.

54 For more on what Billey likely observed at the Convention, see David O. Stewart, *Madison's Gift: Five Partnerships That Built America* (New York: Simon & Schuster Paperbacks, 2016).

54 For daily events at the Constitutional Convention, see Historians of the Independence National Historical Park, *1787: The Day-to-Day Story of the Constitutional Convention* (New York: Exeter Books, 1987).

84 For Lynne Cheney's detailed description of Billey, see Lynne Cheney, *James Madison: A Life Reconsidered* (New York: Viking, 2014), 94, 225, 271.

Chapter 8: Charles Beard's Economic Interpretation of the Constitution, Part I: Meeting the Framers

85 *"which increasing population would bring"*: Albert Jeremiah Beveridge, *The Life of John Marshall*, Vol. 1 (Boston and New York: Houghton Mifflin Company, 1919), 202.

85 *"a moral and political example to the rest of the world"*: William J. Bennett, *Our Country's Founders* (New York: Aladdin Paperbacks, 2001), 2.

87 *"establishment of the new system"*: Charles A. Beard, *An Economic Interpre-*

tation of the Constitution of the United States (New York: The Macmillan Company, 1921), 324.

87 *"province is now a ravaged survival"*: Richard Hofstadter, *Progressive Historians* (London: Jonathan Cape Ltd., 1969), 344–345. Before there was a Hofstadter, there was historian and law professor Forrest McDonald. In the 1950s, McDonald attacked Beard fiercely and successfully, most notably in his book *We the People: The Economic Origins of the Constitution*, arguing that Beard got the Framers (and their economic interests) all wrong. A notorious archconservative, McDonald downplayed "slavery" among the Framers, while insisting (in a 1987 lecture as reported by the *New York Times*) that slaves in the South were far better off than French peasants or Russian serfs.

88 *"essence of government"*: Charles A. Beard, *The Supreme Court and the Constitution* (Mineola, NY: Dover Publications, Inc., 2006), 86–87.

88 *"outcome of their labors"*: Charles A. Beard, *An Economic Interpretation of the Constitution of the United States*, 324.

88 *meet all fifty-five delegates*: Beard's financial biographies of the Framers form the most controversial and most attacked portion of his book. For what it's worth, Beard's conclusions are based on (1) tax returns of the states, (2) records of local assessors, (3) wills probated and mortgages reported, and (4) unworked records of the Treasury Department in Washington, DC, including the records of the Hamilton administration at the Treasury itself. For further evidence of Beard's scholarship, see *An Economic Interpretation of the Constitution of the United States*, 21–51.

92 *"a man of great fortune"*: Ibid., 82.

95 *"financial systems of the United States"*: Ibid., 91.

98 *"little is known of his economic interests"*: Ibid., 114.

98 *"appreciation of public securities"*: Ibid., 116.

98 *"considerable wealth"*: Ibid.

99 *"operators in securities"*: Ibid., 117.

100 *"to augment their fortunes"*: Ibid., 123.

101 For more on Madison's land speculations, see Lynne Cheney, *James Madison*, 115–116; 324–327.

102 *"great wealth and influence"*: Ibid., 127.

104 *John Francis Mercer*: Facts about John Francis Mercer: See Bruce Bueno de Mesquita and Alastair Smith, *The Spoils of War* (New York: Public Affairs, 2016), 30–31.

104 *"by birth to a powerful, landed aristocracy"*: Ibid., 132–133.

105 *Robert Morris*: A little more on one of the fascinating and generally unknown Founders. This from Ray Raphael's *Founding Myths: Stories That Hide Our Patriotic Past* (New York: The New Press, 2014), 164–165: "Morris ran the confederated government by himself during the winter of 1776–1777 . . . secured supplies and arranged finances for the Conventional Army . . . assumed unprecedented executive powers, rivaling those of future presidents . . . underwriting government notes, essentially offering his own private credit . . . A man who made his fortune in large measure by privateering (legalized piracy), cornering markets, and war profiteering, and who ended his career in debtors' prison."

105 *"closely identified with the new system of government"*: Charles A. Beard, *An Economic Interpretation of the Constitution of the United States*, 135.

107 *"and near 200 negroes"*: Ibid., 139.

108 *"the inconveniences of depreciated paper"*: Ibid., 141.

108 *"largest fees that were usually given"*: Ibid., 141 (Quoting Herring, *National Portrait Gallery*, Vol. IV).

109 *"certificates of issue"*: Ibid., 144.

109 For more on Caleb Strong, see Henry Cabot Lodge, *A Memoir of Caleb Strong*, United States Senator and Governor of Massachusetts, 1745–1818 (Cambridge: Massachusetts Historical Society, 1879).

110 *"paper that steadily depreciated"*: Charles A. Beard, *An Economic Interpretation of the Constitution of the United States*, 145.

110 *"engaged in the West Indies trade"*: Ibid., 146.

110 *"an efficient Federal Government"*: Ibid., 50 (quoting *Documentary History of the Constitution*, Vol. IV, 678).

112 *And there you have all fifty-five delegates*: Historians and scholars can debate Beard's theories all they want, but for my money his case makes sense: it was no coincidence that only the richest, most powerful men in the country ended up in Philadelphia to write the Constitution.

113 *unique national perspective*: Charles A. Beard, *An Economic Interpretation of the Constitution of the United States*, 325.

Chapter 9: Charles Beard's Economic Interpretation of the Constitution, Part II: Following the Money

115 *"an agreement with Hell"*: William Lloyd Garrison, "Mr. Garrison's Address," *New York Times*, January 15, 1862.

115 *"basis of all other positive powers"*: Charles A. Beard, *An Economic Interpretation of the Constitution of the United States*, 170.

116 *$40 million*: Ibid., 35.

117 *"Small wonder that Mrs. Adams bought them"*: David O. Stewart, *Madison's Gift: Five Partnerships That Built America* (New York: Simon & Schuster Paperbacks, 2016), 105.

117 Slavery in 1787: Howard Zinn, *A People's History of the United States* (New York: Routledge, 2013), 28–29.

117 *"At the Battle of Yorktown"*: Thomas Jefferson also had runaway slaves captured and of course sent back to Monticello. For more on Jefferson's runaway slaves, see Cassandra Pybus, "Jefferson's Faulty Math: The Question of Slave Defections in the American Revolution," *The William and Mary Quarterly* 62, 2 (Apr. 2005): 243–264.

118 *one of every three died*: Howard Zinn, *A People's History of the United States* (New York: Routledge, 2013), 28–29.

118 *slaveholder was President of the United States*: "Presidents Who Owned Slaves," factcheck.org.

118 For more on slavery, see Michael J. Klarman, *Framers' Coup: The Making of the United States Constitution* (New York: Oxford University Press, 2016), 257–304.

Chapter 10: The Chapter of Leftovers: Part I

Sources

The US Constitution: A Reader, Hillsdale College, Politics Faculty.

1787: The Day-to-Day Story of the Constitutional Convention, Independence National Historical Park.

James Madison, Lynne Cheney.

Framers' Coup, Michael J. Klarman.

Thomas Jefferson: Author of America, Christopher Hitchens.

John Adams, David McCullough.

Chapter 11: Open Letter to Senator Ted Cruz
Written in the Style of 1787

123 *"nobody would convict you"*: Lindsey Graham, Washington Press Club, February 2016. Quoted in Catherine Treyz, "Lindsey Graham Jokes About How to Get Away with Murdering Ted Cruz," CNN, February 26, 2016, http://www.cnn.com/2016/02/26/politics/lindsey-graham-ted-cruz-dinner/index.html.

123 Browsing the book aisles one day, I came across *US Constitution for Dummies* (Hoboken, NJ: Wiley Publishing, 2009) written by Dr. Michael Arnheim, an English barrister, of all things. More surprising was the foreword written by Ted Cruz, then partner in the billion-dollar law firm of Morgan, Lewis, & Bockius LLP. Naturally, as one of the Dummies, I bought the book. The chapter is a response to his two-page Foreword. (I can only guess Mr. Cruz was not billing by the hour.)

123 *assassination of John F. Kennedy*: J. R. King, "Ted Cruz Father Linked to JFK Assassination," *National Enquirer*, April 20, 2016, http://www.nationalenquirer.com/celebrity/ted-cruz-scandal-father-jfk-assassination/.

124 *The Constitution was written to limit government*: Michael Arnheim, *US Constitution for Dummies* (Hoboken, NJ: Wiley Publishing, 2009), xix.

125 *"Liberty to ourselves and our Posterity"*: US Constitution, Preamble.

125 *"be admitted Powers by Implication"*: James Madison, Annals of Congress, August 18, 1789.

125 *"by sufficient Powers to the Common Government"*: James Madison, quoted in E. H. Scott (ed.), *Journal of the Constitutional Convention*, kept by James Madison (Chicago: Scott, Foresman, and Company, 1893), 592.

125 *James Madison is the "Primary Author" of the Constitution*: Michael Arnheim, *US Constitution for Dummies*, xix.

125 any and all Laws *passed by the State Legislatures*: James Madison, letter to John Tyler, March 1, 1833.

126 *"Work of many Heads and many Hands"*: James Madison, letter to William Cogswell, March 10, 1834.

126 *"Hostility to expressions of Faith"*: Michael Arnheim, *US Constitution for Dummies*, xx.

126 For the full Supreme Court ruling, see *Van Orden v. Perry* (2005) 545 US 677.

126 *"respecting an establishment of Religion . . ."*: US Constitution, Amendment I.

126 *"Wall of Separation between Church and State"*: The complete letter to the Danbury Baptists:

> Gentlemen, The affectionate sentiments of esteem and approbation which you are so good as to express towards me, on behalf of the Danbury Baptist association, give me the highest satisfaction. My duties dictate a faithful and zealous pursuit of the interests of my constituents, & in proportion as they are persuaded of my fidelity to those duties, the discharge of them becomes more and more pleasing. Believing with you that religion is a matter which lies solely between Man & his God, that he owes account to none other for his faith or his worship, that the legitimate powers of government reach actions only, & not opinions, I contemplate with sovereign reverence that act of the whole American people which declared that their legislature should "make no law respecting an establishment of religion, or prohibiting the free exercise thereof," thus building a wall of separation between Church & State. Adhering to this expression of the supreme will of the nation in behalf of the rights of conscience, I shall see with sincere satisfaction the progress of those sentiments which tend to restore to man all his natural rights, convinced he has no natural right in opposition to his social duties. I reciprocate your kind prayers for the protection & blessing of the common father and creator of man, and tender you for yourselves & your religious association, assurances of my high respect & esteem. Th Jefferson, Jan. 1, 1802.

127 *"as of Constitutional principles"*: Garry Wills, "Child of Entitlement," *New York Times*, July 4, 2017.

127 For more on the *Heller* ruling, see *D.C. v. Heller* (2008) 554 US 570.

127 *the original Understanding of the Framers*: Michael Arnheim, *US Constitution for Dummies*, xx.

127 *"Heller is firing blanks"*: Laurence Tribe and Joshua Matz, *Uncertain Justice: The Roberts Court and the Constitution* (New York: Henry Holt and Company, 2014), 179.

128 *as stated in the Fifth Amendment*: Michael Arnheim, *US Constitution for Dummies*, xx.

128 *"Indictment of a Grand Jury"*: US Constitution, Amendment V.

128 *"cruel and unusual Punishments"*: US Constitution, Amendment VIII.

Chapter 12: The Constitution According to Ben Carson, MD

131 *"there's no cure for that, folks"*: Trump quotes from a tirade against Carson. Quoted from Conor Friedersdorf, "Will the GOP Base Tolerate Donald Trump's Attack on Ben Carson?," *The Atlantic*, November 13, 2015.

131 *"to that of child molester!"*: Gregory Krieg, "Trump Likens Carson's 'Pathology' to That of a Child Molester," CNN, November 12, 2015, http://www.cnn.com/2015/11/12/politics/donald-trump-ben-carson-child-molester/index.html.

131 *"communities and families within those communities"*: Trump quoted in Trip Gabriel, "Trump Chooses Ben Carson to Lead HUD," *New York Times*, December 5, 2016.

132 *"when they come out, they're gay"*: Carson quoted from interview, CNN's *New Day*, March 4, 2015. Elsewhere, Carson claimed gay marriage would lead to "mass killings" and "utter chaos." See Michael Fitzgerald, "Ben Carson: Gay Marriage Will Lead to 'Mass Killings' and 'Utter Chaos,'" *Towleroad*, October 13, 2016, http://www.towleroad.com/2016/10/ben-carson-gay-marriage/.

132 not *tombs but* silos *built by Joseph*: Michael E. Miller, "Ben Carson Believes Joseph Built Egypt's Pyramids to Store Grain," *Washington Post*, November 5, 2015.

132 *"the Big Bang Theory are all 'fairy tales'"*: Carson quoted from speech in 2012 at an event called Celebration of Creation.

132 *the blade broke on his friend's belt buckle*: Story told by Carson over and over and over.

133 *"steeped in a Christian understanding of politics"*: Ben Carson and Candy Carson, *A More Perfect Union: What We the People Can Do to Reclaim Our Constitutional Liberties* (New York: Sentinel, 2015), 14.

134 *"secure the blessings of Liberty to ourselves and our posterity"*: Ibid., 83–93.

134 *"children still in the womb"*: Ibid., 89–92.

135 *"their evil intentions with relatively little resistance"*: Ibid., 61.

135 *"equal protection of the laws"*: US Constitution, Amendment XIV.

135 *"domestic tranquility"*: Carson and Carson, *A More Perfect Union*, 53.

135 *Each year, more than 10 million women and men*: "National Statistics," National Coalition Against Domestic Violence, accessed June 14, 2017, http://ncadv.org/learn-more/statistics.

135 *25,000 calls*: "Census: Domestic Violence Counts," National Network to End Domestic Violence, accessed June 14, 2017, http://nnedv.org/re sources/census.html.

136 *three or more women are murdered by their husbands*: "Intimate Partner Violence: Facts & Resources," American Psychological Association, accessed June 14, 2017, http://www.apa.org/topics/violence/partner.aspx.

136 *"into a spotlight that has never dimmed"*: Ben Terris and Stephanie Kirchner, "The Story of the Surgery That Made Ben Carson Famous," *Washington Post*, November 13, 2015.

136 *"Why did I have them separated?"*: Ibid.

136 *"What therefore God hath joined together, let no man put asunder"*: KJV, Matthew 19:6.

Chapter 13: Rewriting the Constitution: Mark Levin and the Asner Amendments

137 *"Get the hell out of here"*: Mark Levin, *The Mark Levin Show*, May 22, 2009.

137 *"mangled"*: Mark Levin, *The Liberty Amendments: Restoring the American Republic* (New York: Threshold Editions, 2013), 1.

137 *"delusional governing elite"*: Ibid.

138 *Levin Article I*: Amendment to restore the Senate: Ibid., 209.

138 *Levin Article II*: Amendment to establish supermajority legislative override: Ibid., 211.

138 *Levin Article III*: Amendment to limit taxes: Ibid., 213.

139 *"the common Defense and general Welfare of the United States"*: US Constitution, Article I, Section 8.

139 *Amendment to protect the vote*: Mark Levin, *The Liberty Amendments: Restoring the American Republic* (New York: Threshold Editions), 218.

143 *"towards more Conservative candidates"*: Jim DeMint, *Allman in the Morning*, FM NewsTalk 97.1, April 27, 2016.

143 *"giddy"*: Michael Wines, "Some Republicans Acknowledge Leveraging Voter ID Laws for Political Gain," *New York Times*, September 16, 2016.

143 For more on the Amendment to grant the states authority to check Congress, see Ibid., 216–217.

143 *Levin Article V*: Amendment to federal laws: Levin, *The Liberty Amendments*, Ibid., 217.

143 *"the security of liberty"*: Alexander Hamilton, *Federalist No. 1.*

144 *"to save the Republic"*: Mark Levin, speech to State Legislature, December 4, 2014.

145 *Richard Nixon*: Rutger Bregman, "The Bizarre Tale of President Nixon and His Basic Income Bill," *Correspondent*, May 17, 2016, https://thecorres pondent.com/4503/the-bizarre-tale-of-president-nixon-and-his-basic -income-bill/173117835-c34d6145.

Chapter 14: Immigration and Ann Coulter: A Review That Was Never Published in the *New York Times Book Review*

147 *"It's yours"*: Ann Coulter, *Hannity & Colmes*, June 20, 2001.

147 *"convert them to Christianity"*: Ann Coulter, "This Is War," *Townhall*, September 14, 2001.https://townhall.com/columnists/anncoulter/2001/09/14 /this-is-war-n865496.

147 *"mutilated bodies from bridges"*: Ann Coulter, *¡Adios, America!: The Left's Plan to Turn Our Country into a Third-World Hellhole* (Washington, DC: Regnery Publishing, 2015), 122.

148 *"Thank a Mexican"*: Ibid., 118.

148 Coulter's fixation with Mexican beheadings can be found in a chapter called "Why Can't We Have Israel's Policy on Immigration?"; Ibid., 121–124.

148 *"women, children, and innocent bystanders"*: Ibid., 122.

148 *"no concept of 'litter' "*: Ibid., 203.

148 *"trash away in their lives"*: Ibid., 206.

148 How Mexicans destroy the environment: Ibid., 204–206.

149 Hmong *immigrants*: Ibid., 138–139.

149 *"He selfish"*: Bobbitt's penis chopping: Ibid., 183; Coulter's endnotes, 338.

150 *especially hard*: For her views on the Hmongs: Ibid., 129–141.

150 *"Thank you, Teddy Kennedy"*: Ibid., 135.

150 the Hmongs' role: The story of the Hmongs and the United States: "Hmong Americans," Wikipedia, last modified June 14, 2017, at https:// en.wikipedia.org/w/index.php?title=Hmong_Americans&action=history.

152 *"an immigrant in La Raza doing any of that!"*: Coulter, *¡Adios, America!* (Washington, DC: Regnery Publishing, 2015), 60.

152 *"cooked up" anchor babies*: Ibid., 35.

152 Coulter on anchor babies: Ibid., 34–36, 38–39.

152 *"abortion, sodomy, gay marriage, and unicorns"*: Ibid., 35.

153 Justice William J. Brennan's footnote: Ibid., 35–38.

153 *"may well be the* legal *alien of tomorrow . . ."*: *Plyler v. Doe* (1982) 457 US 202.

154 *"equal protection of the laws"*: US Constitution, Amendment XIV.

154 For more on Ann Coulter's beef with Ted Kennedy, see Coulter, *¡Adios, America!* (Washington, DC: Regnery Publishing, 2015), 17–18, 54, 60, 70, 76, 78, 82, 95, 98, 104, 138, 172, 203, 210, 226, 274, and 276.

155 *"before we were a country"*: Lyndon Johnson, Remarks at Liberty Island, New York, October 3, 1965, http://www.lbjlibrary.org/lyndon -baines-johnson/timeline/lbj-on-immigration.

155 "I lift my lamp beside the golden door!": Anne Hempstead, *The Statue of Liberty* (Chicago: Heinemann-Raintree Library, 2006), 23.

156 Benjamin Franklin on Germans: Benjamin Franklin, letter to Peter Collinson, May 9, 1753.

156 For an example of Adams's anti-Catholicism, see John Adams, letter to Abigail Adams, October 9, 1774.

156 *"useful mechanics"*: George Washington, letter to John Adams, November 15, 1794.

157 *the Nordic (Aryan) race*: Madison Grant, *The Passing of the Great Race, or the Racial Basis of European History* (Burlington, IA.: Ostara Publications, 2011), 167–178.

157 *"defective strain"*: Ibid., 51.

158 *"above all of rulers, organizers, and aristocrats . . ."*: Ibid., 221.

158 *"future anthropologists to unravel"*: Ibid., 47.

158 *"swarms of Polish Jews"*: Ibid., 46.

158 *"and a long skull"*: Ibid., 85.

158 *"We gave at the office"*: Coulter, *¡Adios, America!* (Washington, DC: Regnery Publishing, 2015), 278.

159 *"age of Pericles"*: Grant, *The Passing of the Great Race*, 131–132.

160 *"saner society in the future"*: From Charles Davenport, *Eugenics: The Science of Human Improvement by Better Breeding*, as quoted in Ladelle

McWhorter, *Racism and Sexual Oppression in Anglo-America: A Genealogy* (Indianapolis: Indiana University Press, 2009), 204.

160 For the full decision, see *Buck v. Bell* (1927) 274 US 200.

161 *"a Jew is a Jew"*: Madison Grant, *The Passing of the Great Race*, 18.

161 *"my Bible"*: Jonathan Peter Spiro, *Defending the Master Race: Conservation, Eugenics, and the Legacy of Madison Grant* (Burlington: University of Vermont Press, 2009), 357.

Chapter 15: The Shocking Truth About the Bill of Rights

In addition to the historian Carol Berkin, I am equally indebted to Ray Raphael's *Constitutional Myths*.

163 *"in an important light"*: James Madison, letter to Thomas Jefferson, October 17, 1788.

163 *"no real security to liberty"*: Noah Webster (using pen name "Pacificus"), letter to James Madison, August 14, 1789.

163 *"most cherished values"*: Carol Berkin, *The Bill of Rights: A Fight to Secure America's Liberties* (New York: Simon & Schuster, 2015), 3.

163 For more on the little fanfare paid to the Bill of Rights, see ibid., 131–151.

164 *"constitution of government"*: Alexander Hamilton, *The Federalist No. 84*. Quoted in Ray Raphael, *Constitutional Myths: What We Get Wrong and How to Get It Right* (New York: The New Press, 2013), 138.

165 *an old condition*: For more on Madison's "piles," see James Madison et al., *The Washington-Madison Papers, Collected and Preserved by James Madison* (Philadelphia: The Bicking Print, 1892).

167 *By the way*: There is no evidence that Patrick Henry ever fell off his horse.

169 There is also no evidence that James Madison ever told a joke or even repeated one, let alone one about a duck's ass.

173 *"temptation to foreign adventure"*: Quoted in Walter Isaacson, *Benjamin Franklin: An American Life* (New York: Simon & Schuster, 2004), 456.

175 *"or rather to deceive"*: Thomas Tudor Tucker, letter to St. George Tucker, October 2, 1789.

175 *"if you can keep it"*: As quoted in Isaacson, *Benjamin Franklin*, 33: "According to a tale recorded by James McHenry of Maryland, Franklin made his point . . . to an anxious lady named Mrs. Powell, who accosted

him outside the hall. 'What kind of government,' she asked, 'have you delegates given us?' To which he replied, 'A republic, madam, if you can keep it.'"

176 *"your Excellency's Most obedient & most humble servant"*: Quoted in Ray Raphael, *Constitutional Myths*, 149.

Chapter 16: The Bill of Rights in the Real World

A word to the reader: The nuts and bolts of the following Supreme Court cases came from Wikipedia.

177 *"you can suspend much if not all of the Bill of Rights"*: Gore Vidal, Q&A chat, *USA Today*, February 4, 2003, https://usatoday30.usatoday.com /community/chat_03/2003-02-04-vidal.htm.

177 *"like you've never got sued before"*: Donald Trump, campaign rally, Fort Worth, Texas, February 26, 2016.

178 *"ridiculous pomp, foolish adulation, and selfish avarice"*: Richard Labunski, *James Madison and the Struggle for the Bill of Rights* (New York: Oxford University Press, 2006), 316.

178 *"repulsive pedant, a gross hypocrite, and an unprincipled oppressor"*: Fawn Brodie, *Thomas Jefferson: An Intimate History* (New York: W. W. Norton & Company, 1974), 322.

180 *"traitor to his country"*: Scott Christianson, *With Liberty for Some: 500 Years of Imprisonment in America* (Boston: Northeastern University Press, 2000), 218.

180 *"I am not free"*: Legislative Documents, vol. 12, issue 35, part 2 (J. B. Lyon Company, 1920), 2244.

180 *"whether the nation will go to war?"*: Erwin Chemerinsky, *The Case Against the Supreme Court* (New York: Penguin Books, 2014).

182 *"shiftless, ignorant and worthless class of antisocial whites of the South"*: Paul Moreno, *The Bureaucrat Kings: The Origins and Underpinnings of America's Bureaucratic State* (Santa Barbara, CA: Praeger, 2016), 78.

182 *"cutting the Fallopian tubes"*: *Buck v. Bell* (1927) 274 US 200, 207.

182 *"Three generations of imbeciles are enough"*: Ibid.

183 *"None had a stove or running water"*: William Manchester, as quoted by Chemerinsky, *The Case Against the Supreme Court*, 54.

184 *"That is their business, not ours"*: *Korematsu v. United States* (1944) 323 US 214, 225.

184 *"a great injustice and it will never be repeated"*: Karen Korematsu, "When Lies Overruled Rights," *New York Times*, February 17, 2017.

184 For more on *Debs* and *Korematsu*, see Chemerinsky, *The Case Against the Supreme* Court, 54–56, 65–66. A Distinguished Professor of Law at the University of California, Irvine School of Law.

185 *"violently beat my wife and children"*: "Ruling Reopens Wound for Bitter Ex-soldier," *New York Times*, June 30, 1987.

185 *"sovereign immunity"*: *United States v. Stanley* (1987) 483 US 669.

186 *"to satisfy the moral, ethical, and legal concepts"*: *United States v. Stanley* (1987) 483 US 669, 710.

186 *"unnatural manner with a man and a woman"*: *Bowers v. Hardwick* (1986) 478 US 186, 201.

187 *"Does the Constitution confer 'a fundamental right to engage in homosexual sodomy?'"*: Ibid., 191.

187 For more on the legal precedents of *Bowers v. Hardwick*: See *Griswold v. Connecticut* (1965) 381 US 479 and *Stanley v. Georgia* (1969) 394 US 557.

188 *"there is no such thing as a fundamental right to commit homosexual sodomy"*: Bowers, 186.

189 *"been subject to state intervention throughout the history of Western civilization"*: Ibid., 186, 196.

189 *"rooted in Judeo-Christian moral and ethical standards"*: Ibid., 186, 196.

189 *"Homosexual sodomy was a capital crime under Roman law"*: Ibid., 186, 196.

189 *"the first English statute criminalizing sodomy was passed"*: Ibid., 186, 197.

189 *"crime not fit to be named . . ."*: Ibid., 186, 197.

189 *"would be to cast aside a millennia of moral teaching"*: Ibid., 186, 197.

190 *"facetious"*: Ibid., 186.

193 *"nor shall private property be taken for public use without just compensation"*: US Constitution, Amendment V.

194 *"transfer property from those with fewer resources to those with more"*: *Kelo v. City of New London* (2005) 545 US 469, 505.

197 *"Congress shall have power to enforce this article by appropriate legislation"*: US Constitution, Amendment XV.

197 *"speaks to current conditions"*: *Shelby County v. Holder* (2013) 570 US 2.

198 *"Blatantly discriminatory evasions of Federal decrees are rare"*: Ibid.

201 *"nor deny to any person within its jurisdiction the equal protection of the laws"*: US Constitution, Amendment XIV.

Chapter 17: The Chapter of Leftovers: Part II

203   *the price of wheat*: James Madison, *The Papers of James Madison, Volume 2*, ed. Henry Dilworth Gilpin (Washington, DC: Langtree & O'Sullivan, 1840), 849.

203   *connected to an overhead fan*: Nancy Russell, "Innovative Benjamin Franklin Rocked," *Columbia Daily Tribune*, April 5, 2012, http://www .columbiatribune.com/cee9f061-e67e-5e42-8f53-fb7d83cbd9d7.html.

203   *"defend the Constitution of the United States"*: US Presidential Oath.

203   *"New Testament to be given by Divine Inspiration"*: Union of American Hebrew Congregations, *Judaism at the World's Parliament of Religions* (Cincinnati: Robert Clarke & Co., 1894), 266.

203   *one thousand five hundred were in German*: Scott Bomboy, "Looking at Two Little-Known Versions of Our Constitution," *National Constitution Center*, August 24, 2015, https://constitutioncenter.org/blog/looking -at-two-little-known-versions-of-our-constitution.

203   *all debts should be forgiven after nineteen years*: Thomas Jefferson, letter to James Madison, September 6, 1789.

204   *George Washington's bill*: See "Entertainment of George Washington at City Tavern, Philadelphia, September 1787." Lloyd Gordon, "The Constitutional Convention." Accessed June 14, 2017, http://teachingamerican history.org/convention/citytavern/.

Chapter 18: The Emperor Has No Robes: Justice Antonin Scalia and *Citizens United*

205   *"divine law"*: Rabbi Shlomo Itzhaki, also known as Rashi, medieval French rabbi. Believing it to be a proverb from the *Talmud*, Justice Scalia misquoted it in his opinion *United States v. Sun-Diamond Growers of California* (1999) 526 US 398, 400.

205   *"glimpse of the great patterns of his jurisprudence"*: Matthew J. Franck, "His Final Two Dissents Reveal Themes of His Jurisprudence," *National Review*, March 14, 2016.

206   For more on Scalia's last playdate, see Jeffrey Toobin, "The Company Scalia Kept," *The New Yorker*, March 2, 2016.

206   *"Deum Diligite Animalia Diligentes"*: Amy Brittain and Sari Horwitz,

"Justice Scalia Spent His Last Hours with Members of This Secretive Society of Elite Hunters," *Washington Post*, February 24, 2016.

206 *"dark green robes emblazoned with a large cross"*: Ibid.

207 *"believed in the Devil"*: Jennifer Senior, "In Conversation: Antonin Scalia," *New York*, October 6, 2013; quoted in Bruce Allen Murphy, *Scalia: A Court of One* (New York: Simon & Schuster, 2014).

207 *Scalia was especially clever when denouncing homosexuality*: Adam Serwer, "Here Are the 7 Worst Things Antonin Scalia Has Said or Written About Homosexuality," *Mother Jones*, March 26, 2013, http://www.motherjones.com/politics/2013/03/scalia-worst-things-said-written-about-homosexuality-court/.

207 *"why not child molesters?"*: Trudy Ring, "Antonin Scalia: If We Protect Gays, Why Not Child Molesters?" *The Advocate*, November 17, 2015, https://www.advocate.com/politics/2015/11/17/antonin-scalia-if-we-protect-gays-why-not-child-molesters.

207 *"'immoral and unacceptable'"*: *Lawrence v. Texas* (2003) 539 US 558, citing the ruling in *Bowers v. Hardwick* (1986) 478 US 186.

207 *"sexual intercourse with someone of the same sex"*: Ibid.

208 *"women's equality is . . . one of the 'smug assurances' of our time"*: I quote here from Jeffrey Toobin's *New Yorker* article, February 16, 2016, in which he paraphrases Scalia's dissent (7–1) in *US v. Virginia* (1996), where Scalia argues against admitting women to the Virginia Military Institute.

208 Definition of originalism: Quoting Antonin Scalia, *A Matter of Interpretation: Federal Courts and the Law*.

208 *"intelligent and informed people of the time"*: Rossum and Tarr, *American Constitutional Law, Volume I: The Structure of Government*, 11.

208 *"prevent corruption or its appearance"*: *Citizens United v. Federal Election Commission* (2010) 558 US 310, 314.

209 *"laws of our country"*: Thomas Jefferson, "The Papers of Thomas Jefferson: Retirement Series, volume 10: 1 May 1816 to 18 January 1817," https://www.monticello.org/site/research-and-collections/papers.

209 *"government will soon be at an end"*: George Mason. Quoted in Robert B. Yates, Notes on the Constitutional Convention, June 23, 1787.

209 *"human nature reared"*: Patrick Henry, Speech to the Virginia convention, June 8, 1787.

209 *"foreign corruption"*: Alexander Hamilton, *The Federalist No. 22.*

209 *"most violent effects"*: Benjamin Franklin, letter to William Strahan, Quoted in Walter Isaacson, *Benjamin Franklin: An American Life* (New York: Simon & Schuster, 2014), 456.

209 *"clamours and combinations"*: James Madison, letter to Thomas Jefferson, August 8, 1791.

209 *"enslave the rest"*: Gouverneur Morris, Madison's Notes. Quoted in Raphael, *Constitutional Myths*, 164.

Chapter 19: Scarier Than Scalia: Introducing Justice Clarence Thomas

211 *"hair on my Coke"*: Anita Hill, testimony to Judiciary Committee, 1991. Quoted by Susan Milligan, "Anita Hill Testifies in Clarence Thomas Hearing," *Daily News*, October 12, 1991.

211 *Justice Thomas also failed to fully report*: See Bruce Allen Murphy, *Scalia: A Court of One* (New York: Simon & Schuster, 2014), 426.

211 *fund-raising seminar*: Eric Lichtblau, "Common Cause Asks Court About Thomas Speech," *New York Times*, February 14, 2011, http://www.nytimes.com/2011/02/15/us/politics/15thomas.html.

211 *"ambassador to the Tea Party"*: "The Thomas Issue," editorial, *New York Times*, February 17, 2011.

212 *"pornography collection"*: Steve Kornacki, "How We Know Clarence Thomas Did It," *Salon*, October 27, 2010, http://www.salon.com/2010/10/27/anita_hill_clarence_thomas/. For more on this subject, see Andrew Peyton Thomas's affectionate biography *Clarence Thomas: A Biography* (New York: Encounter Books, 2001), 144. "The most palpable evidence of Thomas's spiritual drift was his frequenting of pornographic movie houses in New Haven during these years."

212 *"an almost axiomatic truth"*: *Bradwell v. Illinois* (1873) 83 US 130, 132.

212 *"Be fruitful, and multiply"*: KJV, Genesis 1:28.

213 *"to execute wrath upon the evildoers"*: Laurence Tribe, "Clarence Thomas and Natural Law," *New York Times*, July 15, 1991. Professor Tribe goes on to say that Thomas considered abortion murder and its "practice or counseling cannot be permitted by any state."

213 *"derives its authority from God"*: As quoted about Scalia in Margaret Talbot, "Supreme Confidence," *The New Yorker*, March 28, 2005.

213 *"Life, Liberty, and the Pursuit of Happiness . . ."*: US Declaration of Independence, 1776.

214 *"shall be the Supreme Law of the land"*: US Constitution, Article VI.

214 *"cannot take it away"*: Robert Dittmer, ed., *Justice Clarence Thomas Dissents*, 2015, quoting Thomas in *Obergefell v. Hodges* (2015) 135 S.Ct. 2584, 2639.

215 *"submissions on the other"*: Thomas Jefferson, "Notes on the State of Virginia," 1787.

215 *"around the country"*: *Obergefell v. Hodges* (2015) 135, S.Ct. 2584, 2635.

Chapter 20: What in Hell Is a Strict Constructionist?

217 *"nominate a strict constructionist to the Supreme Court"*: Mike Pence speech to House and Senate Republicans, January 2017.

220 *"lay the foundation of a civil war . . ."*: Elbridge Gerry, letter to Ann Gerry, August 26, 1787.

220 *"delivered up"*: US Constitution, Article IV, Section 2, Clause 3.

223 *"we shall act heartily and unanimously"*: William Safire, *Lend Me Your Ears: Great Speeches in History* (New York: W. W. Norton & Company, 2004), 872.

223 *"everywhere excite disgusts"*: David O. Stewart, *Madison's Gift: Five Partnerships That Built America* (New York: Simon & Schuster, 2016), 42.

223 *"whether we shall become a respectable nation"*: Dennis Brindell Fradin, *The Founders: The 39 Stories Behind the US Constitution* (New York: Walker & Company, 2005), 107–108.

223 *"I doubt whether I shall agree to it"*: Richard Beeman, *Plain, Honest Men: The Making of the American Constitution* (New York: Random House, 2009), 329.

223 *"the best that could be obtained at this time"*: Ray Raphael, *Founding Myths*, 154.

224 *"imperfect man"*: Alexander Hamilton, *The Federalist No. 85*.

224 *"lose sight of the change which ages will produce"*: Mark Kozlowski, *The Myth of the Imperial Judiciary: Why the Right Is Wrong About the Courts* (New York: New York University Press, 2006), 59.

225 For more on Hamilton's National Bank: Roger Lowenstein, *America's Bank: The Epic Struggle to Create the Federal Reserve* (New York: Penguin Books, 2015).

225 *"raise and support a standing army"*: US Constitution, Article I, Section 8.

Chapter 21: Anonymous Letter to
Certain Members of the Supreme Court

229 *"No matter whether th' Constitution follows th' flag or not, th' Supreme Court follows th' election returns"*: F. P. Dunne, *The Sunday Chat*, 1901, 6.

229 *"and secure the Blessings of Liberty"*: US Constitution, Preamble.

229 *"all laws which shall be necessary and proper"*: US Constitution, Section 8, Clause 18.

230 *"excessive bail shall not be required"*: US Constitution, Amendment VIII.

230 *"is not necessarily superseded, by the supplemental act"*: James Madison, letter to Alexander White, August 24, 1789.

233 *"the emblem of freedom in its truest best sense"*: *Minersville School District v. Gobitis* (1940) 310 US 586.

233 *"idolatry"*: *West Virginia State Board of Education v. Barnette* (1943) 319 US 624.

235 *"imposes its modern theories concerning expression upon the Constitutional text"*: *McIntyre v. Ohio Elections Commission* (1995) 514 US 334.

235 *"deserve the protection of the Bill of Rights"*: Ibid.

236 *"widespread and long-accepted practices of the American people"*: Ibid.

237 *Pacificus*: Carson Holloway, *Hamilton versus Jefferson in the Washington Administration: Completing the Founding or Betraying the Founding?* (New York: Cambridge University Press, 2015), 188.

237 *Helvidius*: Ibid.

237 *"protected, anonymous speech"*: See Thomas Paine, *Common Sense* (New York: Peter Eckler Publishing Co., 1918).

238 Lincoln's anonymous editorials: See James Oakes, "The Supreme Partisan," *New York Review*, July 13, 2017.

238 *"be the first to throw a stone"*: NIV, John 8:7.

238 *"unto God the things that are God's"*: KJV, Mark 12:17.

239 *"to enter the Kingdom of God"*: NIV, Matthew 19:24.

239 *"who need a doctor but the sick"*: NIV, Matthew 9:12.

239 *"they will be shown mercy"*: NIV, Matthew 5:7.

Chapter 22: The Chapter of Leftovers: Part III

241 For more on Washington and James Madison's writings: Lynne Cheney, *James Madison: A Life Reconsidered*, 188.

241 *"Life, Liberty and the pursuit of Happiness"*: US Declaration of Independence.

241 *"obtaining happiness and safety"*: George Mason, Virginia Declaration of Rights, June 12, 1776. See Hillsdale College Politics Faculty, *The US Constitution: A Reader* (Hillsdale, MI: Hillsdale College Press, 2016), 115–118.

242 For more on Washington's slaves: John Richard Alden, *George Washington: A Biography* (Baton Rouge: Louisiana State University Press, 1984), 237.

242 For more on Jefferson's slave quarters: Werner Sollors, *Interracialism: Black-White Intermarriage in American History, Literature, and Law* (New York: Oxford University Press, 2000), 396.

242 Slave state delegates: *Success Library, Volume 10, Parts 28–30* (New York: Success Company, 1902), 6060.

242 Franklin's state dividing: Alan Craig Houston, *Benjamin Franklin and the Politics of Improvement* (New Haven: Yale University Press, 2008), 186.

242 Slave dog owners: Arnold Arluke and Robert Bogdan, *Beauty and the Beast: Human-Animal Relations as Revealed in Real Photo Postcards, 1905–1935* (Syracuse: Syracuse University Press, 2010), 14.

Chapter 23: The Second Amendment: Guns and the NRA

For this chapter, I relied on Iain Overton's *The Way of the Gun: A Bloody Journey into the World of Firearms*, Saul Cornell's *A Well-Regulated Militia: The Founding Fathers and the Origins of Gun Control in America*, and Michael Waldman's *The Second Amendment: A Biography*.

243 *"People kill people"*: Slogan of the NRA, "This Day in Quotes," April 13, 2016.

243 *"before it's done"*: *Assassins*, music and lyrics by Stephen Sondheim (1990).

243 *There are 300 million guns in the United States*: Scott Horsley, "Guns in America, by the Numbers," National Public Radio, January 5, 2016, accessed June 14, 2017.

244 *Between the years*: See preface of Iain Overton, *The Way of the Gun: A Bloody Journey into the World of Firearms* (New York: HarperCollins, 2016); Everytown for Gun Safety, "Gun Violence by the Numbers," accessed June 14, 2017, https://everytownresearch.org/gun-violence-by-the-numbers/; Linda Qiu, "Fact-checking a Comparison of Gun Deaths and Terrorism Deaths," PolitiFact, October 5, 2015, accessed June 14, 2017; and Christopher Mele, "Road Rage Cases with Guns More Than Double in 3 Years, Report Says," *New York Times*, April 25, 2017.

245 *"shall not be infringed"*: US Constitution, Amendment II.

245 *"A well-regulated Militia"*: Ibid.

245 *"keep and bear Arms"*: Ibid.

246 *"capital . . . crime"*: US Constitution, Amendment V.

246 *"render military service in person"*: James Madison, cited in *Appendix to the Congressional Record* (1893), 598. See the Library of Congress, https://memory.loc.gov/ammem/amlaw/lwcr.html.

248 *"arms, ammunition and camp equipage"*: Articles of Confederation, Article VI, March 1, 1781.

248 *"be governed by the civil powers"*: Michael Waldman, *The Second Amendment: A Biography* (New York: Simon & Schuster, 2015), 197.

248 *"real danger of public injury from individuals"*: Ibid.

249 *"Standing Armies"*: Thomas Jefferson, letter to James Madison, December 20, 1787.

249 *Library of Congress*: Michael Waldman, *The Second Amendment: A Biography* (New York: Simon & Schuster, 2005), 63.

249 For more on Shays's Rebellion: Leonard L. Richards, *Shays's Rebellion: The American Revolution's Final Battle* (Philadelphia: University of Pennsylvania Press, 2014).

250 *"anarchy and confusion must prevail"*: George Washington, letter to Henry Knox, February 3, 1787.

252 *"efficiency of a well-regulated militia"*: *United States v. Miller* (1939) 307 US 174.

253 For more on Scalia's logic: *District of Columbia v. Heller* (2008) 554 US 570.

253 *"shall not be infringed"*: Ibid.

254 *Eddie Eagle*: NRA Explore, "Eddie Eagle," *NRA Explore*, accessed June 16, 2017, https://eddieeagle.nra.org/.

255 *One professor*: See John R. Lott Jr., *More Guns Less Crimes* (Chicago: Uni-

versity of Chicago Press, 2010), 126, in which Mr. Lott firmly denies any collusion between Chicago University, the Olin Foundation, and himself. In his own words: "Many of the attacks from groups like Handgun Control, Inc., and the Violence Policy Center focused on claims that my study had been paid for by gun manufacturers or that the *Journal of Legal Studies* was not a peer-reviewed journal and that I had chosen to publish the study in a 'student-edited journal' to avoid the close scrutiny that such a review would provide. These attacks were completely false, and I believe that those making the charges knew them to be false."

255 *"the gun crowd's guru"*: Matt Bai, "The Gun Crowd's Guru," *Newsweek*, March 11, 2001.

255 *"footnote in the history of piffle"*: Christopher Hitchens, *God Is Not Great: How Religion Poisons Everything* (New York: McClelland & Stewart, 2008), 249.

255 *pseudoscientific conclusions*: Overton, *The Way of the Gun* (New York: HarperCollins, 2016) 86–87, 99, 137, 155–167.

256 *John M. Olin*: "John M. Olin Foundation," Wikipedia, last modified May 19, 2017, https://en.wikipedia.org/wiki/John_M._Olin_Foundation.

256 *"belongs to all Americans"*: *District of Columbia v. Heller* (2008) 554 US 570.

256 *gory picture*: Overton, *The Way of the Gun* (New York: HarperCollins, 2016), preface.

258 *"unless whilst performing military duty"*: Stephen P. Halbrook, *A Right to Bear Arms: State and Federal Bills of Rights and Constitutional Guarantees* (Westport, CT: Greenwood Publishing Group, 1989), 56.

258 For the record: I first became aware of the gun lobby and its paranoia in 1976 when *The Mary Tyler Moore Show* did a story about the easy accessibility of guns in Minneapolis. It was the first and only time the show received hate mail of any sort.

Chapter 24: In Conclusion

259 *"the more glorious the triumph"*: Thomas Paine, *Common Sense* (New York: Peter Eckler Publishing Co., 1918).

259 *"neither power nor rights over it"*: Thomas Jefferson, letter to James Madison, September, 6, 1789.

260 *Wise men*: Christopher Hitchens defines wisdom as "knowing what you do not know."

260 *"I am not sure that it is not the best"*: Benjamin Franklin, *The Life and Miscellaneous Writings of Benjamin Franklin* (W. and R. Chambers, 1839), 84.

261 *"like the Ark of the Covenant, too sacred to be touched"*: Thomas Jefferson, letter to Samuel Kercheval, June 12, 1816.

262 *"the first and only legitimate object of good government"*: Thomas Jefferson, letter to the Republican Citizens of Washington County, Maryland, *The Writings of Thomas Jefferson*, H. A. Washington, ed., vol. 8 (1871), 165.

Bibliography

Books

Alden, John Richard. *George Washington: A Biography.* Baton Rouge: Louisiana State University Press, 1984.

Alexander, Michelle. *The New Jim Crow: Mass Incarceration in the Age of Colorblindness.* New York: The New Press, 2012.

Amar, Akhil Reed. *America's Unwritten Constitution: The Precedents and Principles We Live By.* New York: Basic Books, 2012.

———. *The Constitution Today: Timeless Lessons for the Issues of Our Era.* New York: Basic Books, 2016.

Amar, Akhil Reed, and Les Adams. *The Bill of Rights Primer: A Citizen's Guidebook to the American Bill of Rights.* New York: Skyhorse Publishing, 2013.

Andersen, H. Verlan. *The Book of Mormon and the Constitution.* Edited by Hans V. Andersen Jr. Orem, UT: SunRise Publishing, 1995.

Arluke, Arnold, and Robert Bogdan. *Beauty and the Beast: Human-Animal Relations as Revealed in Real Photo Postcards, 1905–1935.* Syracuse: Syracuse University Press, 2010.

Arnheim, Michael. *US Constitution for Dummies.* Hoboken, NJ: Wiley Publishing, Inc., 2009.

Aron, Paul. *Founding Feuds: The Rivalries, Clashes, and Conflicts That Forged a Nation.* Naperville, IL: Sourcebooks, Inc., 2016.

Beard, Charles A. *An Economic Interpretation of the Constitution of the United States.* Mineola, NY: Dover Publications, Inc., 2004.

———. *The Supreme Court and the Constitution.* New York: Macmillan, 1912.

Beck, Glenn. *The Original Argument: The Federalists' Case for the Constitution, Adapted for the 21st Century.* New York: Threshold Editions, 2011.

Beck, Glenn, and Joseph Kerry. *Glenn Beck's Common Sense: The Case Against an Out-of-Control Government, Inspired by Thomas Paine.* New York: Threshold Editions, 2009.

Beeman, Richard. *Plain, Honest Men: The Making of the American Constitution.* New York: Random House, 2009.

Beliles, Mark A., and Jerry Newcombe. *Doubting Thomas: The Religious Life and Legacy of Thomas Jefferson*. New York: Morgan James Publishing, 2015.

Bennett, William J., ed. *Our Country's Founders: A Book of Advice for Young People, Adapted from "Our Sacred Honor."* New York: Aladdin Paperbacks, 1998.

Berkin, Carol. *The Bill of Rights: A Fight to Secure America's Liberties*. New York: Simon & Schuster, 2015.

———. *A Brilliant Solution: Inventing the American Constitution*. New York: Mariner Books, 2003.

Beveridge, Albert J. *The Life of John Marshall*. Frederick, MD: Beard Books, 2000.

Blassingame, John W., ed. *Slave Testimony: Two Centuries of Letters, Speeches, Interviews, and Autobiographies*. Baton Rouge: Louisiana State University Press, 1977.

Brodie, Fawn M. *Thomas Jefferson: An Intimate History*. New York: W. W. Norton & Company, 1974.

Brookhiser, Richard. *James Madison*. New York: Basic Books, 2013.

Bowers, Claude G. *Jefferson and Hamilton: The Struggle for Democracy in America*. New York: Houghton Mifflin Harcourt, 1972.

Butterfield, L. H., ed. *Diary and Autobiography of John Adams*. Cambridge, MA: Belknap Press, 1961.

Carson, Ben, and Candy Carson. *A More Perfect Union: What We the People Can Do to Reclaim Our Constitutional Liberties*. New York: Sentinel, 2015.

Carson, Ben, and Cecil Murphey. *Gifted Hands: The Ben Carson Story*. Grand Rapids, MI: Zondervan, 1996.

Charles, Joshua. *Liberty's Secrets: The Lost Wisdom of America's Founders*. New York: WND Books, 2015.

Chemerinsky, Erwin. *The Case Against the Supreme Court*. New York: Penguin Books, 2014.

———. *The Conservative Assault on the Constitution*. New York: Simon & Schuster, 2010.

Cheney, Lynne. *James Madison: A Life Reconsidered*. New York: Penguin Books, 2014.

Chernow, Ron. *Alexander Hamilton*. New York: Penguin Books, 2004.

———. *Washington: A Life*. New York: Penguin Press, 2010.

Christianson, Scott. *With Liberty for Some: 500 Years of Imprisonment in America*. Boston: Northeastern University Press, 2000.

Church of Jesus Christ of Latter-day Saints. *The Book of Mormon*. Salt Lake City: 1840.

———. *The Doctrine and Covenants*. Salt Lake City: 1921.

Connor, Michal. *The Slave Letters*. Trumbull, CT: Janssen Publishers, 2003.

Cornell, Saul. *A Well-Regulated Militia: The Founding Fathers and the Origins of Gun Control in America*. New York: Oxford University Press, 2006.

Cost, Jay. *A Republic No More: Big Government and the Rise of American Political Corruption*. New York: Encounter Books, 2015.

Coulter, Ann. ¡*Adios, America! The Left's Plan to Turn Our Country into a Third-World Hellhole*. Washington, DC: Regnery Publishing, 2015.

———. *In Trump We Trust: E Pluribus Awesome!* New York: Sentinel, 2016.

Coyle, Marcia. *The Roberts Court: The Struggle for the Constitution*. New York: Simon & Schuster, 2014.

Cruz, Ted. *A Time for Truth: Reigniting the Promise of America*. New York: Broadside Books, 2015.

Davidson, James West. *A Little History of the United States*. New Haven: Yale University Press, 2015.

Davis, Kenneth C. *Don't Know Much About History: Everything You Need to Know About American History but Never Learned. Anniversary Edition*. New York: Harper, 2012.

De Mesquita, Bruce Bueno and Alastair Smith. *The Spoils of War: Greed, Power, and the Conflicts That Made Our Greatest Presidents*. New York: Public Affairs, 2016.

Dittmer, Robert, ed. *Justice Clarence Thomas Dissents*. San Bernardino, CA: CreateSpace Independent Publishing Platform, 2017.

Fea, John. *Was America Founded as a Christian Nation?: A Historical Introduction*. Louisville, KY: Westminster John Knox Press, 2011.

Ford, Paul Leicester, ed. *The Works of Thomas Jefferson in Twelve Volumes, Volume 1, Federal Edition*. New York: G. P. Putnam's Sons, 1904.

Fradin, Dennis Brindell. *The Founders: The 39 Stories Behind the U.S. Constitution*. New York: Walker & Company, 2005.

Franken, Al. *Lies and the Lying Liars Who Tell Them: A Fair and Balanced Look at the Right*. New York: Plume Books, 2004.

———. *Rush Limbaugh Is a Big Fat Idiot and Other Observations*. New York: Dell Trade, 1996.

Franklin, Benjamin. *The Autobiography of Benjamin Franklin*. Carlisle, MA: Applewood Books, [Reprint] 2008.

———. *The Life and Miscellaneous Writings of Benjamin Franklin.* W. & R. Chambers, 1839.

Fritz, Jean. *Where Was Patrick Henry on the 29th of May?* New York: Puffin Books, 2010.

Gilpin, Henry Dilworth. *The Papers of James Madison, Volume 2.* Washington, DC: Langtree & O'Sullivan, 1840.

Gingrich, Newt, and Callista Gingrich. *Rediscovering God in America: Reflections on the Role of Faith in Our Nation's History and Future.* New York: Center Street, 2016.

Glover, Lorri. *Founders as Fathers: The Private Lives and Politics of the American Revolutionaries.* New Haven: Yale University Press, 2014.

Graetz, Michael J., and Linda Greenhouse. *The Burger Court and the Rise of the Judicial Right.* New York: Simon & Schuster, 2016.

Grant, Madison. *The Passing of the Great Race, or the Racial Basis of European History.* Burlington, IA: Ostara Publications, 2011.

Greenawalt, Kent. *Religion and the Constitution, Volume I: Free Exercise and Fairness.* Princeton: Princeton University Press, 2006.

Griffiths, Trevor. *These Are the Times: A Life of Thomas Paine* (screenplay). Nottingham, UK: Spokesman, 2005.

Halbrook, Stephen P. *The Founders' Second Amendment: Origins of the Right to Bear Arms.* Chicago, IL: Ivan R. Dee, 2008.

———. *A Right to Bear Arms: State and Federal Bills of Rights and Constitutional Guarantees.* Westport, CT: Greenwood Publishing Group, 1989.

Hamilton, Alexander, John Jay, and James Madison. *The Federalist: A Commentary on the Constitution of the United States.* Edited by Robert Scigliano. New York: Modern Library, 2001.

Hempstead, Anne. *The Statue of Liberty.* Chicago: Heinemann-Raintree Library, 2006.

Hillsdale College Politics Faculty. *The US Constitution: A Reader.* Hillsdale, MI: Hillsdale College Press, 2016.

Hitchens, Christopher. *God Is Not Great: How Religion Poisons Everything.* New York: McClelland & Stewart, 2008.

———. *Thomas Jefferson: Author of America.* New York: Harper Perennial, 2005.

———. *Thomas Paine's Rights of Man: A Biography.* New York: Grove Press, 2006.

Hofstadter, Richard. *The Progressive Historians: Turner, Beard, Parrington.* New York: Knopf Doubleday, 2012.

Holloway, Carson. *Hamilton versus Jefferson in the Washington Administration: Completing the Founding or Betraying the Founding?* New York: Cambridge University Press, 2015.

Holowchak, Mark Andrew. *Thomas Jefferson: Moralist.* Jefferson, NC: McFarland & Company, 1858.

Houston, Alan. *Benjamin Franklin & the Politics of Improvement.* New Haven: Yale University Press, 2008.

Independence National Historical Park, National Park Service. *1787: The Day-to-Day Story of the Constitutional Convention.* New York: Exeter Books, 1987.

Isaacson, Walter. *Benjamin Franklin: An American Life.* New York: Simon & Schuster, 2004.

Jacoby, Susan. *Freethinkers: A History of American Secularism.* New York: Henry Holt and Company, 2005.

Jordan, Mark D. *The Invention of Sodomy in Christian Theology.* Chicago, IL: University of Chicago Press, 1997.

Kauffman, Bill. *Forgotten Founder, Drunken Prophet: The Life of Luther Martin.* Wilmington, DE: ISI Books, 2008.

Kaye, Harvey J. *Thomas Paine and the Promise of America.* New York: Hill and Wang, 2006.

Kidd, Thomas S. *Patrick Henry: First Among Patriots.* New York: Basic Books, 2011.

Klarman, Michael J. *The Framers' Coup: The Making of the United States Constitution.* New York: Oxford University Press, 2016.

Knott, Stephen F., and Tony Williams. *Washington & Hamilton: The Alliance That Forged America.* Naperville, IL: Sourcebooks, Inc., 2015.

Kozlowski, Mark. *The Myth of the Imperial Judiciary: Why the Right Is Wrong about the Courts.* New York: New York University Press, 2006.

Kramnick, Isaac, and R. Laurence Moore. *The Godless Constitution: The Case Against Religious Correctness.* New York: W. W. Norton & Company, 1997.

Labunski, Richard. *James Madison and the Struggle for the Bill of Rights.* New York: Oxford University Press, 2006.

Lengel, Edward G. *First Entrepreneur: How George Washington Built His—and the Nation's—Prosperity.* Boston, MA: De Capo Press, 2016.

Levin, Mark R. *The Liberty Amendments: Restoring the American Republic.* New York: Threshold Editions, 2013.

————. *Rediscovering Americanism and the Tyranny of Progressivism*. New York: Simon & Schuster, 2017.

Levy, Leonard W. *The Establishment Clause: Religion and the First Amendment. Second Edition, Revised*. Chapel Hill: University of North Carolina Press, 1994.

Lippincott, Horace Mather. *Early Philadelphia: Its People, Life, and Progress*. Philadelphia, PA: J. P. Lippincott Company, 1917.

Lippy, Charles H. *Seasonable Revolutionary: The Mind of Charles Chauncy*. Chicago, IL: Nelson-Hall, 1981.

Lodge, Henry Cabot. *A Memoir of Caleb Strong: United States Senator and Governor of Massachusetts, 1745–1818*. Cambridge: Massachusetts Historical Society, 1879.

Lott, John R., Jr. *More Guns, Less Crime: Understanding Crime and Gun Control Laws. Third Edition*. Chicago, IL: University of Chicago Press, 2010.

————. *The War on Guns: Arming Yourself Against Gun Control Lies*. Washington, DC: Regnery Publishing, 2016.

Lowenstein, Roger. *America's Bank: The Epic Struggle to Create the Federal Reserve*. New York: Penguin Books, 2015.

Madison, James. *Writings*. Edited by Jack N. Rakove. New York: The Library of America, 1999.

Madison, James, et al. *The Washington-Madison Papers, Collected and Preserved by James Madison*. Philadelphia: The Bicking Print, 1892.

Maier, Pauline. *Ratification: The People Debate the Constitution, 1787–1788*. New York: Simon & Schuster, 2010.

Manchester, William. *The Glory and the Dream: A Narrative History of America, 1932–1972*. Boston: Little, Brown and Company, 1974.

Mapp, Alf J., Jr. *The Faiths of Our Fathers: What America's Founders Really Believed*. Lanham, MD: Rowan & Littlefield Publishers, 2005.

————. *Thomas Jefferson: Passionate Pilgrim*. Lanham, MD: Rowman & Littlefield Publishers, 2009.

Marshall, Peter, and David Manuel. *From Sea to Shining Sea: For Young Readers. Book Two, 1787–1837*. Grand Rapids, MI: Revell, 2011.

Matthews, Marty D. *Forgotten Founder: The Life and Times of Charles Pinckney*. Columbia, SC: University of South Carolina Press, 2004.

Mayyasi, Kim A. *Call to Virtue: Republics of Character from Rome to 1776*. Minneapolis: Hillcrest Publishing Group, 2016.

McCullough, David. *John Adams*. New York: Simon & Schuster, 2001.

McDonald, Forrest. *We the People: The Economic Origins of the Constitution.* New Brunswick, NJ: Transaction Publishers, 1991.

McGaughy, J. Kent. *Richard Henry Lee of Virginia: A Portrait of an American Revolutionary.* New York: Roman & Littlefield Publishers, Inc., 2004.

McGuire, Robert A. *To Form a More Perfect Union: A New Economic Interpretation of the United States Constitution.* New York: Oxford University Press, 2008.

McWhorter, Ladelle. *Racism and Sexual Oppression in Anglo-America: A Genealogy.* Indianapolis: Indiana University Press, 2009.

Miller, Melanie Randolph. *An Incautious Man: The Life of Gouverneur Morris.* Wilmington, DE: ISI Books, 2008.

Moreno, Paul D. *The Bureaucrat Kings: The Origins and Underpinnings of America's Bureaucratic State.* Santa Barbara: Praeger, 2016.

Murphy, Bruce Allen. *Scalia: A Court of One.* New York: Simon & Schuster, 2014.

Notes of Debates in the Federal Convention of 1787 Reported by James Madison. Athens: Ohio University Press, 1985.

Overton, Iain. *The Way of the Gun: A Bloody Journey into the World of Firearms.* New York: HarperCollins, 2016.

Paine, Thomas. *Collected Writings: Common Sense, The Crisis, Rights of Man, and the Age of Reason.* San Bernardino, CA: Pantianos Classics, 2017.

Parry, Edwin F., ed. *Joseph Smith's Teachings: A Classified Arrangement of the Doctrinal Sermons and Writings of the Great Latter-day Prophet.* Salt Lake City: Deseret News, 1913.

Paulsen, Michael Stokes, and Luke Paulsen. *The Constitution: An Introduction.* New York: Basic Books, 2015.

Rabin-Havt, Ari, and Media Matters for America. *Lies, Incorporated: The World of Post-Truth Politics.* New York: Anchor Books, 2016.

Raphael, Ray. *Constitutional Myths: What We Get Wrong and How to Get It Right.* New York: The New Press, 2013.

———. *Founders: The People Who Brought You a Nation.* New York: The New Press, 2009.

———. *Founding Myths: Stories That Hide Our Patriotic Past.* New York: The New Press, 2014.

Rhodehamel, John. *George Washington: The Wonder of the Age.* New Haven: Yale University Press, 2017.

Richards, Leonard L. *Shays's Rebellion: The American Revolution's Final Battle.* Philadelphia: University of Pennsylvania Press, 2014.

Richman, Sheldon. *America's Counter-Revolution: The Constitution Revisited.* Ann Arbor, MI: Griffin & Lash, 2016.

Rossum, Ralph A., and G. Alan Tarr. *American Constitutional Law, Volume I: The Structure of Government.* Boulder: Westview Press, 2016.

Rutland, Robert A., et al. *The Papers of James Madison. Volume 10, 1787–1788.* Chicago: University of Chicago Press, 1977.

Safire, William. *Lend Me Your Ears: Great Speeches in History.* New York: W. W. Norton & Company, 2004.

Sargent, Epes, ed. *The Select Works of Benjamin Franklin.* Boston: Phillips, Sampson and Co., 1853.

Scalia, Antonin. *A Matter of Interpretation: Federal Courts and the Law.* Princeton, NJ: Princeton University Press, 1997.

Scott, E. H., ed. *Journal of the Constitutional Convention, Kept by James Madison.* Chicago, IL: Scott, Foresman and Company, 1893.

Sehat, David. *The Jefferson Rule: How the Founding Fathers Became Infallible and Our Politics Inflexible.* New York: Simon & Schuster, 2015.

Simon, James F. *What Kind of Nation: Thomas Jefferson, John Marshall, and the Epic Struggle to Create a United States.* New York: Simon & Schuster, 2002.

Simpson, Henry. *The Lives of Eminent Philadelphians, Now Deceased.* Philadelphia, PA: W. Brotherhead, 1859.

Smith, Billy G., ed. *Life in Early Philadelphia: Documents from the Revolutionary and Early National Periods.* Philadelphia, PA: Penn State University Press, 1995.

Smith, Gary Scott. *Faith & the Presidency: From George Washington to George W. Bush.* New York: Oxford University Press, 2006.

Smith, James Morton, ed. *The Republic of Letters: The Correspondence Between Thomas Jefferson and James Madison, 1776–1826. Volume I: 1776–1790.* New York: W. W. Norton & Company, 1995.

———. *The Republic of Letters: The Correspondence Between Thomas Jefferson and James Madison, 1776–1826. Volume II: 1790–1804.* New York: W. W. Norton & Company, 1995.

———. *The Republic of Letters: The Correspondence Between Thomas Jefferson and James Madison, 1776–1826. Volume III: 1804–1836.* New York: W. W. Norton & Company, 1995.

Smith, Jean Edward. *John Marshall: Definer of a Nation.* New York: Holt Paperbacks, 1996.

Sollors, Werner. *Interracialism: Black-White Intermarriage in American History, Literature, and Law*. New York: Oxford University Press, 2000.

Sparks, Jared, ed. *The Works of Benjamin Franklin*. Chicago: T. MacCoun, 1882.

Spiro, Jonathan Peter. *Defending the Master Race: Conservation, Eugenics, and the Legacy of Madison Grant*. Burlington, VT: University of Vermont Press, 2009.

Stewart, David O. *Madison's Gift: Five Partnerships That Built America*. New York: Simon & Schuster, 2016.

———. *The Summer of 1787: The Men Who Invented the Constitution*. New York: Simon & Schuster, 2008.

Storing, Herbert J., and Murray Dry. *The Anti-Federalist: Writings by Opponents of the Constitution. An Abridgement of the Complete Anti-Federalist*. Chicago, IL: University of Chicago Press, 1985.

Success Library, Volume 10, Parts 28–30. New York: Success Company, 1902.

Taylor, Alan. *American Revolutions: A Continental History, 1750–1804*. New York: W. W. Norton & Company, 2016.

Thomas, Andrew Peyton. *Clarence Thomas: A Biography*. New York: Encounter Books, 2001.

Thomas Jefferson Memorial Association of the United States. *The Writings of Thomas Jefferson, Volume 16*. Washington, DC: Thomas Jefferson Memorial Association, 1904.

Toobin, Jeffrey. *The Nine: Inside the Secret World of the Supreme Court*. New York: Anchor Books, 2008.

Toth, Michael C. *Founding Federalist: The Life of Oliver Ellsworth*. Wilmington, DE: ISI Books, 2011.

Trachtman, Michael G. *The Supremes' Greatest Hits: The 44 Supreme Court Cases That Most Directly Affect Your Life*. New York: Sterling, 2016.

Tribe, Laurence, and Joshua Matz. *Uncertain Justice: The Roberts Court and the Constitution*. New York: Henry Holt and Company, 2014.

Tyler, Moses Coit. *Patrick Henry*. San Bernardino, CA: [Reprint], 2017.

Union of American Hebrew Congregations. *Judaism at the World's Parliament of Religions*. Cincinnati: Robert Clarke & Co., 1894.

United States. *The Declaration of Independence and the Constitution of the United States of America*. Introduction by Pauline Maier. New York: Bantam Books, 2008.

Waldman, Michael. *The Second Amendment: A Biography*. New York: Simon & Schuster, 2014.

Wilson, B. *Memoir of the Life of the Right Rev. William White.* Philadelphia: C. H. Kay & Co., 1839.

Woodward, Bob, and Scott Armstrong. *The Brethren: Inside the Supreme Court.* New York: Avon Books, 1979.

Wright, Louis B., and Elaine W. Fowler. *Everyday Life in the New Nation.* New York: G. P. Putnam's Sons, 1972.

Zinn, Howard. *A People's History of the United States.* New York: Harper Perennial, 2015.

Journal Articles

Morrison, Larry R. "The Religious Defense of American Slavery Before 1830." *Journal of Religious Thought* 37, 2 (Fall 80/Winter 81), 16–29.

Pybus, Cassandra. "Jefferson's Faulty Math: The Question of Slave Defections in the American Revolution." *The William and Mary Quarterly* 62, 2 (April 2005): 243–264.

Singleton, Madilyn M. "The Science of Eugenics: America's Moral Detour." *Journal of American Physicians and Surgeons* 19, 4 (Winter 2014), 122–125.

Newspaper and Magazine Articles

Bai, Matt. "The Gun Crowd's Guru." *Newsweek*, March 22, 2001.

Bartlett, Bruce. "Immigration: The Real Cost of a Closed Door Policy." *The Fiscal Times*, November 25, 2011.

Beinart, Peter. "Glenn Beck's Regrets." *The Atlantic*, December 8, 2016.

Brittain, Amy, and Sari Horowitz. "Justice Scalia Spent His Last Hours with Members of This Secretive Society of Elite Hunters." *Washington Post*, February 21, 2016.

Cohen, Adam. "Scalia Mouths Off on Sex Discrimination." *Time*, March 2010.

Cooper, Matthew. "Antonin Scalia's 2008 Ruling Set Parameters for Today's Gun Control Reform Debate." *Newsweek*, June 20, 2016.

Dunne, F. P. *The Sunday Chat*, 1901.

Franck, Matthew J. "His Final Two Dissents Reveal Themes of His Jurisprudence." *National Review*, March 14, 2016.

Friedersdorf, Conor. "Will the GOP Base Tolerate Donald Trump's Attack on Ben Carson?" *The Atlantic*, November 13, 2015.

Fuller, Jaime. "How Has Voting Changed Since *Shelby County v. Holder?*" *Washington Post*, July 7, 2014.

Gabriel, Trip. "Trump Chooses Ben Carson to Lead HUD." *New York Times*, December 5, 2016.

Hickey, Walter. "How the NRA Killed Federal Funding for Gun Violence Research." *Business Insider*, January 16, 2013.

"Justice Brennan's Vision." *New York Times*, July 25, 1997.

Korematsu, Karen. "When Lies Overruled Rights." *New York Times*, February 18, 2017.

Miller, Michael E. "Ben Carson Believes Joseph Built Egypt's Pyramids to Store Grain." *Washington Post*, November 5, 2015.

Milligan, Susan. "Anita Hill Testifies in Clarence Thomas Hearing." *Daily News*, October 12, 1991.

"Mr. Garrison's Lecture." *New York Times*, January 15, 1862.

Oakes, James. "The Supreme Partisan." *New York Review*, July 13, 2017.

Schwartz, John. "Between the Lines of the Voting Rights Act Opinion." *New York Times*, June 25, 2013.

Senior, Jennifer. "In Conversation: Antonin Scalia." *New York*, October 6, 2013.

Singleton, Madilyn M. "The Science of Eugenics," *Journal of American Physicians and Surgeons* 19, 4 (Winter 2014), 122–125.

Talbot, Margaret. "Supreme Confidence." *The New Yorker*, March 28, 2005.

Terris, Ben, and Stephanie Kirchner. "The Story of the Surgery That Made Ben Carson Famous." *Washington Post*, November 13, 2015.

"The Thomas Issue." *New York Times*, February 17, 2011.

Toobin, Jeffrey. "The Company Scalia Kept." *The New Yorker*, March 2, 2016.

Tribe, Laurence. "Clarence Thomas and 'Natural Law.'" *New York Times*, July 15, 1991.

Websites and News Outlets

American Psychological Association. "Intimate Partner Violence: Facts & Resources." Accessed June 14, 2017, http://www.apa.org/topics/violence/partner.aspx.

Bomboy, Scott. "Looking at Two Little-Known Versions of Our Constitution." National Constitution Center, August 24, 2015, https://constitutioncenter.org/blog/looking-at-two-little-known-versions-of-our-constitution.

Bregman, Rutger. "The Bizarre Tale of President Nixon and His Basic Income Bill," *The Correspondent*, May 17, 2016, https://thecorrespondent.com/4503 /the-bizarre-tale-of-president-nixon-and-his-basic-income-bill/173117835 -c34d6145.

Cobabe, George. "The White Horse Prophecy." Foundation for Apologetic Information & Research. Accessed July 14, 2017, https://www.fairmor mon.org/wp-content/uploads/2011/12/cobabe-whitehorse.pdf.

Coulter, Ann. "This Is War." *Townhall*, September 14, 2001, https://townhall .com/columnists/anncoulter/2001/09/14/this-is-war-n865496.

"Eugenics in the United States." Wikipedia. Last modified June 11, 2017, https://en.wikipedia.org/w/index.php?title=Eugenics_in_the_United_States &action=history.

Everytown for Gun Safety. "Gun Violence by the Numbers." Accessed June 14, 2017, https://everytownresearch.org/gun-violence-by-the-numbers/.

Federation for American Immigration Reform. "History of US Immigration Laws." Accessed June 14, 2017, http://www.fairus.org/facts/us_laws.

Fitzgerald, Michael. "Ben Carson: Gay Marriage Will Lead to 'Mass Killings' and 'Utter Chaos.'" *Towleroad*, October 13, 2016, http://www.towleroad .com/2016/10/ben-carson-gay-marriage/.

Freedman, Milton. Financial Page. *The New Yorker*, June 20, 2016.

Gordon, Lloyd. "The Constitutional Convention." Accessed June 14, 2017, http://teachingamericanhistory.org/convention/citytavern/.

"Hmong Americans." Wikipedia. Last modified June 14, 2017, https://en.wiki pedia.org/w/index.php?title=Hmong_Americans&action=history.

Horsley, Scott. "Guns in America, by the Numbers." National Public Radio, January 5, 2016. Accessed June 14, 2017, http://www.npr.org/2016/01/05 /462017461/guns-in-america-by-the-numbers.

Jackson, Brooks. "Presidents Who Owned Slaves." Last modified December 18, 2007, http://www.factcheck.org/2007/12/presidents-whoNew-owned -slaves/.

Jefferson, Thomas. "The Papers of Thomas Jefferson: Retirement Series." Volume 10, 1 May 1816 to 18 January 1817, https://www.monticello.org/site /research-and-collections/papers.

"John M. Olin Foundation." Wikipedia. Last modified May 19, 2017, https:// en.wikipedia.org/wiki/John_M._Olin_Foundation.

Kornacki, Steve. "How We Know Clarence Thomas Did It." *Salon*, October 27, 2010, http://www.salon.com/2010/10/27/anita_hill_clarence_thomas/.

Krieg, Gregory. "Trump Likens Carson's 'Pathology' to That of a Child Molester." CNN, November 12, 2015, http://www.cnn.com/2015/11/12/politics/donald-trump-ben-carson-child-molester/index.html.

Lichtblau, Eric. "Common Cause Asks Court about Thomas Speech." *New York Times*, February 14, 2011, http://www.nytimes.com/2011/02/15/us/politics/15thomas.html.

Mele, Christopher. "Road Rage Cases with Guns More Than Double in 3 Years, Report Says." *New York Times*, April 25, 2017, https://www.nytimes.com/2017/04/25/us/road-rage-guns.html.

Milbank, Dana. "Mormon Prophecy Behind Glenn Beck's Message." *Huffington Post*, October 5, 2010.

National Coalition Against Domestic Violence. "National Statistics." Accessed June 14, 2017, http://ncadv.org/learn-more/statistics.

National Humanities Center. *Becoming American: The British Atlantic Colonies, 1690–1763*. Accessed June 10, 2017, http://nationalhumanitiescenter.org/pds/becomingamer/growth/text7/indianlands.pdf.

National Network to End Domestic Violence. "Census: Domestic Violence Counts." Accessed June 14, 2017, http://nnedv.org/resources/census.html.

NRA Explore. "Eddie Eagle." Accessed June 16, 2017, https://eddieeagle.nra.org/.

Oaks, Dallin H. "The Divinely Inspired Constitution." Church of Jesus Christ of Latter-day Saints, 1992. Accessed July 1, 2017, https://www.lds.org/ensign/1992/02/the-divinely-inspired-constitution?lang=eng.

Qiu, Linda. "Fact-Checking a Comparison of Gun Deaths and Terrorism Deaths." *PolitiFact*, October 5, 2015. Accessed June 14, 2017, http://www.politifact.com/truth-o-meter/statements/2015/oct/05/viral-image/fact-checking-comparison-gun-deaths-and-terrorism-/.

Ring, Trudy. "Antonin Scalia: If We Protect Gays, Why Not Child Molesters?" *The Advocate*, November 17, 2015, https://www.advocate.com/politics/2015/11/17/antonin-scalia-if-we-protect-gays-why-not-child-molesters.

Russell, Nancy. "Innovative Benjamin Franklin Rocked." *Columbia Daily Tribune*, April 5, 2012, http://www.columbiatribune.com/cee9f061-e67e-5e42-8f53-fb7d83cbd9d7.html.

Serwer, Adam. "Here Are the 7 Worst Things Antonin Scalia Has Said or Written About Homosexuality." *Mother Jones*, March 26, 2013, http://www.motherjones.com/politics/2013/03/scalia-worst-things-said-written-about-homosexuality-court/.

Taylor, J. R. "Ted Cruz's Father—Caught with JFK Assassin." *National*

Enquirer, April 20, 2016, http://www.nationalenquirer.com/celebrity/ted-cruz-scandal-father-jfk-assassination/.

Treyz, Catherine. "Lindsey Graham Jokes About How to Get Away with Murdering Ted Cruz." CNN, February 26, 2016, http://www.cnn.com/2016/02/26/politics/lindsey-graham-ted-cruz-dinner/index.html.

Vidal, Gore. Talk Today. *USA Today*, February 4, 2003, https://usatoday30.usatoday.com/community/chat_03/2003-02-04-vidal.htm.

Wills, Garry. "Child of Entitlement." *New York Times*, July 4, 2017.

Wines, Michael. "Some Republicans Acknowledge Leveraging Voter ID Laws for Political Gain." *New York Times*, September 16, 2016, https://www.nytimes.com/2016/09/17/us/some-republicans-acknowledge-leveraging-voter-id-laws-for-political-gain.html.

Zephyr Teachout. *The Anti-Corruption Principle* 94. *Cornell Law Review*, 341 (2009), http://scholarship.law.cornell.edu/clr/vol94/iss2/8.

Court Cases

Bowers v. Hardwick, 478 US 186 (1986).

Bradwell v. Illinois, 83 US 130 (1873).

Buck v. Bell, 274 US 200 (1927).

Citizens United v. Federal Election Commission, 558 US 310 (2010).

Debs v. United States, 249 US 211 (1919).

District of Columbia v. Heller, 554 US 570 (2008).

Griswold v. Connecticut, 381 US 479 (1965).

Kelo v. City of New London, 545 US 469 (2005).

Korematsu v. United States, 323 US 214 (1944).

Lawrence v. Texas, 539 US 558 (2003).

McCreary County v. American Civil Liberties Union, 545 US 844 (2005).

McIntyre v. Ohio Elections Commission, 514 US 334 (1995).

Minersville School District v. Gobitis, 310 US 586 (1940).

Obergefell v. Hodges, 576 US (2015).

Plyler v. Doe, 457 US 2002 (1982).

Shelby County v. Holder, 570 US 2 (2013).

Stanley v. Georgia, 394 US 557 (1969).

United States v. Miller, 307 US 174 (1939).

United States v. Stanley, 483 US 669 (1987).

United States v. Sun-Diamond Growers of California, 526 US 398 (1999).

Van Orden v. Perry, 545 US 677 (2005).

West Virginia State Board of Education v. Barnette, 319 US 624 (1943).

Other Sources

Adams, Abigail. Letter to John Adams. March 31, 1776.

Adams, John. Letter to Benjamin Rush. November 11, 1806.

———. Inaugural Address of John Adams. March 4, 1797.

———. Letter to Abigail Adams. October 9, 1774.

———. Letter to James Warren. July 7, 1777.

Bachmann, Michele. Speech to Values Voter Summit. September 9, 2016.

Beck, Glenn. *The Glenn Beck Program.* April 5, 2016.

Buchanan, Pat. Speech to Christian Coalition. *ADL Report.* September 1993.

Carson, Ben. Speech at Celebration of Creation. 2012.

Coulter, Ann. *Hannity & Colmes.* June 20, 2001.

Cruz, Ted. Keynote Address to Conservative Political Action Conference. March 16, 2013.

———. Speech After Iowa Caucus. February 1, 2016.

DeMint, Jim. *Allman in the Morning.* FM NewsTalk 97.1. April 27, 2016.

Elbridge, Gerry. Letter to Ann Gerry. August 26, 1787.

Falwell, Jerry. *The 700 Club.* September 13, 2001.

Franklin, Benjamin. Letter to Ezra Stiles. March 9, 1790.

———. Letter to John Franklin. May 1745.

———. Letter to Peter Collinson. May 9, 1753.

———. Letter to Robert Livingston. July 22, 1783.

Hamilton, Alexander. Letter to James McHenry. May 18, 1799.

Henry, Patrick. Speech to Virginia Convention. June 8, 1787.

Hinckley, Gordon B. Weber State University Commencement Speech. August 1999.

Jefferson, Thomas. Circular to the Governors of the States. March 1, 1792.

———. Letter to Danbury Baptists. January 1, 1802.

———. Letter to Horatio G. Spafford. March 17, 1814.

———. Letter to James Madison. December 20, 1787.

———. Letter to James Madison. September 6, 1789.

———. Letter to John Adams. August 30, 1787.

———. Letter to Richard Henry Lee. May 8, 1825.

———. Letter to Samuel Kercheval. June 12, 1816.

———. Notes on the State of Virginia. 1787.

Johnson, Lyndon. Remarks at Liberty Island. October 3, 1965.

Levin, Mark. *The Mark Levin Show*. May 22, 2009.

———. Speech to State Legislature. December 4, 2014.

Madison, James. *Annuls of Congress*. August 18, 1789.

———. Letter to Alexander White. August 24, 1789.

———. Letter to John Tyler. March 1, 1833.

———. Letter to Thomas Jefferson. October 17, 1788.

———. Letter to Thomas Jefferson. August 8, 1791.

———. Letter to William Cogswell. March 10, 1834.

———. Speech at Virginia Convention. December 2, 1829.

———. "The Preservation of Deer." June 18, 1779.

Nugent, Ted. *All Access* Interview. July 14, 2014.

"Pacificus" [Noah Webster]. Letter to James Madison. August 14, 1789.

Palin, Sarah. *The O'Reilly Factor*. May 6, 2010.

Sondheim, Stephen (music and lyrics), and John Weidman (book). *Assassins* (musical), 1990.

Trump, Donald. Speech at Fort Worth, Texas Rally. February 26, 2016.

Tucker, Thomas Tudor. Letter to St. George Tucker. October 2, 1789.

Washington, George. Letter to Henry Knox. February 3, 1787.

———. Letter to John Adams. November 15, 1794.

Yates, Robert B. Notes on the Constitutional Convention. June 23, 1787.

Acknowledgments

Amateurs like ourselves, approaching the mysteries of the Constitution for the first time, are inevitably dependent on the scholarship of those who do it for a living. The brilliant historians and legal scholars we must thank in particular—whether they want us to or not—are:

Ray Raphael, *Constitutional Myths: What We Get Wrong and How to Get It Right.*

David O. Stewart, *Madison's Gift: Five Partnerships That Built America* and *The Summer of 1787: The Men Who Invented the Constitution.*

Carol Berkin, *The Bill of Rights: A Fight to Secure America's Liberties* and *A Brilliant Solution: Inventing the American Constitution.*

Isaac Kramnick and R. Laurence Moore, *The Godless Constitution: The Case Against Religious Correctness.*

Michael J. Klarman, *The Framers' Coup: The Making of the United States Constitution.*

Saul Cornell, *A Well-Regulated Militia: The Founding Fathers and the Origins of Gun Control in America.*

Michael Waldman, *The Second Amendment: A Biography.*

Lynne Cheney, *James Madison: A Life Reconsidered.*

Howard Zinn, *A People's History of the United States.*

Erwin Chemerinsky, *The Case Against the Supreme Court.*

We are gratefully indebted to their research, perspectives, and invaluable opinions.

In addition, we would like to thank:

Bob Bender, our scrupulous and diligent editor, and his associate Johanna Li. You should have seen the manuscript before they got their hands on it. The remaining clichés, run-on sentences, and blunders (should they exist) are all our own.

Bob Barnett, our lawyer, who read the book proposal, agreed to represent it, then made the deal with Simon & Schuster quicker than most men can get dressed in the morning. None of the many lawyer jokes in the book is directed at him.

Jonathan Karp, our publisher, and fan of *The Mary Tyler Moore Show*, who took the chance that two of its alumni still knew what they were doing.

Jon Kukla, historian and author, for his generosity in reviewing the manuscript and giving us his expert notes and suggestions.

Janis Uhley, our editorial associate, who did everything there is possible to do to get a book ready for publication except write it.

Our crack team of researchers, Matthew Seymour, Alejandra Seymour, and Katrina Denman.

Liza Asner, who believed in the project even before its authors did.

Carlene Weinberger, who not only read all of the early drafts but made sure the wife jokes were at a minimum.

All the many little Asners who helped by staying out from underfoot.

And, finally, to the Right-Wingers and their henchmen—politicians, pundits, and apologists—without whose lies and misrepresentations this book would not have been necessary.